MEDIEVALIA ET HUMANISTICA

MEDIEVALIA ET HUMANISTICA
New Series, Number 1
Edited by Paul Maurice Clogan

Katherine Zell *Roland H. Bainton* • Wyclif and the Augustinian Tradition with Special Reference to His *De Trinitate* *Gordon Leff* • A Collection of Decretal Letters of Innocent III in Bamberg *Stephan Kuttner* • The Tale of the Captive Bird and the Traveler: Nequam, Berechiah, and Chaucer's *Squire's Tale* *Albert C. Friend* • Rhythmic Architecture in the Music of the High Middle Ages *Theodore Karp* • The Tuscan Town in the Quattrocento: A Demographic Profile *David Herlihy* • The University and the Church: Patterns of Reform in Jean Gerson *Steven E. Ozment* • *Epistola Cuthberti De Obitu Bedae*: A Caveat *W. F. Bolton* • The Hussite Revolution and the German Peasants' War: An Historical Comparison *Frederick G. Heymann* • Number Symbolism and Medieval Literature *Edmund Reiss* • Some Common Features of Italian Urban Experience (c. 1200–1500) *Marvin B. Becker* • Flavio Biondo's *Roma Instaurata* *Dorothy M. Robathan* • *The Kambriae Descriptio* of Gerald the Welshman *Urban T. Holmes* • The *Planctus* of Oedipus: Text and Comment *Paul Maurice Clogan* • Verses on the Life of Robert Grosseteste *Richard W. Hunt*

MEDIEVALIA ET HUMANISTICA

STUDIES IN MEDIEVAL & RENAISSANCE CULTURE

Founded in 1943 by S. Harrison Thomson

NEW SERIES
NUMBER 2

MEDIEVAL AND RENAISSANCE STUDIES IN REVIEW

Edited by Paul Maurice Clogan

CASE WESTERN RESERVE UNIVERSITY

The Press of
Case Western Reserve University
Cleveland & London
1971

Editorial Note

FOUNDED IN 1943 by S. Harrison Thomson and now under new editorship and management, *Medievalia et Humanistica* continues to publish, in a series of annual volumes, significant scholarship, criticism, and reviews in all areas of medieval and Renaissance culture: literature, art, archaeology, history, law, music, philosophy, science, and social and economic institutions. *Medievalia et Humanistica* encourages the individual scholar to examine the relationship of his discipline to other disciplines and to relate his study in a theoretical or practical way to its cultural and historical context. Review articles examine significant recent publications, and contributing editors report on the progress of medieval and Renaissance studies in the United States and Canada.

Medievalia et Humanistica is sponsored by the Medieval Interdepartmental Section of the Modern Language Association of America, and publication in the series is open to contributions from all sources. The editorial board welcomes interdisciplinary critical and historical studies by young or established scholars and urges contributors to communicate in an attractive, clear, and concise style the larger implications in addition to the precise material of their research, with documentation held to a minimum. Texts, maps, illustrations, and diagrams will be published when they are essential to the argument of the article.

Books for review, inquiries regarding Fasciculi I–XVII in the original series, and manuscripts (which should be prepared in conformity with the second edition of *The MLA Style Sheet* and accompanied by a stamped, self-addressed envelope) should be addressed to the Editor, *Medievalia et Humanistica*, P.O. Box 2567, Cleveland, Ohio 44112. Inquiries regarding single or standing orders for the New Series should be addressed to The Press of Case Western Reserve University, Quail Building, Cleveland, Ohio 44106.

Preface

THIS SECOND VOLUME in the new series of *Medievalia et Humanistica* explores from different points of view the general topic of "Medieval and Renaissance Studies in Review," and each article makes a significant and original contribution to this topic. The first three articles (by Francis R. Walton, Charity C. Willard, and Paul J. Alexander, with a Foreword by Paul J. Alexander and Mary E. Giffin) constituted a symposium on "Byzantine Studies and Western Literatures." This symposium was included in the program of the Modern Language Association of America's December, 1970 annual meeting in New York City and marked the introduction of Byzantine studies into the Association's medieval section. *Medievalia et Humanistica* is pleased to publish a revised version of this symposium. Six review articles analyze important recent publications in Latin palaeography, cataloguing of medieval manuscripts, *Corpus der italienischen Zeichnungen 1300–1450*, political and legal theories, Lord Berners, and the future of medieval history. Three critical articles examine significant aspects in the scholarship of *The Praise of Folly*, the concept of "the wise ruler," and Walahfrid's "Metrum Saphicum." This volume also contains, for the first time, a complete Table of Contents and a Cumulative Index for Fasciculi I–XVII of the original series. As a new feature of the series, review articles about important publications in medieval and Renaissance studies are inaugurated in this second volume.

In compiling and editing the articles in this volume, the editor is most grateful to the members of the editorial board for their expert criticism, as well as to Milton V. Anastos (University of California at Los Angeles), Peter Charanis (Rutgers University), Frederick R. Goff (the Library of Congress), John L. Grigsby (Washington University), Clarence H. Miller (St. Louis University), Dorothy Miner (the Walters Art Gallery), Karl Morrison (University of Chicago), Anthony Mortimer (Case Western Reserve University), and Richard S. Sylvester (Yale University). Marie Oemler (Ashland College) labored long and hard in the preparation of the Cumulative Index for

vii

Fasciculi I–XVII of the original series. The editorial board is pleased to appoint Julie Sydney Davis as Managing Editor of the new series. Forthcoming volumes in the new series will explore from different perspectives the topics of social contexts and of spirituality in the Middle Ages and Renaissance.

P.M.C.

MEDIEVALIA ET HUMANISTICA

Paul Maurice Clogan, Editor
CASE WESTERN RESERVE UNIVERSITY
Julie Sydney Davis, Managing Editor

EDITORIAL BOARD

Contents

MEDIEVALIA ET HUMANISTICA

Byzantine Studies and Western Literatures

A FOREWORD

Paul J. Alexander and Mary E. Giffin

THE APPEARANCE IN *Medievalia et Humanistica* of three essays on Byzantine literature and its importance in relation to the literature of Western Europe marks the present interest in extending American scholarship in medieval languages and literatures eastward to Byzantium. In 1968 the Modern Language Association announced the formation of the Modern Greek Studies Association, to be affiliated with the American Historical Association, the American Council of Teachers of Foreign Languages, and the Modern Language Association. A symposium of the Modern Greek Studies Association, centering attention on contemporary Greek literature, took place in 1969. The officers of the Medieval Section of the Modern Language Association, planning in their program for 1970 to welcome the Byzantinologists of the Modern Language Association to the Medieval Interdepartmental Section, concluded to include papers by a classical scholar, a literary scholar, and an historical scholar. Dr. Francis R. Walton, director of the Gennadius Library, Athens, was invited to present the incunabula of that important collection; Professor Paul J. Alexander of the University of California at Berkeley, whose interest in the history of Byzantium extends to the literature as well, was to assist in combining the disciplines of the program; and Professor Byron C. P. Tsangadas, representing the Modern Greek Studies Association, was to deliver a comment at the close of the program.

Earlier versions of the following three essays by Dr. Francis R. Walton, Professor Charity C. Willard, and Professor Paul J. Alexander were read before the Medieval Section of the Modern Language Association at the annual meeting of the association in December, 1970, and have been revised for publication in *Medievalia et Humanistica*. They have served to introduce Byzantine studies into the Modern Language Association, and each essay makes a significant contribution to scholarship.

Dr. Francis R. Walton's paper on "Incunabula in the Gennadius Library" represents a classical approach to the common theme of Byzantine studies and Western literatures. Essentially, the paper is a survey of the incunabula printed in the Greek language and preserved in the remarkable Athenian library founded by the Greek diplomat and bibliophile Joannes Gennadius (✝ 1932). It so happens that all the extant incunabula were printed in Italy. Dr. Walton's contribution, therefore, illustrates the interests of Italian printers and publishers, and indirectly of the Italian literati, of the last quarter of the fifteenth century in Greek literature, and here lies the great value of his article. The texts represented in the Gennadius Library span the entire range of Greek literature from Homer to the Turkish conquest and beyond. The Greek poets of the pre-Byzantine period (Homer, Hesiod, Theocritus) account for several of the thirty-nine incunabula in the library, as do prose authors such as Aristotle, Theophrastus, and Lucian. Works of Byzantine literature, properly speaking, appear rather rarely in Dr. Walton's survey, presumably because the Italian reading public of the late fifteenth century was not interested in medieval Greek literature. Apparent exceptions, such as a copy of the *Greek Anthology*, only confirm this impression, for the main value of this tenth-century collection lies in the classical poems contained therein. Byzantine civilization is represented in this survey of incunabula exclusively by the Greek scholars who compiled the grammars and edited the classical texts with the aid of which Italians and other Westerners of the late fifteenth and sixteenth centuries gained access to the treasures of classical Greek literature.

Unlike Dr. Walton, Professor Charity C. Willard approaches the theme of Byzantine studies and Western literatures from a Western rather than an Eastern starting point in "A Fifteenth-Century Burgundian Version of the *Roman de Florimont*." In her introductory remarks she sketches the interest of the fifteenth-century Burgundian court in the Alexander cycle. She then concentrates on two literary works concerned with Florimont, the legendary grandfather of Alexander, namely Aimon de Varennes' versified *Florimont* of the twelfth century and a prose version, composed in the fifteenth century and contained in a manuscript of the Bibliothèque Nationale at Paris, *fonds français* 12566. Professor Willard marshals a considerable body of evidence in favor of the hypothesis that both the poetic and prose versions may derive from a Byzantine tradition of the eleventh century, via a Latin translation made in the East at the time of the Crusades. She also shows that the matter of Florimont had further repercussions in Western literature, notably in *Mélusine* and in Rabelais.

Finally, in an essay on "Byzantium and the Migration of Literary Works and Motifs: The Legend of the Last Roman Emperor," Professor Paul J. Alexander follows the migration of a literary motif from its origin in Syriac-speaking seventh-century Mesopotamia, through its emergence in a text translated into Byzantine Greek in the same century, to its role in the Latin Middle Ages and its revival in nineteenth-century Germany.

It had been the hope of the planners of the Medieval Interdepartmental Section that the program would convey an impression of the wealth and sophistication of Byzantine literature and of its meaning for students of Western literature. The contributors have done much to justify these hopes, but undoubtedly much remains to be done and must be left to similar occasions. The contributors illustrate, each in his own way, aspects of the influence of Byzantine literature on the literatures of France, Italy, and Germany. Little, however, is said in these papers of Byzantine influence on English literature and nothing at all of the enormous formative impact on the Slavic literatures. Furthermore, there remain many literary genres, represented by a great quantity of Byzantine works, that have not been tapped at all by the contributors. We are thinking particularly of the twin jewels of Byzantine literature, theology and historiography, but also of many other kinds of literature in which Byzantium excels: the epigram, the saint's life, and the like. Above all, the acknowledged masterpieces of Byzantine literature and their influence remain to be presented: the Pseudo-Dionysian corpus, the religious poetry of Romanos, the *Life of the Emperor Basil* by his grandson Constantine Porphyrogenitus, or the epic poem *Digenis Akrites*, to mention only a few of the many bright stars in the Byzantine literary firmament. There is clearly a great deal of work to be done in the field of Byzantine literature and its influences.

So far as American scholarship is concerned, there can be no doubt that Byzantine literature is a neglected field of study. The Center for Byzantine Studies at Dumbarton Oaks, for example, while it has made notable contributions to the study of Byzantine history, archaeology, art, religion, and even science, has paid relatively little attention to Byzantine literature and philology. Not even the most indispensable tools, such as a handbook of Byzantine literature written in the English language, not to speak of a comprehensive and adequate dictionary of Byzantine Greek, presently exist. The initiative of the Modern Language Association to include Byzantine literature in its program and the willingness of *Medievalia et Humanistica* to open its pages to contributions relating to Byzantine literature will therefore be applauded not only by Byzantinists but also by students of medieval and modern literature who realize that Byzantium played an important role in the Western literary tradition and that this tradition must be studied in its entirety.

The time is ripe for American scholars, especially younger persons still in the formative periods of training and study, to fill the gap left by their elders and to rediscover and analyze the role played by Byzantine civilization in the formation of Western literatures. If the present program of the Medieval Interdepartmental Section of the Modern Language Association should have made a modest contribution to a development of this kind, the labors of the organizers and participants would be amply rewarded.

Incunabula in the
Gennadius Library

Francis R. Walton

THE GENNADIUS LIBRARY in Athens is a specialized collection, the subject of which is, in a word, Greece. First and foremost a research library, it is also a bibliophile's delight and a rare-book library of considerable distinction. It owes its existence to the Greek diplomat Joannes Gennadius (1844–1932), a man of modest means but great vision and ability. It was always his intention that his library should find its permanent home in Greece, and in 1922 he presented his beloved books, the fruit of a lifetime of discriminating collecting, to the American School of Classical Studies, in trust for the Greek people and for the scholars of all nations.[1]

As a devoted patriot, Mr. Gennadius wished his collection to represent the history and achievement of Greece in its entirety, from earliest times down to his own day. Within this framework, however, his interests were thoroughly catholic. The dark centuries of Turkish domination concerned him no less than the splendors of Byzantium, and the political pamphlets of mid-nineteenth century Athens were sought out as zealously as any choice editions of Demosthenes. He realized the collective value, as documentation, of ephemeral materials. And being by temperament a perfectionist, he sought to make his collection as comprehensive as possible. He was not content with a representative edition or two of each Greek author. Ideally he must have them all, and though he was nearly seventy before he acquired the first edition of Homer, the series of printed Greek texts down to, say, 1550 is remarkably complete. By the time of his death the collection amounted to some 26,000 volumes. Today it has nearly double that number, but its growth has faithfully followed the lines of the original pattern, and it remains a specifically Greek library.

Among its many treasures is a small but important group of incunabula. Few as these are, they provide a good twofold sampling of the

7

collection as a whole: first as representing several of its areas of major interest and strength, and again as including a number of choice examples of the fine and distinctive copies that so delighted Gennadius the bibliophile.

Appropriately, well over half of the incunabula in the Gennadius Library are Greek — thirty-nine of a total of seventy. The figure is more impressive than it may at first sound, for while from the invention of printing $\pm$ 1450 to the end of the century forty thousand books (i.e., separate titles or editions) were published, fewer than seventy Greek books had been printed by 1500.[2]

According to Proctor the first attempts at printing bits of Greek were made in 1465, at Mainz and at Subiaco. The German effort was a disastrous failure, and the effective development of Greek printing took place in Italy. By the early seventies presses that employed some Greek types existed in Rome, Venice, Milan, Padua, Ferrara, Treviso, and Vicenza, and what is perhaps the earliest entire Greek text ever printed is assigned to Brescia, ca. 1474.[3]

The earliest in our series of Greek books is the *Epitomē tōn oktō tou logou merōn*, the *Summary of the eight parts of speech*, compiled by Constantine Lascaris of Byzantium and printed at Milan by Dionysius Paravisinus 30 January 1476 (Goff, L-65).[4] The foreword, in Greek and in Latin, is addressed by Demetrius the Cretan to the "noble and studious youths" whose desire to learn Greek he has long admired. Wishing both to help them and to benefit himself, he says, he has finally, after much experimentation, solved the technical difficulties of printing Greek and as the first product of his types he offers them this useful compendium of Greek grammar.

The 1476 Lascaris is, indeed, generally cited as the earliest printed Greek book, and the claim is not unjustified, provided its terms are made clear. The Lascaris is without question the earliest *dated* Greek book, and this holds true whether the date 30 January places it in the year 1476 or 1477 by our reckoning. It is also the first book printed *wholly* in Greek. But any absolute claim to priority can be disputed by at least two undated publications (both, moreover, belonging to the Graeco-Latin class): the book ascribed to Brescia 1474, the mock-heroic *Battle of the Frogs and Mice*; and the *Erotemata* of Chrysoloras, printed in parallel columns with a Latin translation and ascribed to Vicenza 1475 or 1476.[5] An even earlier rival is an adaptation of Guarino's abridgement of the *Erotemata* of Chrysoloras, printed with a Latin translation and commentary at Venice ca. 1471.[6] To judge by

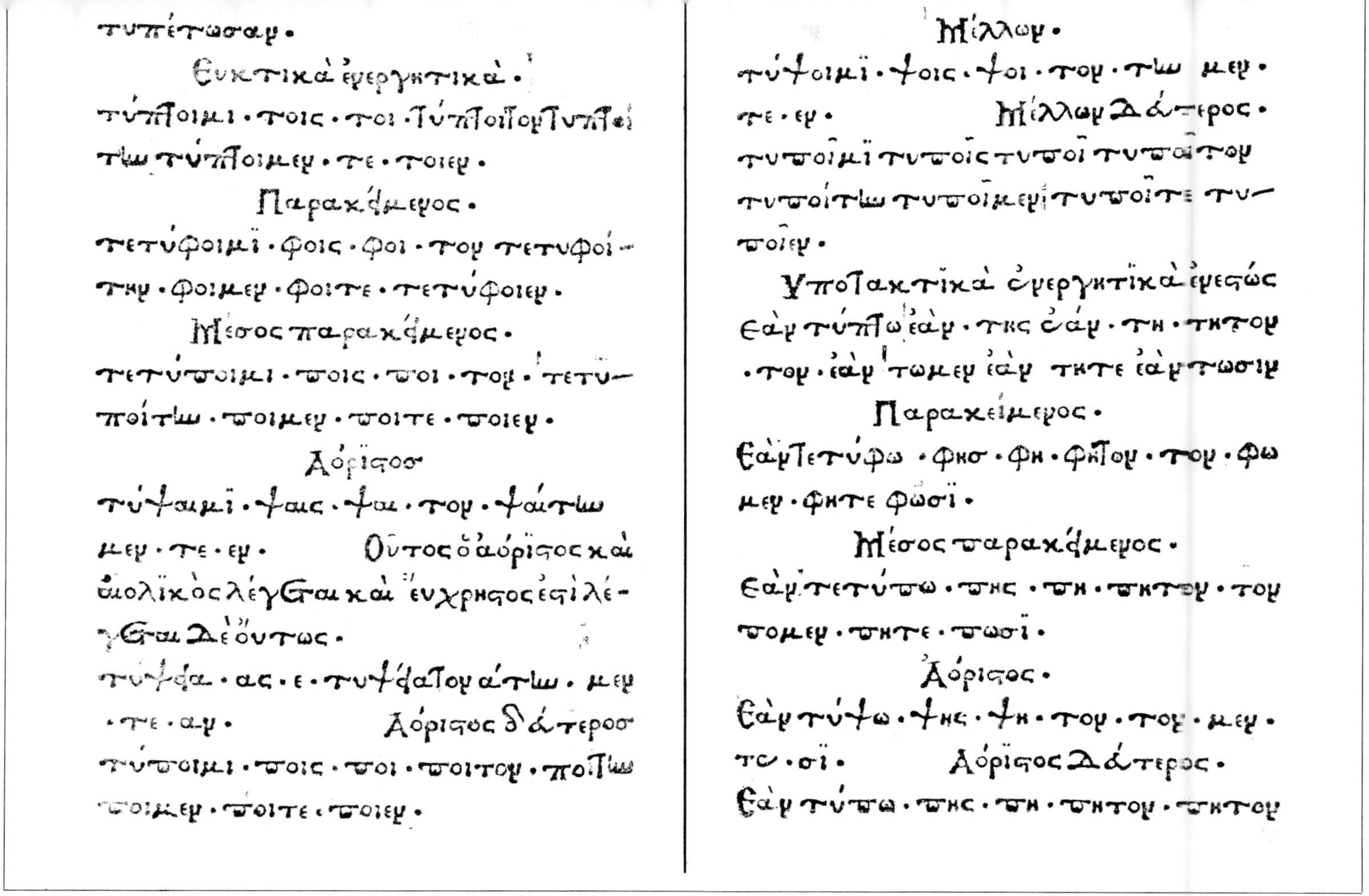

τυπτετωσαν·

Μέλλων·

τύ·τοιμὶ·τ̣οις·τ̣οι·τ̣ου·τ̣ω μεν·
τε·εν·   Μέλλων ἁπλούστερος·
τυπτοιμι·τυπτοιστυποι τυπτοιτου
τυπτοιτυ·τυπτοιμεν·τυπτοιτε·τυ·
ποιεν·

Παρακείμενος·

Ὑποτακτικὰ ἐνεργητικὰ ἐρέσθως
ἐὰν τυπτῶ ἐὰν τῆς ἐὰν τῆ·τη·τιτον
τον·ἐὰν τω μεν ἐὰν τητε ἐαρτυπτον

Παρακείμενος·

ἐὰν τετύφω·φης·φη·φιτον·τον·
μεν·φητε φωσι·

Μέσος παρακείμενος·

ἐὰν τετύφωσι·φης·φη·φητον·του·
φωμεν·φητε·φωσι·

Ἀόριστος·

ἐὰν τύ·της·τη·φ̣τον· —
το·οι·

Εὐκτικὰ ἐνεργητικὰ·
τυπτοιμι·τοις·τοι·τυπτοιον τυπτοι
τω τυπτοιμεν·τε·τοιεν·

Παρακείμενος·

τετυφοιμι·φοις·φοι·φου τετυφοι—
τημ·φοιμεν·φοιτε·τετυφοιεν·

Μέσος παρακείμενος·

τετυφοιμι·τοις·τοι·τοι·τον·τον· τετυ—
ποιτω·τοιμεν·τοιτε·τοιεν·

Ἀόριστος·

τύ·φαιμι·φαις·φαι·τον·φαιτην
μεν·τε·εν· Οὗτος ὁ ἀόριστος και
μολιχος λεγεται και ἐνχρησος ἐστι λε—
γεται·ἐχ ἐοντως·

τυπτφαι·αις·αι·ε·τυτψαι αν·τψην·μεν
τυπτφαι·τε·εν·

λοιπ...·λοιπω·μα·σης·σητε·λυπισε·
·σει·δεταγχαισιδου·
·δε·μ̣·φωτο·δη·δηκ̣·τον·τον·
·δεμ·δου·δου·μ̣·ψ·ενε·κτενκτε·τον
·δεμ·δοτ·μ̣·τ̣ης·σ̣·τωκττε·τωσι·
Ἀόριστος ἁπλούστερου·
τε·οι·

Ἀόριστος·
ἐὰν τύ·τ·της·τ·η·ωτη·του·
ποιμεν·ποιτε·ποισι·

Μέσος παρακείμερος·

ἐὰν τετύψωσι·σης·ση·σητε·του·
ψωμεν·σητε·σωσι·

Ἀόριστος·
ἐὰν τύ·ψω·φης·φι·φιτον·τον·
μεν·φιτε φωσι·

μω...·λοιτον·ποιτ̣μι·
ρους·λοιτω·τοιτον·ποιτ̣μι·
τυπτοιμι·τοις·οιοι·ιποιπι

Ἀόριστος δεύτερος·
τυπτοιμι·λοιτω·τοιτον·ποιτμι·

PLATE I

PLATE II

ΗΛΙΟΣ ΚΥΑΝΕΑΙ ΠΕΤΡΑΣ ΥΠΟΝ. ΟΙ ΤΑ ΒΟΛΗΖΑΝ
ΛΗΤΟΙΔΗ ΚΑΤΑ ΝΗΙΟΝ Ο ΔΙΕΞΙΗΣ ΕΝΙΟΝΤΟΣ
ΘΕΛΓΕΤ ΑΚΟΥΗ ΘΥΜΟΝ. ΑΧΟΣ ΔΕ ΛΙΝ ΗΡΑΚΛΗΙ
ΛΕΙΠΟΜΕΝΟΙ· ΚΑΙ ΤΟΙΟΝ ΕΠΟΣ ΠΑΝΤΕΣΣΙ ΜΕΤΗΥΔΑ.
Ω ΦΙΛΟΙ· ΟΙΟΥ ΥΠΟΙ ΑΠΟΠΛΑΓΧΘΕΝΤΕΣ ΑΡΓΗΣ
ΡΕΙΠΕΤΕ ΔΗ ΤΗΝ ΤΟΞΙΟΝ ΠΛΟΟΝ· ΕΙ ΓΑΡ ΙΤΑ ΜΙΝ
ΔΑΙΚΤΑΛΟΥ ΙΝ ΜΕΓΑΡΟΙΣΙ ΚΑΤΑΥΤΟΘΙ ΠΑΤΡΟΙ ΕΜΙΟ
ΟΙ ΔΕ ΕΙΔΑΝ. ΟΤΕ ΔΕΒΡΟ ΔΙ ΑΙΔΟΣ ΗΡΕΙΟΙΟ
ΠΕΖΟΣ ΕΒΗ ΖΩΣΤΗΡΑ ΦΙΛΟΥ ΤΟ ΛΕΜΟΙΟ ΚΟΜΙΖΩΝ
ΙΡΠΟΛΥ ΤΗΣ ΙΕΜΙ ΔΕΥΡΕ ΝΕΟΝ ΧΝΟΛΟΝΤΑΣ ΙΟΥΛΟΥ.
ΕΝΘΑ ΔΙ ΕΠΙ ΦΡΙΟΛΑΟ ΚΑΣΙΓΝΗΤΟΙΟ ΘΑΝΟΝΤΟΣ
ΗΜΕΤΕΡΟΥ. ΜΥΘΟΙ ΙΝ ΥΠΑΝΔΡΑΞΙΝ. ΟΝΤΙΝΑ ΛΑΟΣ
ΟΙΚΤΙΣΤΟΙΣ ΕΛΕΓΟΙΣΙΝ ΟΔΥΡΕΤΑΙ ΕΞΕΤΙ ΚΕΙΝΟΥ
ΑΘΑΚΥΑΝ. ΤΙΤΗΝ ΑΠΕΚΑΙΝΥΤΟ ΠΥΓΜΑΧΕΟΝΤΑ
ΚΑΡΤΕΡΟΝ ΟΙ ΠΑΝΤΕΣΣΙ ΜΕΤΕΠΡΕΠΕΝ ΗΙΘΕΟΙΣΙΝ
ΕΙΔΟΣ ΙΝΑΔΕ ΒΙΗΝ· ΧΑΜΑΔΙΣ ΔΕ ΟΙ ΗΛΑΣΟΔΟΝΤΑΣ,

ΚΑΙ ΜΑΡΙΑΝ ΑΥΝΟΥ ΣΙ ΛΑΘΩΝ ΑΝΕΡΑΣ ΟΡΜΗΘΕΝΤΕΣ
ΛΥΘΕΝΤΑΙ ΑΜΥΚΟΙΟ ΚΑΤΑ ΚΛΕΟΣ Ο ΠΡΙΝ ΑΚΟΥΟΝ.
ΑΛΛΑ ΚΑΙ ΑΡΟΜΩΝ ΕΘΕΝΤΟ ΜΕΤΑ ΣΦΙΣΙ ΤΟΙΟ ΕΚΗΤΙ.
ΑΥΤΟΝ ΔΕΙ ΤΕ ΘΕΟΝ ΠΟΛΥΑΕΥΚΕΑ ΔΕΞΙΟΑΝΤΟ.
ΠΑΝΤΟΘΕΝ ΑΓΡΟΜΕΝΟΙ. ΕΠΕΙΗ ΜΑΛΑ ΤΟΙ ΓΕΡΙΑΗΡΟΝ
ΑΝΤΙΒΙΗΝ ΒΕΒΡΥΣΙΝ ΥΠΕΡΦΙΑΛΟΙΣ ΠΟΛΕΜΙΖΩΝ.
ΚΑΙ ΑΗ ΠΑΣΧΥΑΙΗ ΜΕΓΑΡΟΝ ΕΝΤΟΣ ΟΣ ΛΥΚΙΟ
ΚΕΙΝ ΜΑΡ ΦΙΛΟΤΗΤΙ ΜΕΤΑ ΠΤΟΛΙΕΘΡΟΝ ΙΟΝΤΕΣ.
ΔΑΙΤΗΝ ΑΜ ΦΙΕΡΟΝ ΤΕΡΠΟΝΤΟ ΤΕ ΘΥΜΟΝ ΕΔΕΣΣΙΝ.
ΑΙΣΟΝΙΔΗΣ ΜΕΝ ΟΙ ΓΕΜΕΝΗ ΚΑΙ ΟΥΝΟ ΜΕΚΑΣΤΟΥ
ΣΦΙΤΕΡΩΝ ΜΥΘΕΙΤ ΑΙΤΑΡΩΝ ΠΕΛΙΑΟ ΤΕ ΦΕΤΜΑΣ.
ΗΔΙ ΛΗΜΝΙΑ ΔΕΞΙΣΙΝ ΕΠΕΣΕΙΝ ΟΝΤΟ ΓΥΝΑΙΞΙΝ
ΟΣΣΑ ΤΕ ΚΥΖΙΚΟΝ ΑΜΦΙ ΔΟΛΟΙΟΝ ΙΗΝ ΕΤΕΛΕΣΣΑΝ.
ΜΥΣΙΔΑ ΤΟΙ ΑΦΙΚΟΝΤΟ ΚΙΟΝ ΟΘΟΙ ΚΑΛΛΙΡΟΝ ΗΡΑ
ΗΡΑΚΛΕΗΝ. ΛΕΚΟΝΤΙ ΝΟΗ. ΓΛΑΥΚΟΙΟ ΤΕ ΒΑΞΙΝ.
ΓΕΦΡΑΔΕ ΚΑΙ ΒΕΒΡΥΚΑΣ ΟΠΟΙ ΑΜΥΚΟΝ ΤΕ ΔΑΙΞΑΝ.
ΚΑΙ ΦΙΝΗΟΣ ΕΕΙΠΕ ΘΕΟΠΡΟΠΙΑΣ ΤΕ ΔΥΗΝ ΤΕ·

Dātes quantū pzofe ₹ siue familie victu cōter confecuerūt eₓpendere in vsū codonata vel quantū cum ōmissario cuₓ ₹ familia habeāt pleniffimā peccatoₓ remiffionē soli tam dari tam in anno iubilei ₡ euni᷑bus cōtra faracenos pzo occupatione terre sancte aut contra Turcos.

Jtem ₡ tale₃ dātes ₹ quilibet de eoₓ familia poffint fibi eligere vnū ₹ done nū pfeffozem sacerdote₃ ſcͮarem vel religioſum cuiuſcū₡ regionis ₡ poffit eos abſoluere ab ōmibus peccatis quanticū₡ grauibus etiā fi talia effiet pzo per ₡ fedes aplica effet merito cōfulenda.

Dcͤio ₹ a cēſuris ₹ penis ōmibus a iure vel per ſtatuta quecū₡ inflictis ſcdi aplicͤ relenate femel in vita.

De nō referuatis aplicͤe ſcͮd totiē₃ quotiens id petierint.

₹ in moztis articulo plenariā remiffionē dare valeat.

Jtem piatem babeat pſtatus confeffoz electus cōmutandi ōia ₹ora pzetereᵃ re religionis ₹ tͤuente emiffa per pfacͤe in iſtam ſanctā expeditionē acͮ boc eſt ₡ ſtanti tribuunt vltra pfatam ſummā quantū vota eoₓ merito ſint eſtimanda.

Suſpendunt oēs indulſcͤtie plenarie ₹ pͤales in vita vel immote conceffe eccleſiis monaſteriis piis locis viuerſitatibus ₹fraternitatis ac ſingulariter₃ perſo nis vl₡ ad triennid ſe₡uens. exceptis pzo cruciata aut inſula jſbodi vel in re₃ no Sicilie citra fanum.

Dtur facultas pfato fratri Angelo cōmiffario aplico ab eo deputatis ₹ pellen cͮ oēs pzedicatoz₃ ad pͤdicandū fupaſcriptas bullas.

Jtem componendi ſup incertis ₹ vſuris.

Jtem fup ſymoniacie in ordine vel beneficiis.

Jtem diſpenſandi in ōnibus irregularitatibus exceptis pzo bomicidio volūta rio ₹ bigamia.

Jtem diſpenſandi in foro ₹ſcͤentie in ₃͠ibus affinitatis ₹ pͤa₃uinitatis vel ad terius impedinenti fecͤeti exſiſtente poſt ₹ͤtactū matrimoniū excepto pͤmo ₃͠n affinitatis recto vel tranſuerſali ₹ recta linea aſcendenti ₹ deſcendentiᵃ.

Jtem cōponendi in foro ₹ſcͤente fuper certis mobilibᵘ₃ monaſteriis eccleſiis aut eccleſiaſticis pſonis debitis qui repetii indicialiter nō poffint.

Jtem cōponendi fup quibuſlibet maleficiis in terriis eccͤie excepto bomicidiū voluntariū ₹ reſtituendi bona cōfiſcata nondū diſfracta.

Jtem pſtatus cōmiffariue pͤt quecū₡ dubia interpͤrtari et declarare qui de mͤte pontificis eſt certus.

Jtem cͤ oͤfcͤe quoſcū₡ pͤdicatoz₃ ee indulſcͤntionis ₹ maledictionis eterne nequiᵘ₃ dircͤte vel indirecte in toto vel in parte ₹mittat fraudem vel retrabatᵘ volente ₹pone re aut dare adam ſanctū opus.

---

iūniolabiliter obſeruari. Et ₃eneraliter quicquid per ipm nuncii ₹ ₹mifſariū urū et deputandos ab eo in ₹miffie fuerit quolibet oзdinaum. ₂los enim ōni bus ₹ ſingulis cuiuſcū₡ ſtatus gradus oзdinis vel ₹ditionis exſtant diſtrictius p cipiendo fub excoͤe late ſine ₹ eterne maledictionis ac pecuniaria ipſius nuncii ₹ cōmiffarii arbitrio qualitate facti ₹ pſone attenta moderanda ₹ de facto a ₹tra faciecͤibus exi₃enda pena Jubibemus ne in ₹miffie ₹ circa ea fraudem aut do lum ₹mittant nicue pzoponentie in capfie feu traͤicie pͤlicͤie oзdinata ſuffra₃ta immittere feu fup male ablatie ₹ vſurie aut aliis bonie incertis ac penis ₹pone re vel alie quolibet ad boc fanctū opus defenſionie fidei aliqua auxilia pſtare ab bmōi eoₓ pzopofito in toto vel pzo parte directe vel indirecte tacite vel expſſe retrabere quoquō pſunant. ₂ion obſtantibus fris nrͤis per quas dudum voluiᵬ mus ut piciˢtam facultatiſ eliŭŭendi pͤfeffozem ₹ abſoluendi ut pͤferuͤr in certie caſ bus inibi expſſie talͤ facultaͤe ſuffulti nemini poffent de abſoluͤis bnͤificio pzo uidere. quibus illarū ₹ derogatoz₃ in eis inferuͤi clauſulaͤi tenozem enu₃ fi de verbo ad verbū mentio fieri deberet ₹ in illis caͤeretur expͤiſe ₡ per quaſ cun₃ clauſulas ₹ derogaͤiones eis nō intelli₃ereͤur dero₃aͤi pzo expͤffo ₹ in ſerto bͤiͤe quo ad ₹miffa nominatim ₹ ſpecifice dero₃aͤ₃ acͮ aliis aplicͤe cͮ ſtitutionibus ₹ oзdinatͤⁱbus ₹ꝛariis quibuſcū₡. ſeu fi aliquibuſ vel eoₓ oзdi nibus cͤ ter vel diuiſim a dicta ſiͤfede indultum ₡ ipi aut dicͤoₓ oзdinum pſo ne ad publicandū aliquaꝩ fras feu indulſcͤntiaꝩ bmoi inuͤ cōpelli feu ₡ inͤ dici ſuſpendi vel excͤoͤiari nͤo poffint per fras aplicͤe nͤo facientͤe plenā et expͤffam ac de verbo ad verbū de indulto bmͤoi mentionem. ₂lulli er₃o ōniͤo bͤoim licͤeat bͤanc pa₃inͤam nͤre volunͤaͤie pͤſtitutionis pͤenſionis pzobibitio nie applicaͤionis ₹cefſionie inbibitionis ₹ derogaͤionie infrin₃ere vel ei auſu temͤario ₹traire. Siquis auͤt boc artͤempͤare pͤfumpferit indi₃nauͤem ōniͤpo tentis dei ac beaͤoₓ ₂etri ₹ ₂auli apłozum eiᵘ ſe nouͤit incurſurū. Datum ₂ome apud Sanctumpetri. Anno incarnaͤionis dnͤice ₂ͤilleſimoquadrin ₃enteſimooctua₃eſimo ₡nͤo pzidie non. decͤembris. ₂ontificaͤᵘ nͤri anno decimo.

PLATE III

INCIPIT TRACTATVS QVIDAM DE

turcis put ad p̄sens ecclesia sancta ab eis af
fligitur collect9 diligenti discussione scrip
turaƶ a quibuſdá fratrib9 p̄dicatoƶ ordi
nis qui etiam de tribus principaliter trac/
tat·ſ·de auꞇenticatione scripturaƶ loqué/
tiũ de p̄ſenti afflictione ecclesie ſcꝺo de cul
pis et cauſis huius afflictionis·Tercio de ei
us duratione et termino q̃tuƺ uidelieƺ té
poris ecclesia ab eis affligetur

IRCA amariſſimam afflictionem eccle
ſie put a perfidis turcis iam noſtris in
tempꝑibus·ipſa mater ecclesia affligiꞇ·
Quatuor ꝑ ordineƺ ſunt declaranda iuxta
quatuor dubia que circa eandé afflictioneƺ
poſſut oriri·Primo an ipſa preſens affilctio
ſit auꞇéticis ſanctoƶ ſcripturis quo ad quá
titatem ſue duratóis preſignata·Scꝺo an
ipſa diuine puidentie pariter et gubernató
ni immediate ſit ſubiecta·Tercio an etiá ac
tóibus et influéciis corpum celeſtiũ ſit ſub/
iecta· Quarto an ipſa valeat fato·i ·ordina
tioni et diſpoſitói cauſaƶ ſecundaƶ aliquo/
mó eſſe ſubordinata·Prima aút ꝑs priuci/
paliter diuiditur in tria membra·cú circa
cá maior et utilior uideꞇ eſſe difficultas

PLATE IV

the single page I have seen reproduced, one might question whether the amount of Greek is enough to allow its consideration, and it is probably on this account that Proctor does not include it in his list of Graeco-Latin incunabula.

More interesting than the question of priority, and more significant, is the fact that three of the four books under discussion are grammars. This is not mere accident. However eager the young humanists were for Greek texts, it is clear that they were even more eager for grammars and dictionaries, the basic tools that would open to them the treasures of Hellenic literature. The works of the fifteenth-century Greek grammarians, above all Chrysoloras and Lascaris, and of the lexicographer Craston, account for a full third of all the Greek books printed in this period. And well into the middle of the sixteenth century, grammars, whether by Greek or Western scholars, continued to make up a significant part of the Greek book trade.

Ten of our thirty-nine Greek incunabula are grammars, and one of them, a Chrysoloras ascribed to a Florentine press of ca. 1498–1500 (Plate I) has the distinction of being the only copy recorded in American ownership (Goff, C-491).[7] These ten incunabula are, further, the nucleus of an important collection of early Greek grammars and of the closely related collection of treatises on the still-vexed Pronunciation Question.

The second oldest Greek book in the Gennadeion (which is also the second oldest dated Greek book) is the Greek and Latin Psalter (Goff, P-1035) printed at Milan 20 September 1481 by Bonus Accursius. This is the first printing in Greek of any portion of the Bible, in a fine copy with unusually wide margins. The library has also the undated Greek Psalter printed in red and black by Aldus ca. 1496–1498 (Goff, P-1033), but unfortunately lacks the earlier Venetian Greek Psalter of 1486. With these two volumes we may class the only other religious text among the Greek incunabula, a charming miniature (11.5 cm.) book of *Hours*, printed by Aldus 5 December 1497 (Goff, H-391).

These three books again provide the starting point for important collections, one of liturgical books (predominantly, of course, those of the Eastern Orthodox Church) and the other of the Greek Bible. The latter collection picks up early in the next century with the polyglot Psalter of Genoa 1516 (which incidentally contains the first printed biography of Christopher Columbus), the first printing of the

Greek New Testament (Basel 1516, edited by Erasmus), and the first complete Bible in Greek, the Aldine of 1518.[8]

The third oldest Greek book in the Library fittingly introduces the largest and most important group of Greek incunabula, works of Greek literature. This is the *editio princeps* of Homer (Goff, H-300), printed at Florence in 1488, by far the most extensive Greek work yet undertaken and a veritable masterpiece. The Gennadeion copy, in two volumes, is handsomely illuminated. The Homer is by no means the rarest of Greek incunabula (according to Goff there are more than thirty copies in American collections alone), but it has always been in demand as one of the landmarks in the history of printing (how satisfying that it was published in Florence rather than Venice!), and it is interesting to note that when Mr. Gennadius finally acquired a copy, in 1913, he paid the then-princely price of £425, nearly four times as much (to judge by the available record) as he paid for any other single item in his whole career. The text was edited by Demetrius Chalcondyles (or Chalcocondyles), a native of Athens who was professor of Greek at the Studio Fiorentino from 1475 to 1491. The two Nerli brothers, of whom we know only that they were of gentle birth and were deeply interested in Greek letters, provided the funds to have it published. And, as the colophon tells us, it was put into print by the "toil and dexterity" of Demetrius of Milan, the Cretan — the very man who had designed the types for the 1476 Lascaris.

Homer is not, as we might have wished, the first classical Greek text to be printed, though only an Aesop and a volume of Theocritus and Hesiod (both Milan, ca. 1480), and two printings of the *Batrachomyomachia* (Brescia, ca. 1474; Venice, 1486) preceded it. More surprising, it had no successor until 1493, when Chalcondyles, by now in Milan, had his edition of Isocrates printed there (Goff, I-210). From this point on, however, there was to be a steady stream of Greek books (at least thirty-seven in the years 1494–1500), mostly of classical authors. In Florence a remarkable series began to appear in 1494. The man responsible was Janus Lascaris,[9] who had succeeded Chalcondyles in the chair of Greek. One of the most versatile, able, and attractive of the Greek exiles who found refuge in Italy, it was he who persuaded Lorenzo di Medici to form a Greek library, and to this end he himself made two journeys to the East to collect manuscripts. It was undoubtedly his study of these, and his lectures on them, that led him eventually to edit and publish some of their treasures.

The first to appear was the *Greek Anthology*, 11 August 1494

(Goff, A-765). The Gennadeion copy is beautifully illuminated but unfortunately lacks the final seven leaves, which contained the dedicatory epistle and the colophon. History is the culprit here, not mere carelessness or vandalism. The book was dedicated to Piero, the hapless son of Lorenzo, who three months later, in November 1494, found it expedient to flee from Florence. As a futile gesture of *damnatio memoriae* the dedicatory leaves were excised in all copies of the *Anthology* still unsold. Ours is one of these. It takes only a glance to see that here is something new, unlike the work of any preceding Greek press or, indeed, of any that was to follow.[10] The text is printed solely in capitals, and from his own dedicatory letter we know that it was Janus himself who designed them. He had certainly seen Greek inscriptions on his travels and, when faced with the problems of printing, it was perhaps this that suggested to him a ready alternative to the variety of letter forms and ligatures found in manuscript texts. Two complete sets of capitals, large and small, together with movable accents and the necessary marks of punctuation, required a font of only 61 sorts — compared with 223 for the types of the 1476 Milan press and an even larger number in some others, notably the early Aldines. The capitals had also the advantage of greater legibility, above all (one would think) for tyros who were not accustomed to the complexities of Greek scribal hands.

Yet the experiment was not a success. Only two more books appeared wholly in capitals: the first edition of Euripides (four plays only) and a small collection of one-line proverbs followed by the *Hero and Leander* of Musaeus. So far the only extensive passage in prose was his own dedicatory epistle in the *Anthology*, but perhaps this was enough to convince him that capitals, however suited to the dignity of verse, were less satisfactory for prose. His next two authors were to be Callimachus (an undated edition) and the 1496 Apollonius Rhodius (Goff, A-924). In both cases the poems were accompanied by ancient commentaries, and he now added a font of minuscules for the scholia, reserving the capitals for the text of the poems. In the Callimachus, scholia and text are printed separately, but the Apollonius combines the two on a single page, the text being centered on the inner margin and the scholia surrounding it on three sides. The effect is striking, and since the ratio of text and notes constantly varies each page is a new esthetic experience (Plate II).

The last major production of Lascaris and his Florentine press was the complete works of the prose satirist Lucian, also 1496 (Goff,

L-320). Capitals would have been totally impracticable for an undertaking of this magnitude, and even in minuscules it makes a folio volume of 524 pages. The Gennadeion copy, once the property of a Cardinal Trivulzio and later at Blenheim Palace, is one of two printed on vellum.[11]

Late in 1496, soon after the completion of the Lucian, Lascaris left Florence to serve under Charles VIII of France, and for the next twelve years and more his career was to be diplomatic. There was no one in Florence to carry on his work and there were no further experiments in the printing of Greek in capitals — none, so far as I know, for nearly three hundred years, until revived by Bodoni in Parma.[12]

In less than three years Lascaris, as editor and publisher, had more than doubled the number of classical Greek texts available in print. At almost the same time, in Venice the most famous of all Greek presses, that of Aldus Manutius, was being established. In five years, 1495–99, the Aldine press produced nineteen works, nearly a third of all Greek incunabula. Of these, three were grammars (including the first Greek grammar composed in Latin) and one a dictionary; two others, the Psalter and *Hours* already mentioned, were religious. The rest were literary or scholarly texts: Theocritus-Hesiod (of which we have two copies, one a variant); Aristophanes; a collection of Greek letters; two minor literary texts (Musaeus and the *Galeomyomachia*); a collection of grammatical writings; the works of Aristotle and Theophrastus (in five folio volumes); a collection of writers on astronomy; and the herbalist Dioscorides. Of the nineteen volumes the Gennadeion lacks only four: Craston's *Lexicon*, the Dioscorides, and the two minor poems. Several volumes of our Aristotle are copiously annotated, apparently in the hand of Nicolò Leoniceno, the famous Hellenist and physician who provided Aldus with at least one of the manuscripts used in the printing. And one of our copies of the Theocritus-Hesiod belonged to Pope Pius VI and is stamped with his arms.

The printing establishment of Aldus and his successors lasted till the closing years of the sixteenth century, and in the annals of Greek printing no name is more honored. Yet for all their services to Hellenism one cannot but regret that the early Aldine types, which effectively determined the course of Greek topography for several centuries, were among the least attractive of the fifteenth-century fonts. As Proctor bluntly says: "In truth, in spite of all his estimable qualities, Aldus seems to have been a man of phenomenally bad taste for his time" (p. 103).

Only one other Greek press requires separate mention, that of Zacharias Callierges, who, we are told, labored five years to perfect his types, for which on 21 September 1498 he secured a privilege stating "that he has caused to be cut a fount of most beautiful Greek letters, united with their accents, as has not been done before either so well or so beautifully" (Proctor, p. 120). With these types four folio volumes were printed in the years 1499 and 1500. These are generally considered among the most beautiful Greek books known, and the library is fortunate in having fine copies of three of them: the *Etymologicum Magnum*, dated 8 July 1499 (Goff, E-112); the Simplicius, issued only three months later, 27 October 1499 (Goff, S-535); and the last of the series, the Galen of 5 October 1500 (Goff, G-38).[13]

Mr. Gennadius was little interested in translations, even those made by Greek scholars, and his collection of incunabula included only two examples: Theodore Gaza's translation of Aristotle, *De animalibus* (Goff, A-973), printed at Venice in 1476, and an illuminated copy of Joannes Argyropoulos' translation of Aristotle, *Ethica ad Nicomachum* (Goff, A-981), printed at Florence ca. 1480. Several others have been added in recent years,[14] and more attention is now being given to strengthening this aspect of Renaissance Greek humanism in our collection.

Modern Greek literature finds at least token representation in a slender volume of great rarity, the poem of Demetrius Moschus, *Helen and Alexander*, published with a Latin translation by the author's friend Ponticus Virunius at Reggio Emilia "not before 1500" (Goff, M-865). It is of some interest (as the translator points out in his dedicatory preface) that the poet, like Helen herself, is a native Spartan. Only this copy and one at the Huntington Library are recorded in American collections. With this work we may perhaps class the *Epigrammata et Hymni* of Michael Marullus, published, probably under his own supervision, at Florence 26 November 1497 (Goff, M-342). Though the poems are all in Latin the poet himself was Greek, born in Constantinople in the year of the city's capture. He was drowned in 1500, and his early death, widely and sincerely mourned, was commemorated in verse by Janus Lascaris and by Ariosto among others.

Our extensive travel collection, which embraces not only Greece but the entire Near East, again has only minimal representation: a Cologne printing, ca. 1495, of Sir John Mandeville's *Itinerarius* (Goff, M-162). The alleged author is a rather shadowy figure, perhaps even a fabrication. This may justify our placing beside his volume what

13

might be called a "courtesy" incunabulum, i.e., a sixteenth-century imprint that passes muster because it has been described in one of the standard bibliographies of incunabula. The book in question is a charming edition of Joannes de Hese, *Itinerarius a Hierusalem . . . per diversas partes mundi* (Goff, H-148), printed at Paris by Robert Gourmont for Olivier Senant, and hence not before 1505. Apparently all editions are rare, and of this Paris edition (not in the British Museum or the Cambridge libraries)[15] the only other copy in American ownership is at the Boston Public Library.

The remaining group of incunabula all relate in one way or another to Eastern affairs and to the aftermath of the Fall of Constantinople in 1453. The West was deeply shaken by this calamity that its own blindness and bigotry had helped to produce, and among those most concerned were Aeneas Sylvius Piccolomini (Pius II, pope 1458–64) and the great cardinal Bessarion, born at Trebizond. From the hand of Aeneas Sylvius we have a brief but moving narrative of the Fall itself, *De captione urbis Constantinopolitane Tractatulus* (Goff, P-659), an undated printing ascribed to Rome 1488–90. Both this and the opening pages of the *Dialogus de somnio quodam* (Goff, P-669),[16] written soon after the event, show the deep impression that it made on him. More important, however, is the *Epistola ad Mahumetem*, the letter — actually a treatise — that he addressed to Mehmet the Conqueror, expounding the teachings of Christianity and seeking to convert the Sultan. We have two editions of this: the relatively common Treviso edition of 1475 (Goff, P-700) and one of the four printings, all of them rare, ascribed to Cologne, Ulrich Zel, 1469–72 (Goff, P-697; another copy in the Morgan Library). A collection of Mehmet's own letters, *Epistolae Magni Turci*, was evidently very popular. The Gennadeion has an edition of Padua, ca. 1475 (Goff, M-58).

Cardinal Bessarion, scholar, statesman, and patron-in-chief to the Greek refugees from the East, was second only to Pius II in his zeal for a crusade. In 1470 the aged prelate was deeply stirred by the Turkish capture of Euboea (or Negroponte) and wrote a series of impassioned appeals to the princes of Italy, urging them to lay aside their fraternal strife and unite against the common enemy of Christendom, the Turk. The Latin text was published at Paris in April 1471, and in the same year an Italian translation by Lodovico Carbone was printed in Venice (Goff, B-521). An interesting feature of the work is that it incorporates a translation of one of Demosthenes' orations against Philip of Macedon, the *First Olynthiac*, here provided with marginal notes by Bessarion to point up the analogy. So far as I can discover, this (and its Latin counterpart) are the first appearances in print of any work of Demosthenes. The Greek text was not published until 1504.

The Spanish bishop Rodriguez Sanchez de Arevalo, resident in Rome, as a gesture of sympathy addressed to his friend Bessarion an *Epistola lugubris et consolatoria de infelice expugnacione insule Euboye dicte Nigropontis*. It was printed at Rome in 1470, and within the year reprinted at Cologne (Goff, R-213) in a handsome folio volume of ten leaves. The contents, alas, are disappointing, hardly more than a series of pious and edifying banalities, with little or nothing of factual interest.

For over a hundred years Negroponte had been Venice's most cherished Eastern possession, her "pearl of the Orient," and the cruelty displayed by the victorious Mehmet, who had led the siege personally, was appalling even to that hardened age. Having promised to spare the *bailie*'s neck he had him sawn in two, and most of the male inhabitants, even children, were put to the sword. Europe, though it had done nothing to prevent the disaster, was alarmed, and for a while it looked as though a united front was possible. In the spring of 1471 a papal legation was sent to Ratisbon, where the Emperor himself was expected to attend the Diet. He did appear, though he was long in coming. There was much talk, including a surviving oration by the assistant legate, Giannantonio Campani, the shepherd boy who rose to be bishop and who edited Quintilian and Suetonius. The Gennadeion has an edition of the speech, printed at Rome ca. 1488–90 (Goff, C-76). The Diet proved inconclusive, and no action was taken.

The next major crisis in Turkish affairs was the siege of Rhodes in the summer of 1480. The Turks were finally beaten off, and Rhodes won a reprieve of forty-two years. Guillaume Caoursin, vice-chancellor of the Order of St. John, wrote an account of the siege, and this was published, perhaps before the year was out, at Venice and again in Parma. Of the Parma edition (Goff, C-109) the only American copies recorded are those in the Huntington Library and the Gennadeion.

Rhodes was safe, but only a few weeks later a Turkish force landed in southern Italy and seized Otranto, which it managed to hold for a year. The immediacy of the threat could no longer be ignored. Sixtus IV set a good example by patching up his quarrel with Florence and by contributing generously to the Armada. He also issued, on 4 December 1480, a *Bulla indulgentiarum pro expulsione Theucri de Italia*

(Goff, S-553).[17] This may well be our rarest incunabulum, though there is at least one other copy, in Stockholm. Hain 14805 records three leaves only; ours has a fourth, containing, on the recto, a "Summarium bulle precedentis" (Plate III).

Three weeks later, 27 December 1480, in a sermon preached at St. John Lateran on the Feast of St. John,[18] Stephanus Thegliatus, archbishop of Bar (and later of Patras), ends up a list of cities captured and sacked by the Turks with mention of Otranto. Our copy is one of two editions printed at Rome (Goff, T-126). The purport of the discourse is indicated by the heading: *Sermo in materie fidei contra Turcorum persecutionem.*

Finally, there are two works, both anonymous, that deal with the Turkish question in a broader, more general sense, historically and factually in the one case, theologically in the other.

The more important of these is commonly ascribed to a certain "George of Hungary," but all we know of the author is what he himself tells us, that as a youth in 1438 he was taken captive by the Turks at Sebeş in southeast Hungary (now in Rumania), spent many years in Turkey, and eventually escaped to Rome where, ca. 1475–80, he composed his *Tractatus de ritu et moribus Turcorum.* He wrote from first-hand knowledge, and while he was no great admirer of the Turks he never descends to the hysterical name-calling that is typical of so much of the anti-Turkish polemics. It is interesting that at the end he transliterates (and translates) several passages of Turkish literature, probably the first printing of Turkish. The book, not undeservedly, was popular and was still being printed, in the original Latin and in translation, at least as late as 1530. Of the early editions the Gennadeion has three: Rome, ca. 1481 (Goff, G-152); Cologne, ca. 1488 (Goff, G-153); and Cologne, ca. 1500 (Goff, G-154).

The theological work, composed in 1474 and first published in Rome, was perhaps never intended for more than a limited audience and apparently had only three printings. Of the Rome edition, ca. 1474/75 (Goff, T-501), we have the only American copy recorded (Plate IV). We have also the Nuremberg 1481 edition (Goff, T-503), in a fine copy stamped with the arms of Charles III of Spain. The short title, *Tractatus quidam de Turcis,* usually cited for the work is misleading. The subject is not the Turks, but rather "The present affliction of the Church at the hands of the Turks, showing that these sufferings were foretold in reliable prophecies, what sins of the Christians provoked them, and when they will end."

The Dominican authors examine a number of prophecies, ancient and modern, and demonstrate their relevance to the present situation. It is axiomatic to them that afflictions are visitations for sin, and hence that the greater the afflictions the greater must be the sins. The present afflictions are unprecedented. In a short period of time the Turks have overthrown two empires (Constantinople and Trebizond), four kingdoms, twenty provinces, and two hundred cities. The sins responsible must therefore be the most heinous, and by scrutiny of the authorities these are shown to be sodomy (said to be prevalent) and some irregularity in the administration of the Eucharist. Incidentally, the question is raised whether the Preaching Friars should denounce sodomy in their public sermons or whether this would only arouse greater interest in the vice. As to the duration of the affliction the prophecies reveal that it will last "eight weeks," i.e., fifty-six years (of which some few only remain to run) and that a minor Christian king will then arise who will recover all the lands lost to Christendom and will destroy both the Turkish power and Islam itself. The prophecy was not fulfilled. Prince Charming did not appear, or perhaps fresh sins provoked further afflictions. The *Tractatus* was quietly shelved and all but forgotten.

There are a few of our incunabula not accounted for in this survey: other Greek texts; three additional "courtesy" incunabula (one the only copy in Goff); and the *Genealogiae* of Boccaccio, a work that is tangential — but not irrelevant — to our areas of major interest and strength.[19]

The Gennadius Library cannot aspire to a large collection of incunabula, though we have acquired a half dozen in recent years and there are others that we hope some day to possess. Yet this small body of books, a tiny fraction of the output of their time, have an amazing power, the power of all "first things," to speak to us directly and to evoke a whole world of man's endeavors: his dreams, his disappointments, and his delusions — and not least his achievements.

NOTES

1. For a general account of the Library, which was dedicated in 1926, see Peter Topping, "La Bibliothèque Gennadeion, son histoire et ses collections," *L'Hellénisme contemporain*, N.S. IX (1955), 121–48. On the collector himself, see my article "Portrait of a Bibliophile XII: Joannes Gennadius, 1844–1932," *The Book Collector*, XIII (1964), 305–26.
2. Robert Proctor, *The Printing of Greek in the Fifteenth Century*, Bibliographical Society Illustrated Monographs, VIII (Oxford, 1900) is still the

17

standard work. For a useful supplement, with excellent plates, see Victor Scholderer, *Greek Printing Types 1465–1927* . . . (London, 1927). Proctor, pp. 49–51, lists 63 Greek books, but does not include the undated Demetrius Moschus (pp. 109–10) or the *Erotemata* printed at Venice about 1471, which he calls "the nearest approach to a Greek book made up to that time" (pp. 34–35). It should be noted that he counts the five volumes of Aristotle, 1495–98, as separate items. I do the same in my count but, unlike Proctor, am considering the three parts of his no. 14 as three separate items. This reckoning gives a total of 67.

3. Scholderer, p. 3. The text is the pseudo-Homeric *Batrachomyomachia*, crudely printed with an interlinear Latin prose translation and with a metrical version on the facing page. The only known copy is in the John Rylands Library at Manchester.

4. The reference, to be used throughout for volumes represented in the Gennadeion, is to Frederick R. Goff, *Incunabula in American Libraries: A Third Census of Fifteenth-Century Books Recorded in North American Collections* (New York, 1964). The G. L. copy of the 1476 Lascaris is exceptionally fine and was used by Adolf M. Hakkert for his facsimile edition (Amsterdam, 1966).

5. For the Brescia item see above, note 3. The Vicenza Chrysoloras is Goff, C-493, citing only the University of Illinois Library copy.

6. Goff, C-492, citing only the Pierpont Morgan Library copy. See also above, note 2, end, and Agostino Pertusi, "Per la Storia e le Fonti delle prime Grammatiche greche a Stampa," *Italia medioevale e umanistica*, V (1962), 321–51.

7. Another in the group is the first Greek grammar written in Latin, by Urbano Bolzanio, which was printed by Aldus Manutius at Venice in January 1497 (Goff, U-66). The G.L. copy is in mint condition and was once the property of the great French bibliophile A. A. Renouard, who had it handsomely bound; it was later in the collection of Baron de Seillière at the Château de Mello.

8. We unfortunately lack the great Complutensian Polyglot Bible, which though dated 1514–17 was not completed and issued before 1520.

9. Janus Lascaris (1445?–1534) is apparently unrelated to Constantine Lascaris, his somewhat older contemporary, though the two are often confused, even by scholars who should know better. The most recent study of Janus is by Börje Knös, *Un Ambassadeur de l'Hellénisme: Janus Lascaris et la Tradition greco-byzantin dans l'Humanisme français* (Uppsala and Paris, 1945). I have a monograph on him in preparation.

10. Curt F. Bühler, *The Fifteenth-Century Book: The Scribes, the Printers, the Decorators* (Philadelphia, 1960), Plate VII, reproduces a page of the Morgan Library copy, an elaborately illuminated copy on vellum.

11. The other is in Florence, in the Laurentian Library, and is magnificently illuminated throughout. Our copy has the illuminator's designs, in ink, on the first page only, but without color. Probably the work was interrupted by Trivulzio's death. Both the Apollonius and the Lucian are dated simply 1496, but Proctor (pp. 79–80) argues effectively for the sequence: Callima-

chus (undated) — Apollonius — Lucian. Two minor publications, in minuscules, of which the G.L. has only the Cebes (Goff, C-356), seem to belong to the same period as the Lucian.

12. The Florentine types reappear in Rome in 1517 at the Greek College founded
by the Medici Pope Leo X and headed by Janus Lascaris. But except for the
epigrams of Lascaris prefixed to several of the volumes and the lemmata
in the editions of the scholia to Homer and to Sophocles, the capitals are
not used for the printing of consecutive texts.

13. There is a good chapter on Callierges in Deno John Geanakoplos, *Greek
Scholars in Venice* . . . (Cambridge, Mass., 1962), pp. 201–22. Scholderer,
Plate 22, reproduces in color a page of the *Etymologicum Magnum*.

14. Poggio's translation of Diodorus Siculus, the 1476/7 and 1496 Venice editions (Goff, D-211 and D-213); Georgius Trapezuntius' trans. of Eusebius,
De evangelica praeparatione, Venice, 1497 (Goff, E-122); and Ficino's trans.
of Hermes Trismegistus, Treviso 1471 (Goff, H-77).

15. For the latter see H. M. Adams, *Catalogue of Books Printed on the Continent of Europe, 1501–1600, in Cambridge Libraries*, 2 vols. (Cambridge,
1967).

16. Printed at Rome, 11 September 1475.

17. Goff wrongly gives the date as 4 November.

18. In the printed text the sermon is dated to the Feast of St. John, 1481, in the
tenth regnal year of Sixtus IV, i.e., 9 August 1480–8 August 1481. Assuming that the feast day is dated according to the Roman curial calendar, in
which the New Year began at Christmas, the feast of St. John falls, by our
calendar, on 27 December 1480. This not only reconciles the apparently
conflicting dates but makes the reference to Otranto more timely.

19. To provide a complete check list of the Gennadeion incunabula, I append
a record of volumes not previously mentioned or for which the Goff numbers were not given.

Besides the three Greek grammars already cited the Library has: Lascaris,
Vicenza 1489 (Goff, L-67), the Aldine edition of 1494/5 (Goff, L-68), and
the *De nomine et verbo* ascribed to Vicenza, ca. 1489 (Goff, L-69); the
Chrysoloras of Vicenza 1491 (Goff, C-496); the Theodorus Gaza printed
by Aldus in 1495 (Goff, G-110); and the *Erotemata* of Demetrius Chalcondyles and of Manuel Moschopoulos, Milan, ca. 1493 (Goff, D-139), lacking
however the third section by Gregorios of Corinth.

The Goff numbers for our Aldines not previously noted are: Aristophanes,
1498 (Goff, A-958); Aristotle, 5 vols., 1495–98 (Goff, A-959); *Epistulae
Graecae*, 1499 (Goff, E-64); *Scriptores Astronomici*, 1499 (Goff, F-191);
Theocritus, 1495/6, 2 copies (Goff, T-144); and *Thesaurus Cornucopiae*,
1496 (Goff, T-158).

Additional Greek texts in the collection are: Aesop, Reggio Emilia 1497
(Goff, A-104), and a badly defective copy of a Venice edition, ca. 1498
(Goff, A-97); Orpheus, Florence 1500 (Goff, O-103); Phalaris, Venice 1498
(Goff, P-545); and Suidas, Milan 1499 (Goff, S-829).

Miscellaneous texts are: *Reportorium dictorum Aristotelis, Averoys, ali-
orumque philosophorum*, Bologna 1491 (Goff, A-1204); Boccaccio, *Genealo-*

19

giae, Venice 1494/5 (Goff, B-753); and Georgios of Trebizond, *Commentarii in Philippicas Ciceronis,* Venice, ca. 1475 (Goff, G-155).

Finally, there are the three additional "courtesy" incunabula: Marcus Montanus, *Oratio pro Rhodiorum obedientia* (Goff, M-825), an edition ascribed by the *Gesamtkatalog* and the British Museum to the 16th century; the *Donatio Constantini,* assigned to Rome, not before the end of 1503 (Goff, C-864, recording this copy and one in the Library of Congress); and Riccoldus Florentinus, *Confutatio Alcorani,* ascribed to Basel, after 1500 (Goff, R-190a, recording only this copy).

A Fifteenth-Century Burgundian Version of the Roman de Florimont

Charity C. Willard

It HAS BEEN GENERALLY RECOGNIZED that the Byzantine world exercised an important influence in such fields as Venetian architecture, certain early schools of Italian painting, religious music, monasticism, and humanism in the West,[1] but the nature of Byzantine influence on medieval literature has been less well understood. To be sure, there have been numerous discussions of the "matière d'antiquité," of which the Alexander and Troy cycles are notable examples, but the actual manner of transmission, as well as the various modifications of even these themes, present a number of unsolved problems. One especially interesting question is why these particular stories continued to inspire succeeding generations of writers and adapters throughout Europe in spite of obvious changes in literary styles.

For a long time it has been the custom with respect to medieval French literature to regard the twelfth-century forms of this legendary material as being vastly superior to later versions, especially those written in prose. These latter works have frequently been disdained as representing a decline in literary quality, although relatively little effort has been made until quite recently to understand why such modifications might have seemed preferable to those who created or read them.

George Cary, for instance, speaks in his *The Medieval Alexander*[2] of a revival of interest in the Alexander legend at the Burgundian court in the course of the fifteenth century, but he does not really account for all of its manifestation in spite of the abundant evidence of its popularity. Aside from copies of several versions of the *Roman d'Alexandre* in the Burgundian library,[3] there was a *chambre* of Alexander tapestries ordered from Pasquier Grenier of Tournai by Philip the Good

21

in 1459,[4] and in 1468, at the celebration of the marriage of Charles the Bold to Margaret of York in Bruges, there was a pageant representing the marriage of Alexander the Great with the daughter of the King of Egypt.[5]

Even before then, around 1448, a new version of Alexander's exploits had been composed to correspond to the particular interests of the Burgundian courtiers. This was Jean Wauquelin's *Livre des conquestes et faits d'Alexandre*, undertaken at the suggestion of the duke's cousin, John, Count of Estampes and Nevers, and Lord of Dourdan. A luxurious copy of the text was prepared for Philip the Good, and the Prologue refers to his particular interest in the subject. Of the five manuscripts known today, four were prepared for the duke's relatives, although the text was never printed. It should be noted that Wauquelin's sources were more French than Latin and that his Alexander was little more than Charlemagne in eastern guise.[6]

Around the middle of the fifteenth century Alexander also appeared as a protagonist in a sort of "dialogue des morts." This was the *Débat d'honneur*, written by Jean Miélot, one of the duke's secretaries, based on a text by the Italian humanist Giovanni Aurispa, who was in turn inspired by an earlier text of Lucian. The debate purports to have been carried on by Alexander, Hannibal, and the Roman consul Scipio as to which of them enjoyed the greatest renown during his lifetime. Interestingly enough, the referee of the discussion, Minos, ruler of the Underworld, awards the prize to Scipio.[7]

A growing interest in the historical, as opposed to the legendary, Alexander is indicated by the French translation of the Quintus Curtius life of Alexander, finished in 1468 by Vasco de Lucena, a Portuguese courtier in the entourage of the Burgundian duchess, Isabel of Portugal. There is a noteworthy attempt here to separate history from fiction, and the translation appears to have met with considerable success, to judge by the fact that there are still twenty-five manuscripts in existence along with six editions published during the first half of the sixteenth century.[8]

Vasco de Lucena's translation, based on the Latin text of Poggio Bracciolini rather than on the Greek original, however, was dedicated to Charles the Bold, who had only recently inherited his father's dukedom. In the Introduction there is the inevitable comparison between the young prince and the hero of antiquity, couched in the following terms:

Grant temps a que voulenté me print de assembler et translater de latin en françois les faitz d'Alexandre, a fin de en vostre jone aage, vous donner l'exemple et instruction de sa vaillance. Mais pendant le temps que j'ay doubté de translater les gestes, tandiz que je les translate et endementiers que vous estes occupé es guerres de France et de Liege, en la/ destruction de Dynant, et de rechief derrainment, tandis que vous reversés la puissance des Liegeois par terrible bataille, demolissés les murs de leurs citéz, villes, chasteaulx, et finablement tandis que vous leur donnés loix nouvelles, sept ans sont passés ou environ, durant le quel temps voz vertus et euvres chevaleureuses par le monde univers ont esté si avant manifestées que assez est notoire celle doctrine vous estre superflue. Car ainsi comme en toutes aultres vertus de paix de guerre, vous, mon tresredoubté seigneur, pas n'estes gaires seurmonté d'Alixandre, ainsi en devocion, continence, chasteté attemprance l'avez surmonté evidemment, telement, certes, que ycellui Alexandre pas ne vous doit estre exemple de vertus, mais se faire se pouoit qu'il ne retournast en nostre siecle, vous mon tresredoubté seigneur, devriez estre exemple d'Alexandre, que se exemple vous estoit neccessaire il n'estoit ja besoing de plus loing le cerchier, que es vertus, victoires et triumphes de voz ayeulx le duc Phelipe, le duc Jehan, le roy de Portugal, Alexandres de leurs temps, de Monseigneur vostre pere, Alexandre du notre. . . . C'est seulement que aultres y pourront prendre exemple.[9]

Nor is this the only evidence of Charles the Bold's taste for the exploits of antiquity. The duke's literary taste, as recalled by the chronicler Wielant, was such that he "ne prenoit plaisir qu'en histoires romaines et es faitz de Jules Cesar, de Pompée, de Hannibal, d'Alexandre le Grand et de telz aultres grandz et haultz hommes, lesquelz il vouloit ensuyvre et contrefaire."[10]

Alexander was not the only member of his family to attract the interest of the Burgundian court. Florimont, his grandfather according to a certain tradition, was the subject of an *Histoire de quelz gens et de quele maison descendit le treshault emprereur Alixandre le Conquerant*. The only known manuscript, with the Burgundian coat of arms in the first initial, belongs to the French Bibliothèque Nationale, where it is *fonds français* 12566. It bears witness, first of all, to the Burgundian fascination with genealogy, real or fanciful, from about the middle of the fifteenth century onwards, an interest documented by Jean Miélot's translation of a part of Boccaccio's *De Genealogia Deorum* around 1460.[11]

23

The manuscript is far better known to art historians than to literary medievalists, for it was illustrated by an interesting and very original artist who has come to be known as the Wavrin Master because his work is most frequently associated with volumes which once belonged to the library of the Picard knight and chronicler who was the author of the *Anciennes Chroniques d'Angleterre*.[12] Curiously, both the manuscripts attributed to Jean Miélot and those illustrated by the Wavrin Master are thought to emanate from Lille, although they certainly represent the production of two different workshops. Miélot specialized in translations and didactic treatises, whereas the Wavrin group is devoted primarily to romances of adventure, frequently prose versions of earlier narrative poems. Both groups of manuscripts have similar physical characteristics in that they are almost always written on paper rather than on vellum and are illustrated by line drawings, some of them enlivened by touches of watercolor. The work of several different scribes and artists can be observed, but the Wavrin Master is certainly the most talented illustrator of the group.[13]

Because of the 105 rather humorous and racy drawings, which seem to foreshadow the technique of early printed book illustration, f. fr. 12566 has been exhibited several times in recent years, notably in Brussels in 1959, on the occasion of the 400th anniversary of the foundation of the Royal Library. In this particular exhibition, devoted to the literary and artistic patronage of Philip the Good, the manuscript found its place among others attributed to the so-called workshop of the Wavrin Master. Like several others of the group it is written in a script which has come to be associated with a certain Jean d'Ardennay, first identified in a manuscript now in Turin, a copy of Valerius Maximus dated 1446 (MS. L. IV. 13. 15 of the Biblioteca Nazionale) which was unfortunately damaged in the fire of 1904. According to L. M. J. Delaissé, who prepared the catalogue for the Brussels exhibition, the Florimont illustrations are thought to represent an early work of the master. As this is the only volume bearing the mark of the Burgundian ducal library, Delaissé raises the question of why Philip the Good does not seem to have been interested in owning other products of the workshop and suggests the hypothesis that this artist was too much in advance of his contemporaries to appeal to the somewhat flamboyant tastes of the duke and his chief courtiers.[14]

The text has roused far less interest than the format of the manuscripts, although Alfons Hilka, the editor of the twelfth-century versified *Florimont*,[15] pointed out that it merited a special study, primarily because this particular text does not correspond to the other prose versions of Aimon de Varennes' poem. Discussion of both the poem and the later prose version, however, has turned mainly on such problems as Aimon de Varennes' place of origin and the authenticity of certain Greek expressions which appear, with French translations, throughout the text, or whether the poem is not, after all, merely a rather mediocre imitation of the *Partonopeus de Blois*, with an exotic atmosphere created by the author's *souvenirs de voyage.*[16]

Leaving aside for the present these debates which have, on the whole, frequently generated more heat than light, let us turn to an examination of what both Aimon de Varennes and the author, or adapter, of f. fr. 12566 have to say about their source of inspiration.

Aimon de Varennes, who gives the date of composition of his poem as 1188, explains that he translated it from the Latin version of a Greek text which he had seen at Philippopolis (modern Plovdiv). He undertook the project to please a lady he admired. He is quite explicit about these circumstances:

> Lors a sejour a Chastillon
> Estoit Aime une saison
> Et pourpansait soi de l'istoire
> Qu'il avoit eu en memoire
> Il l'avoit en Gresse veue
> Mai n'estoit pas par tot seue.
> A Felipople la trova,
> A Chastillon l'en aporta;
> Ensi qu'il l'avoit empris
> L'ait de latin en romans mis.
> [vv. 27–36]

He even repeated in a later passage of the poem the use he had made of the material he found in Macedonia.

> A siaus qui sevant le clergie
> Contet par ethymelogie
> Que por s'amie Vialine
> Traist de greu l'istoire latine
> Et del latin fist le romans
> Aymes, que fut loials amans.
> [vv. 9211–16]

Philippopolis was a Byzantine metropolis of some importance around the middle of the twelfth century, as is attested by the Arabian geographer Idrisi. In the Byzantine world generally the twelfth century was,

25

of course, a period of considerable intellectual and artistic activity. Not only were the classics still being read with enthusiasm, but new romances were being evolved on the basis of classical themes and new artistic forms were being evolved.[17] There remains, however, the problem of accounting for Aimon de Varennes' presence there in the years preceding 1188.

Although the French Hellenist Jean Psichari considered Aimon's knowledge of the Greek language suspect, he himself insisted that his native language was not French:

> As Fransois veult de tant servir
> Que ma langue lor est salvaige;
> Car ju ait dit en mon langaige
> As muels que ju ai seü dire.
> Se ma langue la lor empire,
> Por ce ne m'en dissent annui;
> Mues ainz ma langue que l'autrui.
> Romans ne estoire ne plet
> A Fransois, se il ne l'on fet.
>
> [vv. 13,614–22]

At least his knowledge of the geography of the region seems quite authentic. Not only does he describe accurately the voyage from Egypt to Greece; he insists that his acquaintance with Gallipoli is first-hand. His description of Durazzo in Albania and of the Via Egnatia, a medieval crusading and pilgrimage route between Belgrade and Constantinople, bears comparison with those of Villehardouin, Foucher de Chartres, or the Arab Idrisi.[18]

In describing Philip of Macedonia's route from Egypt to Greece, for instance, he says:

> Qui veult d'Egipte en Gresce aleir,
> La grant meir li convient passeir;
> Mai s'il veult aleir per Surie,
> Per Anthioche et per Turquie,
> An longue voie, a port de meir
> Porait il bien en Gresce aleir;
> Le Bras Saint Jorge passerait,
> Jai plus de meir n'i trouverait.
> [A] Galipol une citeit,
> Ou Aymes ot jai maint jor esteit,
> Illuec est li bras plus estrois,
> Passeir le puet le jor .III. fois.
>
> [vv. 165–76]

In speaking of the site of Adrianopolis he adds:

> La cytez fut en un pendant
> Dejoste une ewe corrant.
> Aymes le di[s]t qui l'ait veüe
> Et tote la terre seüe.
> [vv. 10,213–15]

Did Aimon travel as a merchant? The important role accorded to Dulfius, the cloth merchant, suggests a sympathy with that section of society, and certainly the episode in which Florimont slips into the royal palace for a secret meeting with the Princess Rommadanapple disguised as a tailor's apprentice is one of the most developed in the whole story in both poem and prose versions. It not only suggests a familiarity with the details of a cloth merchant's operations but scarcely seems the sort of device which would appeal to a nobleman. By the end of the twelfth century the routes from Venice to Constantinople were well traversed by merchants' caravans, but at the same time during the reign of Manuel Comnenus (1143–80) not only trade but also political circumstances brought to the Eastern Mediterranean and to the Byzantine Empire a flood of westerners, many of whom settled there.[19] At the same time, Aimon's expressed devotion to the precepts of chivalry might also indicate that he had been one of the adventurers who took part in the final struggle to prevent the collapse of the Kingdom of Jerusalem in 1187. His sojourn in Châtillon brings to mind the name of Guy de Lusignan's ill-starred companion Renaud de Châtillon. Such a possibility has never even been investigated by the scholars who have undertaken to determine whether the Châtillon in question was the one in Lorraine or another in the region of Lyon, although the evidence in favor of the latter would seem to be more convincing. There were also the Norman knights from Sicily who occupied Corfu and sacked Thessalonica in 1185, thus contributing to the downfall of the Comnenian dynasty, among the many adventurers and other travellers who might have had reason to know the routes described in the poem or to discover the Latin translation of a Greek adventure story. Manuscripts of Aimon's poem are to be found in England and northern Italy as well as in France, but little effort has been made to account for their presence outside of France, or to study the manuscript tradition on other than linguistic grounds.[20]

Whatever circumstances may have led to the discovery of the document which originally inspired the poem, at least the intent is clear.

The tale has to do with the youthful adventures of a hero who is said to be the father of Philip II of Macedonia, and thus the grandfather of Alexander the Great. In both the poem and the later prose versions the interest is divided between genealogy and youthful exploits, although the genealogical aspects are nowhere more fully developed than in f. fr. 12566. It should also be noted that there is a sort of continuation of the prose *Florimont* devoted to the history of the hero's father Madien, King of Babylonia, written by Perrinet du Pin de La Rochelle and dedicated in 1448 to Anne de Lusignan, Duchess of Savoy and Princess of Cyprus, and a member of a celebrated crusading family.[21]

The marriage of Madien to a Greek princess marks the starting point of the episodes which are common to the poem and three prose versions of *Florimont*. This princess, who brought Macedonia as part of her dowry, was also, be it noted, the younger sister of the princess who married Brutus, traditional ancestor of the kings of Britain (an allusion which brings to mind a passage from the beginning of Wavrin's *Anciennes Chroniques d'Angleterre*). After Madien's death, Seloc, the older son, inherited Babylonia, whereas Philip, the second child, set out to claim his mother's territories in Greece. On arriving in Macedonia, he killed a fierce lion which had been ravaging the countryside; it was to commemorate this exploit that he founded the city of Philippopolis. He then married the daughter of Meneus, King of Malta, Sicily, and Barbary. She is called Amordyalé in the poem, but Rommadanapple in f. fr. 12566. Another Rommadanapple was born to this union, a princess so beautiful and talented that at the age of ten she was already besieged by suitors. Thus her father decreed that any pretender who wished to see her even once would have to agree to serve the realm for three years. At the end of this period he might not only see the princess but receive a kiss as a reward for his pains.

It is scarcely surprising that the ultimate winner in this contest for the princess was Florimont, son of Matakars (Mataquas), Duke of Albania, and Edorie, daughter of the King of Persia as well as niece of the King of Slavonia. Florimont's prowess was foretold in a dream (figuring a lion cub) which his father had had before the child's birth. After the account of Florimont's birth, f. fr. 12566 in particular devotes considerable attention to a description of his education, supervised by Master Flocart, and of the knightly training provided by his father.

Florimont's initial feat of valor, the killing of a monster which had the power to restore itself by bathing in the sea, led to an encounter with the Dame de l'Ile Celée, a supernatural creature whom Florimont loved in secret until the charm was broken and the romance spoiled by Master Flocart, who spied on the lovers and revealed their secret to Florimont's mother. A good deal more is made of this episode in the poem than in the prose versions, where it is regarded as a youthful flight of fancy not to be taken too seriously, even if Florimont, in his despair over the loss of the lady, took to behaving in such an eccentric fashion that he came to be called Pauvre Perdu. It was in this guise, accompanied by Master Flocart under the assumed name of Caco-pédie,[22] that he travelled to the court of King Philip, to lend him assistance in his war against Candiobras, King of Hungary.

In the meantime, however, Florimont enhanced his knightly reputa-tion by overcoming Garganeüs, nephew of the Emir of Carthage, the giant who terrorized the region surrounding his stronghold on Monte Gargano in Apulia. This episode is given an extensive development in all versions and is certainly the most celebrated of Florimont's exploits.

While Florimont, disguised as the Pauvre Perdu, was earning a second reputation for valor at King Philip's court, he was lodged at the house of a rich merchant (Delfis in the poem; Dulfis in f. fr. 12566). This merchant's rôle is particularly emphasized in the Burgun-dian version, although all give importance to the episode of the plot whereby he and Rommadanapple's governess, Cyprianne, manage to slip Florimont into the girl's apartments disguised as a tailor's appren-tice, his face hidden by a stack of bolts of fabric arranged on top of his head. The comic possibilities of this situation are emphasized in the Burgundian version, and the realism of the love scene which fol-lows shows a surprising sophistication in a princess who has led such a protected life. It departs considerably from the courtly conventions of the poem.

After Florimont's identity had been revealed at a great May festival, he was naturally enough allowed to marry the princess and thus to become heir to the throne of Macedonia. This was the union which produced a son named Philip, who in due time would become the father of Alexander the Great.

In the meantime Florimont was able to bring about a general pacifi-cation in the region and an alliance for an expedition against the Emir of Carthage. The storming of the stronghold of Clavegris is the final major episode of all versions. The allies, disguised as merchants, were able to kill one of the Emir's minions and to persuade another, Suliman, to deliver the castle into Florimont's hands. The undertaking was complicated by the Emir's wife, Henemedie, daughter of the King of Nubia, who fell in love with Florimont, but he was able tactfully to turn her interest in the direction of Candiobras, King of Hungary, who was unmarried. From the rendition of Clavegris, and the release of the prisoners held there, Florimont proceeded to the capture of Carthage and eventually all of Libya. Thus the Emir of Carthage, in total defeat, was obliged to promise the hand of his daughter, Olympias, to Florimont's son Philip. He did not long survive his ignominy, and thus his widow was free to marry Candiobras and Florimont able to return to Rommadanapple in Philippopolis. He arrived there to find his father-in-law on his deathbed; thus he became the ruler of Macedonia.

The various manuscripts of the poem have different endings, as do the prose versions, some dwelling more than others on Florimont's descendants. It is scarcely surprising to find the genealogical aspects given particular attention in the Burgundian manuscript. In the text which serves as basis for the Hilka edition (Paris, B.N. f. fr. 15101) there is an appeal made by Aimon to his audience:

> [O]r pri a cels qui sont el mont
> [E]t az bonz troveors qui sont
> Et az Fransois pri per amors
> Que ne blasment pas ma labours
> Qui blaiment ceu qu'il doit loeir
> Et loent ceu qu'il doit blaimeir,
> Il ne se puet pas mues honir.
> [vv. 13,607–13]

There follows a brief résumé of Florimont's history; then come a few lines extolling largesse, ending with the following observation:

> Et cil que se repant de bien
> Semble le serf qui vers lez chiens
> Tourne quant a corrut asseis;
> Por ce est mors et afoleis.
> Ja ne[l] prandra sen grant anui
> Li chien[s], s'il ne torne vers lui;
> Por le retour pert il son loz.
> Ce ne fist pas Eleneos,
> Il ne retorna tant ne quant,
> Maix a toz jors aloit avant,
> Ains jors ne fut por avarice
> Ne en prixon ne en justice.
> Cil que elle tient en prison
> N'oze faire conduit ne don.
> Florimont ne prit elle mie.

> Toz jors menoit moult bele vie,
> Per largesce conquist asseis,
> De plusors rois fut rois clameis.
> Quant Aymes en fit le romant,
> .M. et .C. .IIII^{xx}. et .VIII. ans
> Avoit de l'Incarnacion;
> Adont fut retrait per Aymon.
>   [vv. 13,659–80]

The Burgundian prose version likewise ends with an appeal to the audience, but in what a different spirit:

> Et pour ce que j'ay à mon pooir en ceste petite oeuvre mys au mains mal que j'ay peu et au plus pres de la veritey ainsy que je l'ay trouvé par escript les fais et grans proesses du tres victorieulx prinche, le roy Flourimont, en son temps roy de Machedonne, filz du duc d'Albanye, et de la naissance et aulcuns des fais en brief du roy Phlippe de Machedonne son filz, du quel vint et issy le tresvictorieux empereur Alixandre le Grant, dont cy appres porres oir au lonc, je feray prendre fin à ceste petite oeuvre et mal aournee matere. Sy supplye treshumblement en toutte humilité à Dieu mon benoit createur et à sa benoitte Vergo More que ce que j'ay usé et passé temps en oizeuse en moy occupant en ceste matere, en delaissant leur service, qu'il leur plaise le moy pardonner. Et à ceulx quy ce livre liront ou orront lire, prye et requiers que s'ilz y troevent chose ou il y ait faulte, qu'ilz voellent excuser ma simplesse et petit entendement et suppleer à mon ignorance. Et cy fine le livre du roy Flourimont, filz du duc d'Albanye, et de la nais-sance du roy Phlippe, son filz, pere du roy Alixandre le Grant.
>   [f. fr. 12566, fol. 257v°–258r°]

George Cary, in *The Medieval Alexander*, dismisses all this geneal-ogy as fanciful, but Alfons Hilka, on the contrary, calls attention to a work published some time ago by A. H. Veselovskij,[23] which sug-gests the possibility of a connection between this concept of Alexan-der's ancestry and an oriental version of the Alexander saga. The question is thus raised as to what Aimon de Varennes might actually have heard in Macedonia in the middle of the twelfth century. Obviously the author of the version in f. fr. 12566 was troubled by the problem of the ultimate sources of his model, for he says:

> Et disoyent aulcuns qu'il fu engendrés d'un enchanteur quy se nommoit Neptanabus, quy par enchantement fist tant que il coucha avoec la royne Olimpyas. Que il en est ne qu'il en fu je ne le say et m'en rapporte aux clers quy les histoires en ont

faittes, et le porres plus amplement voir ou Livre d'Alixandre
quy de tout ce fait mencyon. [fol. 257v°]

The need becomes evident for a thorough investigation into the non-
European aspects of the Alexander legend, along with a desire to know
what information might lie hidden in a forgotten corner of some Greek
library. Could this version of Alexander's background represent some
legend which was popular at the time of the Hellenic renaissance of
the eleventh century?[24]

Marcel Françon has more recently presented another interesting
hypothesis. Basing his ideas on a series of articles by the Belgian
scholar Henri Grégoire, he has suggested that Florimont may represent a recollection of Vladimir, Prince of Dioclea (Montenegro). His
fight against the giant of Monte Gargano is likewise recorded in the
romance of *Mélusine* as a combat between Geoffroy à la Grant Dent
and the giant Gardon. It would therefore be the wars in the Balkans
during the tenth century which served as inspiration for the adventures of Florimont, conflicts involving the Bulgarians, Montenegrins,
and Greeks as well as the Normans, under the leadership of Robert
Guiscard, between 1081 and 1085.[25]

The Lusignans, whose early history inspired *Mélusine*, were established in Little Armenia in the fourteenth century, but the territory
already existed in 1187. The possibility of a connection between *Mélusine* and *Florimont* is borne out by the fact that Jean d'Arras refers
to Florimont at the beginning of his fourteenth-century version of
Mélusine, saying: "Il est vérité qu'il ot jadis un roi en Albanie qui fut
moult vaillans homs. Et dit l'ystoire qu'il ot de sa premiere femme
pluseurs enfans, dont l'ystoire dit que Mataquas, qui fu pere Florimont, fu ses premiers filz."[26]

Furthermore, the giant of Monte Gargano appears to be the basis
for the name of the Rabelaisian giant Gargantua. He is even referred
to as Gargan in *Les chronique admirables*. Rabelais could easily have
known the adventures of Florimont through an edition of one of the
prose versions published in Lyons (1558) by Olivier Arnoullet. Thus
Professor Françon concludes:

> Le roman de *Mélusine*, comme celui de *Florimont*, illustrent
> donc les événements guerriers qui se sont déroulés aux Xe et
> XIe siècles dans les Balkans ou dans le Proche-Orient. Jean
> d'Arras a transporté à Guérande l'action qui, dans *Florimont*
> avait lieu au Monte Gargano, et il a attribué à Geoffroy la
> Grant Dent les exploits de Florimont. Le géant mis à mort

par ce dernier s'appelait Garganeüs, tandis que celui que
Geoffroy a tué se nommait Gardon. On peut voir là une défor-
mation de Gargan qui d'après Gadioz est le thème dont est
formé le nom Gargantua.[27]

On the whole this theory seems more plausible than the suggestion of
Fourrier and the opinion of Albert Henry that, in spite of all Aimon
de Varennes said to the contrary, he had invented the whole story.[28]
There is further evidence of Florimont's fame at the beginning of
the fifteenth century, when he was cited by Christine de Pisan in her
Débat des deux amants as one of the world's celebrated lovers.[29]

Though far from achieving the popularity of the more common
version of Alexander's genealogy, Aimon de Varennes' poem was
sufficiently admired to have circulated over a considerable territory
throughout the thirteenth and fourteenth centuries. Fourteen manuscripts still exist in France, England, and Northern Italy in addition to
the lost one which is listed in the 1426 inventory of the Visconti
Library in Pavia.[30] There are also three later prose versions, only one
of which claims descent from the poem (B.N. f. fr. 1490 and Arsenal
Ms. 3476), although the five early printed editions which appeared in
Paris, Rouen, and Lyons between 1538 and 1558 also give evidence
of being based on the poem. The two other fifteenth-century manuscripts represent separate versions of the story. In addition to f. fr.
12566, there is also B.N. f. fr. 1488 which, entitled *Le Livre de Florimont filz du duc Jehan d'Orleans et de Helaine, fille du duc de Bre-
tagne*, bears only a very slight resemblance to the other Florimont
versions, but rather seems to show common elements with *Pierre de
Provence et la belle Maguelonne*, a late medieval romance recognized
to have a distinctly Byzantine background.[31]

The author of f. fr. 12566, like Aimon de Varennes, speaks of
having known a Latin text in Greece; in his case he found it in Salonika. He tells of having made a pilgrimage to the Holy Land in the
company of a group of Picard knights during the year 1418, and of
having been detained in Greece by the onset of winter weather. Wishing, as he explained, to learn something of Greek history and customs,
and

en enquerant des choses dessus dittes entre pluiseurs volumes
de livres qui me furent monstré, choisy ung petit livre escrypt,
translaté du grec en latin, lequel traittoit la venue d'aulcuns
rois de Machedonne, desquelx dessendy le treshault empereur
Alixandre le Grant, jadis roy de Machedonne, qui en pau de

33

temps conquist toutes les parties orientalz. Et pour ce que je savoye de certain que en pau de lieux de par decha estoit seu la venue ne de quel gens le tres hault empereur Alixandre estoit dessendus, pris la paine et labeur de translater de latin en franchois le livre qui de ses predicesseurs faisoit mencion. . . .[32]

As the story of Alexander the Great had already been retold at the Burgundian court around 1448 and this manuscript would seem to have been prepared only slightly later, one must conclude that the anonymous author of this prose *Florimont* wanted to correct the more popular version of Alexander's genealogy by a version which seemed to him nearer to the original sources. Wauquelin's account is recognized to have been based primarily on French sources which could well have seemed undependable to someone who had been given the opportunity to know the Greek world at first hand.

The author of this *Florimont* has been tentatively identified as Jean de Wavrin himself by the late Jean Porcher. The theory presents many attractive possibilities and solves a number of problems. Porcher based this identification on the resemblance between f. fr. 12566 and other manuscripts which belonged to Wavrin's personal library, a number of them bearing his signature. Furthermore, it is undeniably true that the author of the *Chroniques d'Angleterre* demonstrated on several occasions a notable interest in the Middle East, not only by the pages he devoted to an account of the crusading expedition to Rhodes and Constantinople in 1444–45 led by his nephew Wallerand de Wavrin, but by his participation in a mission to Pope Pius II in the fall of 1463 which proposed to organize one more crusade against the Turks. The pages describing his nephew's expedition are vivid enough to have been based on an eyewitness account, if not of the action itself, then at least of the terrain where it took place. Moreover, no document has been found to account for Jean de Wavrin's presence elsewhere between August 1417, when he was present at a muster of the Burgundian forces in Beauvais, and 1420, when he is known to have taken part in the crusade against the Hussites in the company of some Savoyard knights.[33] He would have had time to make a pilgrimage in this period. Certainly his library contained an impressive number of books dealing with antiquity, and as an historian he showed a concern for verifying sources which was somewhat in advance of his contemporaries. Doutrepont has mentioned him as one of four courtiers who did the most to encourage the taste for tales of antiquity at the Burgundian court.[34] All of this might be explained in part by a sojourn in Salonika during the fall of 1418.

It is possible to suggest various reasons for the differences between the Burgundian text and others. Certainly it was revised by the author to appeal to the tastes of his audience. There is also the possibility that it was intended to be read aloud and therefore occasionally summarized past action to refresh the memories of his listeners. It still seems important, however, to take seriously the author's claim that he was translating a separate Latin text. This version of a Greek original could have dated from the time when the land formed part of the Roman Empire, or it could have been made in the wake of the Italian influence which preceded the establishment of the Frankish kingdom. One of the other prose versions states quite simply that it is based on the earlier poem:

> Celuy qui a cueur de grand valeur et entend en amour de dame ou damoiselle si entende de bon cueur le livre que Aymes de Varannes fist de gregoys en fransois d'une histoire. . . .
> Or oys seigneurs, Aymez si estoit en amours de celle noble damoiselle Jullienne ainsi comme je vous ay dit et si estoit en Lonris, mais il fist l'istoire à Castillon de Phelippon de Macedoine qui avoit esté en Babiloine et du filz au duc Marquis qui tenoit par heritage Duras et toute Albanie. Et le filz d'iceluy duc de Duras dont l'istoire parle si eust nom Florimond en fransois et Helenois en gregois. Iceluy Florimond fust roy, et si acquiert asses honneur et terre, et eust moult de peine et travail en sa vie. En iceluy temps estoit Aymez à Castillon soubz Abseque; et se pensa d'icelle histoire qu'il avoit en Grece veue. . . .[35]

The first printed edition (1528) does not refer to Aimon de Varennes, but speaks of the discovery of the Latin text in Philippopolis and the subsequent translation into French. The author of f. fr. 12566 makes no mention of Aimon de Varennes either; his version of the tale is considerably longer, however, than either the version in f. fr. 1490 (259 folios as opposed to 186) or the 1528 edition. Both seem to be summaries of the material presented by the poem. The chief episodes, such as the fight with the giant Garganeüs, are developed in considerable detail, but other passages are passed over or recounted in abbreviated form. As Jean Psichari pointed out as early as 1891, "rien ne nous a prouvé que les versions en ont été faites sur les compositions rimées que nous possédons. Elles peuvent par-ci par-là porter la trace des mss. perdus, dont elles émaneraient, et nous mettre ainsi sur une piste."[36]

Rather than hypothesizing lost manuscripts, however, it would seem more logical to consider the possibility of two translations from the Latin version, each somewhat adapted to fit the requirements of two audiences separated by nearly three hundred years. This explanation would seem adequate to explain the differences between f. fr. 12566 and the poem of Aimon de Varennes. A good example of the variations (and similarities) offered by the various reworkings would be the passage where the giant Garganeüs is mentioned for the first time. The poem says:

> "Fils," fait li dus, "bien sai et voi
> Que contre lui nen ais pooir.
> Moult muelz ain ge qu'il ait l'avoir
> Que soie mors ne afolez.
> Moult est grans et fors cist mafeis:
> Il est bien .VII. piés mesurez,
> Plus grans que nus hons que soit nez
> Et seit muelz traire de baston
> Que abelestiers de bouson.
> Son chastel ait fort en un pui
> Dou fait a mainte gent anui.
> Em Pulle est dejoste un plain;
> Le pui noment Mont de Gargain.
> Il nen ait ille desor meir
> C'o galies nen ast rober.
> Quant hons se welt de lui deffandre
> Et il le puet par force prendre,
> En moult male prison le met:
> En une terre le tramet
> Ou il le fait mout bien garder,
> Que il ne s'en puisset embler.
> A l'ore que il doit maingier
> Por pastre le fait envoier:
> De l'erbe maingut, se il puet,
> Ou se se non, morir l'estuet.
> Puels que il met hom em prison,
> Jamais n'en prendrait reanson."
> [vv. 3018–44]

The somewhat pedestrian version in f. fr. 1490 is as follows:

> Quant le duc entendit ce que son filz dist il en fut moult dolent. Si print Florimond par la main et le tira en sa chambre et luy dist: Beau filz, et quesse que vous voullez faire? Nous

36

voulles vous destruire sans cause? Car nul homme ne peut durer contre Garganeüs le grant geant. Il a bien xvj pies de hault et porte ung si grant baston que nul homme n'ourtroient porter et si tir si droit d'une saiecte que nul ne l'ose actaindre. Si a fait ung chastel en une hault montaigne par quoy il tient en subjection toute la contrée, car il n'y a isle d'icy en Chippre que ses galées ne voisent rober. Et la montangne a nom Mont Gargan, et james ne a pitié de homme, ains les envoye en ung sien pais ou il les fait pestir comme bestes, et qui ne vieult mengier de l'erbe, il luy convient mourir. Dont, mon enffant, je vous prie et requiert que vous laisses ceste entreprinse, car mieulx aime qu'il ait votre amour que il eust votre corps, car contre luy ne pourries resister. [fol. 57v⁰–58r⁰]

The passage is even more abbreviated in the 1528 edition:

Filz, respond Mataquas, je scay pour vray que contre luy n'auryes duree, car il te surmonte en cinq piedz de haulteur et est de si faulse vie quant il prent une forte place qui contre luy s'est deffendue il envoye les gens en cruelle prison, ou pour leur vivre ont herbe seullement, ou sinon les fait mourir. Parquoy mieulx ayme estre tenu du truage que pour ce tu soys affollé ne mort.

The version in f. fr. 12566, however, in addition to including the details set forth by the poem, adds to them in some cases. Whereas it is possible that it may be based on the poem, it seems more reasonable to account for the differences as a slightly different interpretation of the Latin text. The differences in a given passage may be slight, but taken as a whole they do not seem directly related to the French poem. The passage which describes the duke's admonition to Florimont says this:

Beaulx fils, ce dist le duc Matacart, asses say que à l'encontre de luy ne porries resister, sy aime mieulx que de mon tresor il me couste que ce que mors ou affolés en soyes, car moult est à merveillez grans et fors Garganeüs, moult est fiers et orguilleux. Il se tient en Puille ou il a fait faire une forteresse sur ung mont qui se nomme Mont Gargain, par lequel il fait maint mal et maint meschief à ses voisins, sy en y a pau autour de luy qui ne soyent sy trebutaire, et n'a nulles isles en ceste mer que par ses galées ne soyent pilées et robées. Car se aulcuns en y a qui à l'encontre de luy se rebellent, et que au dessus en puist venir, moult en prent grant pugnicion, car mourir miserablement et à grant destresse les fait en ses prisons par rage de faim, ne jamais raenchon n'en voelt prendre. [fol. 57v°]

Another interesting passage for comparison, with regard to the poem and to the version in f. fr. 12566, is one which describes Florimont's early education. Of course the exact import of such passages is difficult to judge without knowledge of a Latin source, but it gives some idea of how the two writers adapted their material somewhat to fit the ideas of their contemporaries. Neither here nor elsewhere, however, is there any suggestion that the poem is being adapted into prose, as is often the case in f. fr. 1490. Aimon de Varennes says in this case:

> Bien le fist norir et garder
> Li dus tant que il sot parler.
> Ses peires le mist a l'escole
> Et a Maistre Fouquart le rent.
> Et il l'aprist mout doucement
> Et si dist que a son vivant
> Ne pertiroit mais de l'enfant.
> Florymons mout bien aprenoit
> Tot seu que il savoir devoit.
> Le duc le fist bien doctriner
> De chevacher, d'armes porter,
> De lance roidement ferir
> Et de cheval d'escut courir,
> Jeus des taubles d'eschas mater,
> As dames belement parler,
> Et puels d'esperviers et d'ostors,
> De counoistre faux jugeors,
> Parler en plait cortoissement
> Et conoistre faux jugement,
> D'escremie, de champions,
> De menu ferir de bastons,
> De harpe et de vïele aprist.
>   [vv. 1893–1915]

The prose version lays considerable stress on Florimont's ability to do everything better than his peers, and speaks of his parents' pleasure at his accomplishments:

> Le duc le fist moult bien garder et nourrir tant qu'il vint en l'eage de .vj. ans. Sy le bailla le duc en garde à Maistre Flocart et moult luy pria que l'effant euist en cure de l'apprendre et introduire comme à ung tel effant appartenoit. Le maistre respondy et promist au duc que de l'effant n'euist quelque soing, et que sy bien s'en acquitteroit que à tous jours mais bon gre luy en devroit savoir. Et avec ce promist au duc que jamais de l'enfant ne se deppartiroit. Moult l'apprist bien Maistre Flocart, tellement que de son eage l'effant fut telle-

ment lettrés et introduis en science que de son eage sourmon-
toit les aultres effans en toutes sciences, dont le duc et la ducesse
furent moult contempt. L'effant Flourimont commancha à
croistre, sy le fist le duc introduyre et apprendre à poindre et
galopper le destrier et le faisoit apprendre de l'escremye de l'ecu
et du boucler. Tant et sy bien apprist l'effant que ly maistre n'y
sorrent que amender. Il sot bien escremir de l'espee et ferir, des
jeux de tables et des eschies ne trouvoit qui le surmontast, entre
dames et damoiselles se savoit moult bien contenir, de beau
parler estoit le maistre. Sy congnoissoit flatteurs, lesquelz il
fuiut et haoit sur toutte riens; faulx juges ne pooit amer. En
luy estoyent touttes les taches que en noble homme doivent
estre. De harpes et de tous instrumens melodieux il se savoit
entre-mettre. Nuls n'estoit qui en chel temps l'en passast.
[fol. 29r°–v°]

Two other details of these manuscripts should be mentioned in
passing. The two versions which depend directly on the poem do not
repeat the Greek expressions and their French translations which have
given rise to so much discussion of Aimon de Varennes' place of
origin. They do, however, occur in f. fr. 12566. The other two prose
versions are written in the language of Paris, or perhaps it would be
better to say, are written without any traits which would attach them
to a particular region of France. The text of f. fr. 12566 abounds in
the Picardisms that one would expect in a manuscript copied in Lille
around the middle of the fifteenth century. It seems evident that it
represents a distinctly *northern* version of the tale, a characteristic
which is of course substantiated by the presence of the Burgundian
coat of arms in the first initial.

There remains the problem of accounting for the presence of this
particular *Florimont* in the Burgundian library during the lifetime of
Philip the Good. The manuscript has a very different aspect from the
luxurious volumes known to have been ordered by the duke, including,
of course, his elaborate copy of Wauquelin's *Alexandre* (B.N. f. fr.
9342), whose production is well documented.[37]

The key to the situation might well lie in the fact that *Florimont* is
primarily the story of the youthful adventures of a future ruler of an
extensive kingdom. Taken together with the humorous and rather
dashing illustrations of the Wavrin Master, which do indeed suggest
cartoons more than they resemble the elaborate miniatures so much
in vogue then at the Burgundian court, the ensemble presents the
possibility that this particular copy of *Florimont* may have been des-

tined for the edification of the future ruler as well as the future knights of the Burgundian realm, that is to say, for Charles, the future *Téméraire*, and the young noblemen who were being reared at the court with him. The person most involved in their intellectual formation was Charles' mother, Isabel of Portugal, Duchess of Burgundy and a princess of the Portuguese royal family, who were already noted for their crusaders and travellers. Born in the Portuguese city of Evora, in the shadow of a ruined temple dedicated to Diana which is still a landmark, the duchess was perhaps more aware than many of her contemporaries in the North of the significance of the antique world. There has already been occasion elsewhere to call attention to her patronage of the early humanists in her entourage, including among others Vasco de Lucena.[38] It is tempting to speculate on her association with the Burgundian *Florimont* manuscript, but there is no doubt about her association with Jean de Wavrin on other occasions, nor with his scribe Jean d'Ardennay, who after 1446 was also in Isabel's service as *châtellain* of Montbard, a town she held in apanage.[39] There is thus good reason to suspect that she might even have encouraged the production of this particular version, which would surely have been more to the taste of young noblemen growing up at the court than to that of their more sophisticated elders, a number of whom are associated with the tales of the *Cent Nouvelles nouvelles*.

A particular interest in the classical world emanating from this circle can be substantiated by two further details. In the first place, it was for Antoine Haneron, Charles of Burgundy's tutor, that the first manuscript in the North to be copied in humanistic script was prepared in 1438. One of the texts therein is Xenophon's *Hiero* in Giovanni Aretino's Latin version.[40] Some years later this same text was the basis for a French translation prepared under Charles the Bold's patronage by one of his secretaries, Charles Soillot. The duchess Isabel herself had already encouraged the translation of the Quintus Curtius interpolated life of Alexander by Vasco de Lucena. Soillot also translated into French Xenophon's pedagogical treatise the *Cyropedia*, after Poggio Bracciolini's Latin version, dedicating it too to Charles of Burgundy.[41]

In this context it is quite possible to suppose that the prose *Florimont* from the Burgundian ducal library could have been intended to provide Duke Philip's sons and his companions with a standard of knightly conduct enhanced by examples from antiquity. The obviously interpolated passages give importance to a somewhat different concept of knighthood from the one which pervades Aimon de Varennes' poem, one more concerned with physical courage and moral valor than with theorizing about the precepts of chivalric love. At the same time, Florimont's adventures would have had the additional merit of cultivating an interest in the Middle East. Undoubtedly the hope still existed in some quarters that Charles would ultimately lead a crusade against the menacing Turks and thus avenge the disaster of the Nicopolis crusade, in which his grandfather John the Fearless had taken part. His father, Philip the Bold, had not renounced such a dream until finally overtaken by old age. In any case Charles the Bold, in his mature years, stands out among his contemporaries as one of the early patrons of the sort of new translation of classical texts which foreshadows the Renaissance.

Unfortunately a final judgment of the situation will never be possible until some good fortune brings to light a copy of the Latin text which must have been known to Aimon de Varennes and the later Burgundian translator, possibly Jean de Wavrin, or, better yet, the Greek text which launched this version of Alexander's ancestry. This basic text must surely have been known in more than one place and over a period of several centuries. Perhaps it can still be recovered by students of Byzantium and of the European Middle Ages working together and exchanging information on mutual problems.

NOTES

1. S. Vryonis, *Byzantium and Europe* (London, 1967), p. 193.
2. (Cambridge University Press, 1956; reprinted 1967), pp. 228–30.
3. G. Doutrepont, *La Littérature française à la cour des ducs de Bourgogne* (Paris, 1909), pp. 136–68.
4. G. T. Van Ysselsteyn, *Tapestry: The Most Expensive Industry of the XVth and XVIth Centuries* (The Hague and Brussels, 1969), pp. 39–40; J. P. Asselberghs, *La Tapisserie tournaisienne* (Tournai, 1967). Catalogue of an exhibition held at the cathedral of Tournai, November 1967.
5. Cary, p. 228, and R. Withington, *English Pageantry* (Cambridge, Mass., 1918), I, 152. Doutrepont, p. 186, also calls attention to the fact that in 1469, when the Duke Charles received a delegation from Ghent, where he had just put down a rebellion, the hall was hung with "tres riche tapicerie du grant roy Alexandre, Hanibal et aultres nobles anciens."
6. Doutrepont, pp. 144–46. The most important copies are B.N. f. fr. 1419 (a paper copy similar in format to the Burgundian *Florimont*), 9342, and a MS from the Coll. Dutuit, now at the Petit Palais. See B. Woledge, *Bibliographie des romans et nouvelles en prose français antérieurs à 1500* (Geneva and Lille, 1954), p. 16; also L. M. J. Delaissé, "Les Chroniques de Hainaut et l'atelier de Jean Wauquelin à Mons, dans l'histoire de la littérature

flamande," in *Miscellanea Erwin Panofsky* (Brussels, 1955) pp. 21–55, and *La Miniature flamande, le mécénat de Philippe le Bon* (Brussels, 1959), pp. 51–52. It should be noted that Wauquelin does not claim to translate an early text, but to put into prose an earlier poem: "Selon ce que je l'ay trouvet en ung livre rimet dont je ne say le non del acteur fors que il est intitulé *Histoire Alixandre.* Et pour ce, se de la vraye histoire de ce tant noble et poissant roy je suis aucunement desvoyé que non s'à Dieu plaist, ou s'aucune deffaulte en la poursuilte de la ditte matiere est trouvée . . . elle soit à Dieu atribuée et la deffaulte à ma negligence tournée" (f. fr. 1419, fol. 17).

7. C. C. Willard, "The Concept of True Nobility at the Burgundian Court," *Studies in the Renaissance,* XIV (1967), 38.

8. Cary, p. 63; C. Samaran, *Vasco de Lucène à la cour de Bourgogne* (Lisbon, 1938), and R. Bossuet, "Vasque de Lucène, traducteur de Quinte-Curce," *Bibliothèque d'Humanisme et Renaissance,* VIII (1946), 197–245.

9. B.N. f. fr. 22457, fol. 1. This manuscript is presumed to be the presentation copy prepared for Charles the Bold.

10. J. J. De Smet, *Recueil des antiquités de Flandre de Philippe Wielant* (*Corpus Chronicorum Flandriae*), (Brussels, 1856), IV, 56, cited in Doutrepont, p. 182.

11. G. Mombello, "Per la fortuna del Boccaccio in Francia: Jean Miélot traduttore di due capitoli della Genealogia," in *Studi sul Boccacio I* (Florence, 1963), pp. 415–44.

12. *La Miniature flamande,* pp. 76–83.

13. L. M. J. Delaissé, "Les Principaux Centres de production de MSS. enluminés dans les Etats de Philippe le Bon," in *Cahiers de l'Assoc. int. des Etudes françaises* (June 1956), pp. 11–34; J. Porcher, "Les Peintres de Jean de Wavrin," *Revue française de l'élite européenne,* LXXVII (1956), 17–22; F. Desonay, "Une Oeuvre fort peu connue du Maître de Wavrin," *Gedenkboek A. Vermeylen* (Brussels, 1923), pp. 409–20.

14. *La Miniature flamande,* p. 80.

15. A. Hilka, ed., *Aimon von Varennes: Florimont, ein altfranzösicher abenteuerroman,* Gesellschaft für Romanische Literatur, Band 48 (Göttingen, 1932), Intro. p. cxxxix. The discussion of various linguistic aspects of the poem has continued for more than a century, from P. Meyer's "Essai de restitution de quelques mots grecs cités dans le Roman de Florimont," *BEC,* XXVII (1866), 331–34, to B. Horiot, "Traits lyonnais dans Florimont d'Aimon de Varennes," *Travaux de linguistique et de littérature du Centre de philologie et littératures romanes de l'Université de Strasbourg,* VI, 1 (1968), 169–85. P. Gardette, "Aimon de Varennes, lyonnais," *Romania,* LXXVII (1956), 506–7, has taken up once more the effort to locate the Varennes and the Chastillon referred to in the poem. In evaluating these discussions it should be remembered that of eleven manuscripts in the Bibliothèque Nationale representing four versions of the text, only four can claim to have been copied in the thirteenth century and none even pretends to be earlier. Of these four, two are in compilations of several romances (f. fr. 792 and 1374); one is in a manuscript which also includes

Erec and Enide (f. fr. 1376); and only one (f. fr. 15101) contains this text alone. This last has additions in a later hand, both at the beginning and at the end, and is unfinished in that the capital letters have not been written in except in the middle portion. None of them bears any indication to suggest that it has any close connection with the author.

Although Aimon de Varennes insisted that French was not his native language, and though there are both a Varenna and a Varena in Northern Italy, where there are also several manuscripts of the poem, nobody but F. Novati (see note 20) has even suggested the possibility of an Italian origin for the poet, although this might provide one clue to his presence in Italy before 1188.

16. A. Fourrier, *Le Courant réaliste dans le roman courtois en France au Moyen Age* (Paris, 1960), p. 449; also A. Henry, in his review of the Hilka ed. in *Romania*, LXI (1935), 354: "D'autre part, *Florimont* n'est pas un roman oriental. Sans doute l'action se passe dans un Orient d'ailleurs géographiquement précisé, mais rien, à part une ou deux légendes orientales ou albanaises, n'y serait changé si elle se déroulait ailleurs. Il n'y a rien, dans *Florimont*, de la couleur locale, ni de l'orientalisme (vrai ou faux) qui baigne le récit dans le Roman d'Alexandre par exemple. . . . *Florimont* est donc simplement un roman d'aventures . . . essentiellement une oeuvre de transition." On the other hand it must not be forgotten that G. Paris had said at a somewhat earlier date, *Romania*, XXII (1893), 163, that "les récentes discussions auxquelles *Florimont* a donné lieu, en ramenant l'attention sur l'oeuvre d'Aimon de Varennes, ne peuvent qu'augmenter l'impatience qu'on a de voir paraître l'édition, . . . d'une des oeuvres, à tous égards, les plus intéressantes du XIIᵉ siècle." See also Douglas Kelly, "The Composition of Aimon de Varennes' *Florimont*," *Romanic Philology*, XXIII (1970), 277–92. The quotations from the poem are taken from the Hilka edition, verified by his basic text (f. fr. 1510). His system of adding and subtracting letters obscures what is really written in the manuscript.

17. See K. Krumbacher, *Geschichte der Byzantinischen Literatur von Justinian bis zum Ende des oströmischen Reiches (527–1453)*, 2nd ed. (Munich, 1897), p. 465; D. T. Rice, *Byzantine Painting: The Last Phase* (New York, 1968), p. 37. See especially the comment of J. M. Hussey, *The Byzantine World* (London, 1967), pp. 58–59, on the relations of Manuel Comnenus (1143–80) with the West: "Trade, policy, political circumstances, had brought to the East Mediterranean, to the Byzantine Empire itself, a flood of westerners, many of whom had settled there. Manuel . . . had a great liking for Latins and their customs."

18. In the study cited in note 16, Fourrier has made an extensive study of Aimon de Varennes' geographical references (pp. 471–82); see also Hilka, Intro., pp. xcix–cii.

19. R. Lopez, "L'Extrême Frontière du commerce de l'Europe médiévale," *Moyen Age*, LXIX (1963), 479–90; also Margaret Frazer, "Byzantine Art and the West," in *The Year 1200, II: A Background Survey* (New York, 1970), p. 185.

20. Hilka, pp. ix–xi, lists London, British Museum, Harley 4487 (dated 1295),

and Harley 3983 (dated 1323) as well as Venice, Bibl. Marciana, fondo antico 22 (14th cent.); Turin, Univ. Bibl. L.II.16; and Monza, Bibl. de San Giovanni 6.21.137. This last is the only one which has been the object of a detailed examination. See F. Novati, "Nouvelles Recherches sur le roman de Florimont d'après un Ms. italien," *Revue des langues romanes*, 4e sér., V (1891), 481–504. There was also a MS, now lost, in the library of the Dukes of Milan at Pavia; see A. Thomas, "Les Mss. fr. et provençaux des ducs de Milan au château de Pavie," *Romania*, XL (1911), 588.

21. G. Doutrepont, *Les Mises en prose des épopées et romans chevaleresques du XIVe au XVIe siècle* (Brussels, 1939), pp. 158–60. Woledge, pp. 91–92, lists five MSS of this work.

22. Aimon de Varennes says:

> Floquars respont: G'iria a pié.
> En maintes terres sui estus,
> Ne vodroie estre coneüs.
> Mon nom wel celer a la gent,
> Car ju irai si povrement,
> Si wel que vos mon nom celez.
> Quacopedie m'apalez;
> Quacopedie en grezois
> Di[s]t mavais garsons en fransois.
>   [vv. 4728–36]

MS fr. 12566: "Sire, je iray a piet car en maint pays ay esté. Pour riens ne voldroye estre congneus. Je voel à tous mon non cheler puis que sy povrement suis vestus. Et voel que par non soye nommés Cacopedye, qui à dire est en langage franchoise *malvaix garchon*. Ainsi sera la Povre Perdu acompaignies de malvaix garchon."

This name Cacopédie is one of the elements which led J. Psichari to question Aimon de Varennes' knowledge of Greek. In the first place, he thought that it must have had an oral origin, or that perhaps it was inspired by an expression which really referred to two companions in misfortune and thus rested on a misinterpretation of the Greek text. The fact that the prose version repeats the same expression in the same context would of course suggest that the error could have occurred between the Greek text and the Latin translation. See the comments of G. Paris in *Romania*, XXII, 159.

23. In *Izŭ istorii romana i povêsti* (St. Petersburg, 1886), I, 494–501, summarized in Hilka, p. cviii.

24. A bibliographical notice in *Byzantion*, XXXVIII (1968), 163, calls attention to the need for editions of manuscripts of the Byzantine *Alexander* romance with reference to the recent work by K. Mitsakis, *Der byzantinische Alexanderroman nach dem Codex Vidob. Theol. Gr. 244* (Miscellania Byzantina Monacensia, 7) (Munich, 1967). This same text was edited by A. H. Veselovskij in 1886 (see above), but six others remain unedited.

25. Marcel Françon, *Leçons et notes sur la littérature française au XVIe siècle* (Cambridge, Mass., 1965), pp. 142–50; for the Normans, see David C. Douglas, *The Norman Achievement* (London, 1969).

26. *Mélusine*, ed. Louis Stouff (Paris, 1932), p. 244.
27. Françon, p. 150; also H. Doutenville, "Le Géant Gargan au XII⁰ siècle," *BSMF*, XXIV (1956), 110–14; H. Grégoire and R. de Keyser, "*La Chanson de Roland* et Byzance," *Byzantion*, XIV (1939), 297–98.
28. See note 16.
29. *Oeuvres poétiques de Christine de Pisan*, ed. M. Roy (Paris, 1891), II, 94–95.
30. Hilka, pp. ix–xii.
31. Doutrepont, *Les Mises en prose*, pp. 264–75; Woledge, p. 43. For Greek sources see Krumbacher, pp. 868–70.
32. MS fr. 12566, fol. 1 v°; it is interesting to note in this context the addition to a fifteenth-century MS in Brussels (MS 15702), the only French version of the *Conquête de la Morée*, which states: "C'est le livre de la conqueste de Constantinople et de l'empire de Romme, et dou pays de la princée de la Morée, qui fu trovée en un livre qui fu jadis del noble baron Messire Bartholomée Guys, le grant conestable, le quel livre il avoit en son chastel d'Estives (Thebes)." Krumbacher, p. 834, observes furthermore that the French version follows the Greek text quite closely.
33. *Anchiennes Chroniques d'Engleterre* par Jean de Wavrin, annotés et publiés pour la Société de l'Histoire de France par Mlle Dupont (Paris, 1858), I, Préface, summarizes biographical evidence based on available documents. The master list on which his name occurs is in Dijon, Arch. de la Côte d'Or B, 11788/32 (Aug. 31, 1417).
34. Doutrepont, *La Litt. française*, p. 186.
35. B.N. f. fr. 1490, fol. 1.
36. *Etudes romanes dédiées à Gaston Paris*, p. 515. This would surely be truer of f. fr. 12566 than of f. fr. 1490.
37. Doutrepont, *La Litt. française*, pp. 34–38; see also R. Vaughan, *Philip the Good* (London, 1970), p. 155: "But in the years after 1445 a steady stream of important commissions resulted in the foundation of groups of scribes at Mons, Valenciennes, Hesdin, Lille, Oudenaarde, Bruges, Brussels and Ghent; all of them engaged in producing lavishly illuminated manuscripts for the Burgundian court." Of course this description would scarcely apply to a number of those produced in Lille.
38. C. C. Willard, "Isabel of Portugal, Patroness of Humanism?" *Miscellanea di Studi e ricerche sul Quattrocento francese*, a cura di Franco Simone (Torino, 1966), pp. 519–44. See also G. Peignot, *Choix de testaments anciens et modernes* (Paris and Dijon, 1829), I, 111.
39. Dijon, Arch. de la Côte d'Or, B 5325 (1441–43): "Compte de Jean Dardenay, châtelain, institué par lettres d'Isabelle de Portugal, duchesse de Bourgogne, à qui le duc avait donné, entre autres terres, celle de Montbard, qui lui était advenue par la mort de sa soeur la duchesse de Guyenne, comtesse de Richemont"; B 5334 (1458–60): "Compte d'Antoine Rouselet, écuyer de Montbard en Auxois, institué par lettres du duc Philippe, en replacement de Jean Dardenay 'homme très-ancien, foible et debilité de sa personne, qui avoit résigné son office.'"
40. *La Miniature flamande*, p. 162. This manuscript is now MS Lips. 50 of the Leyden University Library; see fol. 113r°–128v°: "Leonis Aretini versio Hieronis Xenophontei."

41. For Charles the Bold's copy of Soillot's translation, see *Manuscrits et livres du quatorizième au seizième siècle*, Catalogue 60 of Pierre Berès, Paris; also Doutrepont, *La Litt. française*, pp. 179–80. For the *Cyropedia*, trans. by Vasco de Lucena, see "Isabel of Portugal, Patroness of Humanism?" p. 540, and J. Monfrin, "Humanisme et traductions du moyen âge," *Journal des Savants* (July–Sept. 1963), pp. 182–83.

Byzantium and the Migration of Literary Works and Motifs

THE LEGEND OF THE LAST ROMAN EMPEROR*

Paul J. Alexander

THE BYZANTINE EMPIRE, during the more than one thousand years of its existence, was not only the storehouse of classical Greek literature; it was also "the great clearing house of East and West," in folk literature as well as in other branches.[1] Bulgarians, Russians, Armenians, and Georgians received their first literary stimuli from Byzantium, so much so that the early written monuments of these and other peoples are largely translations from Byzantine Greek originals. Furthermore, a considerable number of Byzantine literary works were translated in the Middle Ages into Latin and had a profound influence on the development of literature in western and central Europe.[2] All this is well known, but it is not always stressed sufficiently that Byzantium functioned not only as a literary donor but also frequently as the recipient of literary gifts. This process has so far been studied in its more general aspects only for one field of literature, hagiography, but influences of Syriac, Arabic, Armenian, Coptic, and even Far Eastern literatures upon that of Byzantium are also important in other genres.[3] Particularly interesting are the migrations of works which originated in the Far East and thence travelled via various intermediate stages including Byzantium to western or Slavic Europe. A case in point is the Indian story about Buddha extant in Greek in the guise of the *Romance of Barlaam and Joasaph* as well as in a Latin transla-

*Several friends and colleagues have read an earlier draft of this paper and made valuable comments, especially Professors Fred Amory, Wolfgang Sauer, and Stephen J. Tonsor. Furthermore, I presented it orally to the Collegium Orientologicum at the University of California, Berkeley, and received many suggestions from various colleagues. I take this opportunity to express my sincere gratitude for all this help. I also wish to thank Mr. Stephen Benin, a graduate student in the Department of History at Berkeley, for checking my references, as well as two readers for *Medievalia et Humanistica* for good advice.

tion of the early eleventh century; or the Indian tale of the two jackals Calila and Dimna translated into Greek in the eleventh century and into various Slavic languages, at the latest, in the early thirteenth; or finally the Hebrew story of the wise Achikar which surfaced at Byzantium in the form of a *Life of Aesop* and thence reached the Slavs.[4] What constitutes the peculiar interest of these and of other instances of long-distance literary migration is not only the appeal of these works to the many cultures into whose languages they were translated, but also the fact that, once many philological and historical labors are completed, it should become possible to define more precisely the process of migration and to ascertain the reasons for their spread. In most cases, however, no such precision is as yet attainable, simply because the scholarly problems are too difficult and the work has just begun.

There is, however, one case of literary borrowing for which the process can be studied in some detail and certain conclusions reached: the legend or expectation of a Last Roman Emperor. The story of its spread is by no means typical, but it may serve to illustrate one type of appeal that facilitated long-distance migration: an appeal to religio-political ideology. This legend is not limited to one particular literary work but is a motif that appears in a variety of forms. Normally it emerges in contexts dealing with Christian expectations concerning the end of the world. At some point, during the course of events leading to the end, there emerges a Last Roman Emperor who defeats the national or religious enemy, journeys to Jerusalem, and resides there for a number of years. At the end of this period he hands over the insignia of his office to God. That act is usually followed immediately by a manifestation of Antichrist, who then seduces vast numbers of people but is finally liquidated by Jesus Christ at his Second Coming. The characteristic features of the legend, therefore, are a war of liberation and an imperial abdication.

What is the origin of this story? It will be advisable to begin at the end to define the circumstances under which this legend was first studied by modern scholars. This happened in nineteenth-century Germany.

The historical development of Germany and of much of Europe in the nineteenth century was determined by two series of events: the Napoleonic wars at the beginning of the century and the foundation of the German Empire towards its end. These happenings, separated though they were by a span of seven decades, were of course related.

The Bismarckian unification of the many German states under the authority of the Prussian dynasty owed a great deal to the nationalist feelings aroused or at least released by the foreign invasions. As a result not only political tracts, but also the philosophy, literature, and historiography of nineteenth-century Germany were permeated by the hope for a united effort of the German principalities and peoples against foreign domination and influence.

In Germany these hopes and dreams reinforced apocalyptic expectations of a restored empire current in eighteenth-century Europe. Characteristically, the legends of the medieval Empire had originated in the Late Middle Ages after the Great Interregnum, when the Empire was little more than an empty title and a nostalgic dream, and when sovereignty in Germany was parcelled out among a host of secular and ecclesiastical princes. In this political atmosphere the popular longing for peace, for freedom from oppression by local dynasts, and for the strengthening of the imperial power produced sagas such as that of Mount Kyffhäuser.[5] A Bavarian chronicle of the early fourteenth century, for example, spoke of an Emperor, buried but not dead, who would return with great military power. By 1434 this legend had gradually crystalized around an Emperor Frederick who was expected to await his reappearance in a castle on Mount Kyffhäuser.[6] After the Napoleonic wars had removed the last vestiges of German unity and demonstrated German impotence, the Romantic movement reinvigorated the medieval legends.

In the second decade of the nineteenth century Friedrick Rückert published his famous and influential poem "Barbarossa." Here, the sleeping Emperor with his fiery beard was described sitting in a subterranean castle to which he had descended, taking with him the Empire's glory. There he will sit, on an ivory chair at a marble table, as long as the ravens fly around Mount Kyffhäuser. But one day he will return to restore the Empire to its former splendor:

> Er hat hinabgenommen
> Des Reiches Herrlichkeit
> Und wird einst wiederkommen
> Mit ihr, zu seiner Zeit.

The popular dream of freedom from foreign influences and interventions, and of national unification affected not only poets and publicists but also the world of scholarship and historiography. Characteristic in this respect is one of the outstanding and influential German works on medieval history, Wilhelm von Giesebrecht's *Geschichte der deutschen Kaiserzeit,* of which the first volume was published in 1855. The preface to the first edition of the work is permeated by an awareness of the depth and intensity of national feeling; it stresses the author's "patriotic purpose" and expresses his fervent desire to provide for the best among the young, as he puts it, "the torch illuminating a brighter future for the German nation."[7] It is instructive to compare the preface of 1855 with that of the fourth edition of 1873. In the interval between the two editions Denmark and Austria had been defeated in battle, the Prussian and allied armies had laid siege to Paris, overthrown Napoleon III, and imposed a burdensome peace upon France. Above all, King William of Prussia had been proclaimed German Emperor at Versailles in January, 1871. This was heady wine indeed for German patriots, and Giesebrecht's preface of 1873 shows its effects very clearly. It speaks of "the most miraculous change of circumstances . . . which we have witnessed in wonder" and expresses the hope that a time "when the resurrected names of Emperor and Empire exert their magical power on millions of people" will generate an interest in the subject of medieval German history.[8]

The events of the 'sixties and 'seventies served not only as the justification for the historical study of the medieval Empire, but also seemed the fulfillment of medieval prophecies and oracles about its revival. Indeed, after these prophecies seemed validated on the battlefields of Europe and in the Hall of Mirrors at Versailles, the study of medieval oracular literature became an academically respectable, even a passionate, scholarly concern in Bismarckian Germany. It is, therefore, no accident that in 1871 the *Historische Zeitschrift,* founded and directed by Heinrich von Sybel, who had played an active role in Prussian politics and was later commissioned by Bismarck to write the official history of the foundation of the Empire, published Georg Voigt's important and influential article on "Die deutsche Kaisersage." In it the author defined his topic, somewhat narrowly, as "the legend of the old Emperor who would not die, who would some day return in order to refound the empire."

In the same *annus mirabilis* of 1871 there appeared a study informed by a different and independent spirit, the Roman Catholic theologian Johann Joseph Ignaz von Döllinger's essay entitled "Der Weissagungsglaube und das Prophetentum in der Christlichen Zeit."[9] In this article Döllinger did not join the chorus of nationalistic wonderment and intoxication over recent successes, nor did he, like his German contemporaries, focus primarily on German prophecies. He cast his net wider, both geographically and typologically, distinguishing four types of medieval prophecy (purely religious, dynastic, national, and cosmopolitan) and emphasized in particular the religious and ecclesiastical component in medieval prophecy. German predictions are touched on only occasionally, and Döllinger discusses instead materials ranging from Portugal to England and from Byzantium to papal Rome. In fact, one gains the impression that with this profound essay Döllinger intended to provide a counterfoil to the prevalent exploitation of medieval prophecies for nationalist purposes. The net effect of the essay on the reader is the realization that medieval prophecy had its roots in early Christianity; was by no means a monopoly of the German nation; was very frequently inspired by political motivations; and miscarried as often as it succeeded in predicting later events. Characteristically, Döllinger concluded with a citation from Isaiah 55:8–9: "My thoughts are not your thoughts, neither are your ways my ways, says the Lord," and remarked that this Biblical verse must have occurred to many a reader of his essay. One cannot escape the conclusion that this sceptical and broadminded study of medieval prophecy by a prominent and pious Roman Catholic churchman was meant to serve as a warning against the prevailing spirit of excitement over the military and political successes of the German nation. Döllinger seems to have felt that the excessive impressionability evidenced by German scholars with regard to recent developments required a learned refutation. Indirectly, therefore, even Döllinger's sober and wide-ranging article offers powerful testimony to the widespread and intense fascination of German intellectuals with the legends surrounding the medieval empire.

In the years that followed the proclamation at Versailles German historians, philologists, and theologians vied with each other in attempting to elucidate the origin and development of the legends about the German Emperors. They were patriots as well as scholars, and occasionally interpreted medieval developments in the light of political programmes of the nineteenth century. It should be recognized, however, that, probably under the influence of Döllinger's cosmopolitan approach, they were to a large extent free of another possible bias. With remarkable objectivity they traced the genesis of German imperial ideology to its roots in cultures far distant from either medieval or modern Germany in time, place, and cultural tradition. Indeed, it is no exaggeration to say that they rejoiced in discovering Biblical, classical, or Oriental foundations to the imperial legends, and considered that such "exotic" origins strengthened and authenticated German expectations of imperial splendor, rather than providing an embarrassment for the German patriot.

The first scholar to connect explicitly the German imperial legends of the Middle Ages with foreign sources [10] was a Lutheran theologian at the University of Erlangen, Gerhard von Zezschwitz, in a book published in 1877 and indicating in its subtitle his claim that he had discovered Byzantine sources for the legends concerning the medieval German Emperors.[11] Zezschwitz's point of departure was a play, the *Ludus de Antichristo*, written in the days of Frederick Barbarossa and embodying the far-reaching imperial claims of that period. He published this text from a twelfth-century manuscript and related the ideas contained therein to the realities and claims prevalent in twelfth-century Germany. In this play the stage is set in Jerusalem and shows the Temple and seven royal thrones: those of the kings of Jerusalem, of the Synagogue, the Roman Emperor, and of the German, French, Greek, and Babylonian kings. The Roman Emperor demands that the French king recognize his universal sovereignty. The latter refuses, is defeated in battle, and finally acknowledges the Emperor's authority. The other kings follow suit, with one exception: the king of Babylon, as the spokesman for polytheism, decides to destroy Christianity and to attack it at its place of origin, Jerusalem. The Roman Emperor comes to the aid of the king of Jerusalem, defeats the king of Babylon in war, and enters the Temple. There he takes off his crown and offers it to God at the altar. This is followed by the entry of the Antichrist into the Temple, the establishment of his reign, and his final destruction.

Zezschwitz provided his edition of this play with a series of "introductory treatises." The first of these, significantly entitled "The New and the Old Empire," demonstrates, both by this heading and its content, how closely related in Zezschwitz's view the medieval play and its subject matter were to the electrifying events of the Bismarckian era. He explained that it illustrated in lively colors the theory of universal monarchy as it had been entertained at the court of Frederick Barbarossa, and in its most extreme form by the Emperor's chancellor Reinald von Dassel.[12] He then investigated in depth the political and religious ideas underlying this play and succeeded in relating them to the historical realities of Barbarossa's Germany and to the vast body of historical and legendary materials surrounding the medieval Empire. There was, however, one pivotal feature of the play which he was unable to explain in terms of the German tradition: the voluntary abdication of the Last Roman Emperor in the Temple at Jerusalem, followed by the entry of the Antichrist.[10] It is true that he found this trait in a treatise of the mid-tenth century by Adso, later abbot of Moustier-en-Der, in the diocese of Chalons-sur-Marne. In his *Epistola . . . de Ortu et Tempore Antichristi* Adso had mentioned a tradition according to which a last king of the Franks would journey to Jerusalem and would lay down scepter and crown on the Mount of Olives. Here too this act of abdication was followed by the coming of the Antichrist.[14] Clearly this was the same tradition of a ruler's abdication at Jerusalem as in the *Ludus de Antichristo*. Yet Zezschwitz pointed out that in the West this tradition was attested only in these two documents of the tenth and twelfth centuries respectively, as well as in a few texts dependent upon them, and that the act of abdication in particular was not derived from Adso's usual ninth-century source, Haymo of Halberstadt's Commentary on *Second Thessalonians*. Zezschwitz was thus driven to look beyond the Western tradition for the source of the notion, expressed by Adso and the *Ludus*, that a ruler would lay down his crown at Jerusalem.

He found this source in a Greek Apocalypse attributed to the "martyr" Methodius.[15] True, here the act of abdication at Jerusalem followed upon the Antichrist's first appearance, but it was clearly in all other respects the tradition underlying Adso and the *Ludus*.[16] Zezschwitz had thus discovered a new dimension for the Western legends about the Emperors and he therefore dedicated to the *Apocalypse* attributed to Methodius a lengthy and detailed section of his book.[17] His results were partly invalidated or refined by later research, but there can be no doubt that it was Zezschwitz who gave the new "orientation" to the further investigation of the Legend of the Last Emperor.

This dependence of all later work on that of Zezschwitz can be demonstrated in detail. The connecting link was a review of Zezschwitz's book by the great German classicist and orientalist Alfred von Gutschmid.[18] Zezschwitz's book and Gutschmid's review then provided the impetus for a series of further publications on the German imperial legends and their sources in ancient apocalyptic legends. In 1895 and 1896, respectively, when all Germany was celebrating the twenty-fifth anniversary of the Empire's founding, two important works on the subject appeared: the historian Franz Kamper's *Kaiser-*

53

prophetien und Kaisersagen im Mittelalter [19] and the theologian Wilhelm Bousset's book *Der Antichrist in der Überlieferung des Judentums, des Neuen Testaments und der Alten Kirche.* Three years later was published Ernst Sackur's *Sibyllinische Texte und Forschungen* (1898). All of them show the impact of Zezschwitz's and Gutschmid's work in that they combine a study of the ancient apocalyptic tradition, as represented for example by Pseudo-Methodius' work, with that of German political legends. Wilhelm Bousset quoted the concluding sentence of Gutschmid's review in the preface of his book. Sackur in turn stated in his foreword that he found Gutschmid's remarks the best that had been written on Pseudo-Methodius and that he owed to him the idea of preparing a critical edition of the Latin text. Work on the subject continued with reduced intensity into the twentieth century, but these remarks must suffice to illustrate the close connection between German scholarly work on the legends concerning medieval Emperors and their origins in Early Christian and Byzantine apocalypses on the one hand and the emergence of German nationalism and the unification of the country on the other.

What was this *Apocalypse* of Pseudo-Methodius, which the German scholars of the nineteenth century, to their surprise, found had exerted a strong influence on the German legends concerning their medieval Emperors? The Greek text is a strange, indeed an enigmatic, document.[20] According to the Greek title, the author was Methodius, bishop of Patara, and the book deals with the kingdoms of the barbarians and the Last Times. The first part of the work (chaps. I–VII) is written in the past tense and contains an extremely fanciful history of the world from Adam to the Moslem invasions. It is based to some extent on the Bible, but the Biblical account is generously "improved" by apocryphal additions and combined with a legend about the founding of Byzantium by the hero Byzas, allegedly the second husband of Alexander the Great's mother, the Ethiopian princess Chuseth. In this part (chap. VII) the author quotes prominently II Thessalonians 2:1–8 and interprets the difficult phrase: "only he who now restrains it [the mystery of lawlessness] will do so until he is out of the way" to refer to the Roman or the Byzantine Empire. It followed from this interpretation that the Empire, destined to restrain the Antichrist, would last to the end of time. He also cited for the same purpose I Corinthians 15:24: "Then comes the end when he delivers the kingdom to God the Father."[21] This same objective of proving that the Byzantine Empire will endure to the last days is also evident in the interpretation which the author gives to Psalms 68:31: "let Ethiopia hasten to stretch out her hands unto God," for the author states that in accordance with the parahistorical genealogies developed by him the Byzantine Emperor is the descendant of an Ethiopian princess, and it is therefore a Byzantine Emperor, as the legitimate heir of Ethiopian royalty, who will "stretch out his hands to God."[22] In this interpretation of the psalm the author reveals his purpose in writing the "historical" section and indeed the entire *Apocalypse*: to prove that the Byzantine Empire would last to the end of time and consequently be victorious over all its enemies, the Moslems included.

In the second part (chaps. VII–X), written in the future tense, the apocalyptist "prophesies" the Arab invasions and describes at great length and in lurid detail their destructiveness and cruelty. The third section of the work (chaps. XI and XII) is eschatological and therefore most interesting in the present context. Pseudo-Methodius predicts that at the time when the Moslems are at the height of their power, an Emperor of the Greeks and Romans will arise against them. He will, in the words of the psalmist (78:65), be "awakened as one out of sleep and like a man drinking wine," whom men had considered dead and worthless. He will defeat the Moslems, drive them back into Arabia, and free the lands of the Empire that they had occupied. The Emperor will then proceed to Jerusalem, where he will reside for one year-week and a half (ten and a half years). The Antichrist will be born. Then the Emperor will ascend Golgotha, will take off his diadem, and depose it on the Cross. He will stretch out his hands to heaven and hand over his imperial power to God. Then the Antichrist will seduce many people, but in the end he will be slain by Jesus Christ at the Second Coming.

This very brief summary hardly gives an adequate impression of the strangeness of the document, and it is impossible in the present context to discuss all the many problems which it poses. Here it must suffice to say that the Greek text was written in the seventh or early eighth century, after Syria and Mesopotamia had been occupied by the Arabs, and is therefore half a millennium later than the church father Methodius to whom it was attributed.[23] The earlier parts of the *Apocalypse*, therefore, consist largely of *vaticinia post eventum*. It is also clear that the work, though strange, fanciful, and legendary, is inspired by the Byzantine ideology of empire which it makes the pivot of an impressive and coherent parahistorical construction culminating in the abdication scene on Golgotha — a point that Zezschwitz, once again, was the first scholar to emphasize.[24] In the first place, the transfer of imperial authority from the Last Roman Emperor to God at the end of time reflects the Byzantine idea that the Emperor is God's vice-regent on earth.[25] From this basic concept it followed logically that successful completion of the divine mandate by the defeat of all non-Christian powers by the Last Roman Emperor meant the end of the mandatory's power, i.e., abdication. Secondly, the role of the Cross in the act of abdication is closely bound up with the Byzantine notion, already known to Eusebius, that God had bestowed universal power on the first Christian Emperor Constantine the Great by a vision of the Cross.[26] Finally, the abdication of the Last Roman Emperor on Golgotha is the visual representation and dramatization of Pseudo-Methodius' interpretation of II Thessalonians 2; I Corinthians 15:24; and Psalms 68:31. In this scene, the restraining influence, i.e., the Empire, is shown to be "out of the way" because by the act of abdication the Empire comes to an end. In this scene, also, it is imagined that Christ, represented by his mandatory the Emperor, "delivers the kingdom to God the Father." Finally, in this act of abdication, Ethiopia, i.e., the Byzantine Emperor descended from the Ethiopian princess Chuseth, quite literally is seen "to stretch out her hands to God." In turn this interpretation of Psalms 68:31 presupposes the entire series of parahistorical genealogies in the first part of the *Apocalypse*, for only if the Byzantine Emperor is descended from the Ethiopian rulers can it be maintained that he personifies the "Ethiopia" of the psalmist. It thus becomes clear that in this *Apocalypse* the abdication scene on Golgotha is deeply rooted in the eschatological, theological, and ideological conceptions of Byzantine Christianity. The scene is clearly an invention based on the three Biblical passages mentioned above, as is the parahistorical construction which buttresses it, but it is an invention which expresses in visual imagery the Byzantine theory of imperial power and Byzantine eschatological expectations.

Is the author of the Greek text responsible for this invention? This raises the question of the originality of the Greek text, and in this connection an important discovery was made about a generation ago. A Hungarian Orientalist, the late Michael Kmosko, proved not only that the Greek text was derived from an original written in the Syriac language, but that this critical text actually survives in a Vatican manuscript of the sixteenth century.[27] Kmosko had the intention of studying the Syriac text in detail but unfortunately was not able to carry out his project. I have, however, transcribed and translated the manuscript, and there can be no doubt, for a variety of philological reasons, that the Syriac text is the original and the Greek text its translation.

By and large, the content of the Syriac is very similar to that of its Greek, Latin, and other translations. Like the Greek text, the Syriac original is attributed to Methodius, who is here called "bishop of Olympus and martyr." Its subject matter is defined as "the succession of kings and concerning the end of times." In the Syriac document the revelation properly speaking is introduced by a preamble according to which Methodius "asked God to learn concerning the generations and concerning the kingdoms, how they were handed down from Adam and until today." God then sent to Methodius "one from among his hosts," i.e., an angel, who showed him all the generations and kingdoms. From the point of view of literary history the most interesting detail in this preamble, all of which is missing in the Greek and all other translations, is the statement that the angel's revelation took place on "the mountain of Shenāgar." [28] This remark makes it highly probable, if not certain, that the text was composed in Mesopotamia, to be exact near Tour Shiggar, or Djabal Sindjar, a mountain range about one hundred miles west of modern Mosul on the slopes of which had been situated the ancient city of Singara. So far as the time of composition is concerned, there are rather clear indications that it cannot have been written prior to A.D. 644 or later than 678. [29]

As in the Greek translation, the first part of the Syriac apocalypse is "historical" and reaches from Adam to the Moslem invasions of "Rome," that is of the Byzantine Empire. Here again there is the Biblical story generously expanded by fanciful data from Oriental history and legend; for example the marriage of the hero Byzas with the princess Chuseth, mother of Alexander the Great, as well as the citations from II Thessalonians 2 and Psalm 68. This parahistorical part is followed, again as in the Greek text, by "prophecies" of the Arab invasions and the terrible destruction and suffering inflicted by the enemy. In the third, or eschatological, section of the Syriac text, this mood of despair gives way to one of hope and triumph. Just as the Moslems are at the height of their power and proclaim blasphemously that "there is no deliverer for the Christians," Pseudo-Methodius predicts that a king of the Greeks will defeat them and drive them back into the desert. This king will then proceed to Jerusalem, will deposit his diadem on the Holy Cross, will stretch out his hands to heaven, and surrender his kingship to God. [30]

In general layout, then, the Syriac original resembles closely the Greek translation. There exist, however, a great many differences in detail, such as the preamble omitted in the Greek version. Some of these differences shed light on obscurities in the translation; others, as is usually the case with newly discovered texts, pose new problems. A most revealing feature is the reference, in the parahistorical section of the Syriac text, to Psalms 68:31: "Let Ethiopia stretch out her hands unto God." Here the author attacks "many brethren of the clergy" who, not unnaturally, assumed that the psalmist meant the kingdom of Ethiopia. Not so, says the author, "the kingdom of Greece" was meant, because its ruler was descended from the Ethiopian princess Chuseth.[31] The first conclusion to follow from this passage in which the author calls his unknown opponents "brethren of the clergy" is that he himself must have been a member of the clergy, a priest, or a monk.

The passage allows a further inference. Why should Methodius' opponents, who were priests in Mesopotamia in the seventh century, have expected the Ethiopian kingdom to last until the end of time and the Ethiopian king to play so important a role in the eschatological events? In the distant past there had indeed been strong religious ties between Syriac-speaking Christianity and Ethiopia, and Syrian missionaries had played an important role in the Christianization of Ethiopia. Furthermore, for a short period in the first half of the sixth century Ethiopia had intervened militarily in the affairs of southern Arabia and even played a role in Mediterranean diplomacy. But in 570 the Persian conquest of Yemen had put an end to Ethiopia's role.[32] The only reason why in the seventh century Pseudo-Methodius' opponents could be so concerned to find a Biblical guarantee for the permanence of the Ethiopian kingdom was that Ethiopia was the only country in the world where Monophysitism was the official religion and the ruler himself a Monophysite.

There is one further inference to be drawn from Pseudo-Methodius' statement that "many brethren of the clergy" interpreted Psalms 68:31 to refer to the ruler of Ethiopia. For Mesopotamian Christians under Moslem rule, to rely in the seventh century for liberation upon the Monophysite monarch of Ethiopia was tantamount to saying that the time of delivery lay in the indefinite future and to permitting an interim accommodation with the conquerors. This, indeed, was the policy pursued by the Monophysite religious leader in that area, Marutha, the metropolitan bishop of Tagrit, who opened the gates of the citadel of his city to the Moslems. His example was followed by many Christian individuals and communities. So successful was this policy that Marutha's biographer, his successor Denha of Tagrit (649–59), was able to describe in dithyrambic terms the security, prosperity, good ecclesiastical organization, and charitable activities of the Jacobite Church in Mesopotamia and its submission to the Arab authorities.[33] This description was approximately contemporaneous with the composition of the Syriac *Apocalypse* of Pseudo-Methodius. However, in contrast to his ecclesiastical superior Denha, the anonymous author of the *Apocalypse* paints in the darkest colors the ravages of the invaders and speaks with great bitterness of collaborators and apostates:

> . . . a multitude of members of the clergy will deny the true faith of the Christians and the Holy Cross and the mysteries of power [the sacraments], and without compulsion and blows and harsh words they will deny Christ and will agree with the unbelievers. . . . They will separate themselves from the congregation of the Christians of their own accord. . . . their false words will find credence. And they will listen concerning something that was said to them and they will comply.[34]

Thus all the aspects of Pseudo-Methodius' pamphlet fit together: his terrifying picture of the Moslems' treatment of the Christian population in Mesopotamia, his bitter complaints over priests and laymen collaborating with the conquerors, his rejection of the "Ethiopian" interpretation of Psalms 68:31 as defeatist, or even treacherous, and finally his insistence on a "Byzantine" interpretation of the verse of the Psalmist and his reliance on help from the Byzantine emperor. Pseudo-Methodius' tract thus was a politico-religious manifesto, rejecting any kind of defeatism or collaboration with the Moslems, warning against reliance on the weak and distant ruler of Ethiopia as a will-o'-the-wisp, calling for war to the finish against the conquerors, and preaching that salvation from the Moslem yoke could come from only one source, the most powerful Christian monarch of the time, the *basileus* at Byzantium. In the end this hope of the author was to be disappointed, for Mesopotamia has remained under Moslem rule to the present day, but in the seventh century this outcome was by no means a foregone conclusion. Byzantine rulers had for centuries acted, and were to continue to act, as protectors of Christians everywhere, even of anti-Chalcedonians under foreign rule. There was thus nothing quixotic in Pseudo-Methodius' political doctrine.

It will now be convenient to retrace the course of this enquiry which has led from Bismarckian Germany to seventh-century Mesopotamia. The legend of the Last Roman Emperor is first attested in the Syriac *Apocalypse* of Pseudo-Methodius, composed in northern Mesopotamia during the third quarter of the seventh century. It is impossible to say with certainty whether this first evidence represents at the same time the historical origin of the legend.[35] At any rate, it appears here as the visualization and culmination of an elaborate substructure of parahistory and Biblical exegesis designed to demonstrate the military superiority of the Byzantine Empire over all past, present, and future enemies and, as a result, the certainty of its survival to the end of time. Zezschwitz was therefore right in concluding that the *Apocalypse* of Pseudo-Methodius, such as he knew it, was based on Byzantine imperial ideology, but wrong in assuming that it must therefore have originated in the Byzantine Empire. This pointed formulation of Byzantine imperial claims was conceived, not on the soil of the Empire, but in an area not far removed from its eastern frontier that had only for relatively short periods formed part of the Roman or Byzantine Empires but which contained sizable Christian minorities looking to the Empire for protection and guidance.

It is not difficult to see why this Jacobite priest's call for resistance to the finish against the Moslem invaders of his country and reliance on the might of the Byzantine Emperor was quickly translated from Syriac into Byzantine Greek. In order to make his message palatable to his Mesopotamian coreligionaries the author of necessity ignored the doctrinal differences that separated his church from that of Byzantium. He gave a coherent, if fanciful and extreme, formulation to Byzantine confidence in the Empire's military superiority over all foreign peoples and in its universal Christian mission: the Byzantine Emperor, by virtue of his possession of the relic of the True Cross on which the Savior had suffered, would conquer all his enemies to the end of time and would then be able to hand over his Empire, made safe for Christ's kingdom and cleansed of its Moslem invaders, to God the Father. Pseudo-Methodius' Syriac tract expressed what every Byzantine recognized as the Byzantine ideology of Emperor and Empire. It buttressed with scriptural arguments and an elaborate parahistorical construction the Byzantine claim to a protectorate over Christians everywhere. Nobody can say in whose travel bag this powerful document of politico-religious irredentism crossed the Arab-Byzantine frontier, but it is easy to see why it appealed strongly to the Byzantine public and was translated into Greek soon after its composition in the Syriac language.

And why was it translated into Latin, and why did it exert an influence on the Latin Middle Ages? The Latin manuscripts of Pseudo-Methodius' *Apocalypse* make it certain that the monk Peter did his translation during the late seventh or in the eighth century. He was probably of Eastern extraction and wrote in a monastery in Merovingian Gaul.[36] In his *praefaciuncula* he writes that he performed his labor of love for his brethren in his monastery "because they [Pseudo-Methodius' predictions] have been rather aptly prophesied for our time . . . so that by means of the happenings which we observe with our own eyes we may give credence to what has been predicted by our fathers."[37] Perhaps Peter was alarmed by the Moslem advance through Spain into Gaul that took place at the beginning of the eighth century and considered Pseudo-Methodius' apocalypse a tract for his times inasmuch as it seemed to describe in lively colors the destructiveness of the Arab invasion and held out a hope for delivery. However this may be, it was the monk Peter's Latin translation that first introduced into the Western political consciousness the notion of a "king of the Greeks or Romans" who would defeat the Moslems and surrender his empire to God.[38]

The later destiny of this motif in the West is well known and need only be summarized here. Directly or indirectly, the impact of Pseudo-Methodius' prediction of a Last Emperor is noticeable in the *Letter . . . on the Origin and Time of the Antichrist* composed in the middle of the tenth century by the monk Adso. As stated before (p. 53), Adso himself informs us that for this one particular feature he is departing from his normal source and is relying on another tradition. It is precisely the passage prophesying the coming of the Frankish king who would restore the Roman Empire and lay down scepter and crown on the Mount of Olives at Jerusalem. As Zezschwitz pointed out a century ago, Adso was here following the apocalypse of Pseudo-Methodius.[39] The only important innovation was that a prophecy originally referring to a Byzantine ruler was rewritten to fit a Frankish king.

This tradition about a future restorer of the Roman Empire who would defeat the Moslems, surrender his crown at Jerusalem, and usher in the reign of Antichrist was to play a powerful role in later German developments. Peter Munz has shown recently that "in the period immediately preceding the First Crusade, more and more people began to identify the final emperor's journey to Jerusalem with a crusade for the reconquest of the Holy Sepulchre." He also has pointed out that in the early twelfth century, "by the time Frederick [Barbarossa] was a young man Antichrist speculation was the universal topic of conversation."[40] At least once in Frederick's lifetime, probably at his coronation in 1152, the *Ludus de Antichristo* was performed in his presence. At a climactic point in the play, at the very end of the first part, the Emperor, after having defeated in battle the last of his enemies, the king of Babylon, enters the Temple at Jerusalem, takes the crown from his head, holds it as well as his scepter and the other insignia before the altar and chants:

> Receive what I offer, for with a kindly heart
> I resign the insignia to Thee, King of Kings
> Through Whom kings rule, Who alone mayst be called
> Emperor and Who art the ruler of all men.[41]

In the second half of the thirteenth century and later, these notions about the Last Emperor, ultimately of Eastern provenance, coalesced with legends concerning the return of Barbarossa's grandson Frederick II from death.[42] By the fifteenth century it was believed that Frederick II was living on in Mount Kyffhäuser, and early in the next century there is evidence that Frederick Barbarossa began to replace his grandson as the hero of the legend.[43] In this final form the motif of the Last Emperor exercised, as we have seen at the beginning of this paper, a profound effect on German literature and historiography in the nineteenth century.[44]

Thus the religio-political manifesto of a Monophysite churchman in Mesopotamia, alarmed by the Moslem occupation of his country, was, as it travelled westward, translated and transformed into a powerful and influential formulation of Byzantine imperial ideology and eschatology, then into an expression of Western hopes for an imperial restoration after a long period of Moslem threats, subsequently into an assertion of the medieval German Empire's claim to hegemony over Christendom, and finally into the gradual realization by German scholars of the nineteenth century that the roots of their nation's imperial legends lay to a considerable degree in Biblical and Oriental traditions.

NOTES

1. Franz Dölger, "Byzantine Literature," in J. M. Hussey, ed., *The Cambridge Medieval History*, vol. IV, part II (Cambridge, 1967), p. 263.

2. See, for example, for patristic literature: A. Sigmund, *Die Überlieferung der Griechischen Christlichen Literatur in der Lateinischen Kirche bis zum 12. Jahrhundert* (Munich, 1949).

3. On hagiography, see Paul Peeters, *Orient et Byzance: Le Tréfonds Oriental de l'hagiographie byzantine*, Subsidia Hagiographica 26 (Brussels, 1950). This remarkable book touches on many instances of translations outside the hagiographical genre in the strict sense and raises many general problems concerning intercultural literary borrowings.

4. Dölger, p. 242.

5. Albrecht Timm, *Der Kyffhäuser im deutschen Geschichtsbild*, Historisch-Politische Hefte der Ranke-Gesellschaft, III (Göttingen, n.d. [1960–61?]). The author offers a useful collection and discussion of materials that I have used in the text. Recently F. Graus, "Die Herrschersagen des Mittelalters," *Archiv für Kulturgeschichte*, LI (1969), 65–93, esp. 80–82, made some interesting comments on the typology of royal legends in the Middle Ages, including that of Mount Kyffhäuser. After this paper had been submitted for publication, an anonymous reader for *Medievalia et Humanistica* called my attention to a recent book, Peter Munz' *Frederick Barbarossa: A Study in Medieval Politics* (London, 1969). The first and last chapters of this book contain an interesting discussion of the Kyffhäuser legend, of which I have made grateful use in the revision of this paper.

6. Georg Voigt, "Die deutsche Kaisersage," *Historische Zeitschrift*, 26 (1871), 131–87, esp. 161.

7. Wilhelm von Giesebrecht, *Geschichte der deutschen Kaiserzeit*, 5th ed. (Leipzig, 1881). The preface of 1855 is here reprinted, pp. v–xvi.

8. Giesebrecht, pp. xvii–xx.

9. Now most conveniently accessible in Döllinger's *Kleinere Schriften* (Stuttgart, 1890), pp. 451–557. At the time when he wrote this article, Döllinger was already deeply involved in his conflict with the Papacy over the issue of papal infallibility; see S. J. Tonsor, "Döllinger," *New Catholic Encyclopedia*, IV (New York, etc., 1967), 959 f. By letter Professor Tonsor calls my attention to the lively political and religious interest in Russia, Greece, and the Near East prevailing at Munich during the nineteenth century and suggests that Döllinger and other Munich savants may have hoped seriously to reverse at long last the tide of Islam.

10. In 1871 Döllinger (*op. cit.*; in *Kleinere Schriften*, esp. p. 497 ff.) had discussed Pseudo-Methodius' *Apocalypse* in some detail, but so far as I can see, he did not establish any connection with German imperial legends. As early as 1857 Adolf von Gutschmid, whose later publications were to make decisive contributions to the investigation of the genesis of the German imperial legends (see p. 65 and n. 18), had become acquainted with this *Apocalypse* through the casual use made of it by Franz C. Movers in his *History of the Phoenicians*. In his review of one volume of this work, Gutschmid inserted a lengthy footnote (now reprinted in his *Kleine Schriften*, II (Leipzig, 1890), 1–19, esp. 14–17, n. 1) on Pseudo-Methodius which ranged far beyond the purposes for which Movers had cited this text. He called the *Apocalypse* of Pseudo-Methodius "ein in mehrfacher Hinsicht interessantes und in einer gewissen Beziehung auch historisch wichtiges Doku-

63

ment," pointed out the medieval popularity of the Latin translation in the West, and urged a critical edition. These references to the historical importance of the text are vague, but the suggestion may not be far-fetched that he had guessed its connections with the legends about the medieval rulers of Germany.

11. Gerhard von Zezschwitz, *Vom Römischen Kaisertum Deutscher Nation: Ein mittelalterliches Drama, nebst Untersuchungen über die byzantinischen Quellen der deutschen Kaisersage* (Leipzig, 1877). At the end of the book (pp. 213–41) the author edits the Latin text of what he calls "das Drama vom Römischen Kaisertum Deutscher Nation und vom Antichristen" from the only manuscript of the twelfth century, formerly at Tegernsee. This Latin play was later published, under the more appropriate title of *Ludus de Antichristo* and with many improvements by Wilhelm Meyer, in *Sitzungsberichte der Kgl. Bayerischen Akademie der Wissenschaften, Philosophisch-Philologische und Historische Klasse* (1882), Heft 1, 17–40. There are several later editions, as well as an English translation by J. Wright, *The Play of Antichrist* (Toronto, 1967). See also Zezschwitz's popular lecture "Der Kaisertraum des Mittelalters in seinen religiösen Motiven" (Leipzig, 1877).

12. It is noteworthy that, in spite of all his enthusiasm for the achievement of German unity in 1871, Zezschwitz expresses some reservations with regard to these far-reaching claims of universal monarchy. He states that in the twelfth century the older notion of the Emperor's protectorate (*Schirmherrschaft*) over Christendom was steadily transformed into the idea of universal monarchy (p. 20) and calls this change "the most serious political mistake perpetrated by the imperial government" (p. 23). He even believes that the author of the *Ludus* viewed these claims with some irony (p. 22).

13. Zezschwitz, *Vom Römischen Kaisertum*, p. 37 and passim.

14. The *Epistola* is available in a critical edition by Ernst Sackur, *Sibyllinische Texte und Forschungen* (Halle a.d.S., 1898; now reprinted Turin, 1963), 97–113. See p. 110: "*Quidam vero doctores nostri dicunt, quod unus ex regibus Francorum Romanum imperium ex integro tenebit, qui in novissimo tempore erit. et ipse erit maximus et omnium regum ultimus. qui postquam regnum feliciter gubernaverit, ad ultimum Ierosolimam veniet et in monte Oliveti sceptrum et coronam suam deponet. hic erit finis et consummatio Romanorum christianorumque imperii. statimque secundum predictam Pauli apostoli sententiam* [II Thess. 2:3]. *Antichristum dicunt mox affuturum. . . .*" See Zezschwitz, *Vom Römischen Kaisertum*, pp. 18 and 37 ff. and the English translation of the *Epistola* by J. Wright (n. 11 above), pp. 100–10. The composition of Adso's work may be connected with popular beliefs concerning the year 1000.

15. Zezschwitz, *Vom Römischen Kaisertum*, pp. 43–84 and passim. He, as well as the other older scholars, could use only a most unsatisfactory edition in the anonymous publication *Monumenta S. Patrum Orthodoxographa*, 2nd ed. (Basel, 1569), 93 ff. The Latin translation was edited, after Zezschwitz's publication, by Sackur, *Sibyllinische Texte*, pp. 57–69, and the Greek version by V. M. Istrin, in *Chteniia Obshchestvia Istorii i Drevnostei Rossiisskiikh pri Moskovskom Universitete*, 193 (1897), pp. 4–50.

16. Sackur, *Sibyllinische Texte*, p. 93: "Et cum apparuerit filius perditionis, ascendit rex Romanorum sursum in Golgotha . . . et expandit manus suas in caelum et tradit regnum christianorum Deo et patri et adsumetur crux in caelum simul cum coronam regis"

17. Zezschwitz, *Vom Römischen Kaisertum*, p. 43: "Aber eben von diesem Punkte aus eröffnet sich für jeden, der die einschlagenden morgenländischen Traditionen kennt, eine ganz neue Fernsicht." Pseudo-Methodius' *Apocalypse* is discussed on pp. 43–84.

18. The review is reprinted in Gutschmid's *Kleine Schriften*, V (Leipzig, 1894), 495–506.

19. A second edition of Kampers' book was entitled *Die Deutsche Kaiseridee in Prophetie und Sage* (Munich, 1896). Kampers continued to publish a great deal on this and related subjects, e.g., *Vom Werdegang der Abendländischen Kaisermystik* (Leipzig and Berlin, 1924).

20. There still exists no critical edition of the Greek text, but Istrin's edition (see n. 15, above) prints the Greek text from a Vatican manuscript of the sixteenth century and records the variants of several others. Sackur's edition of the Latin translation (n. 15, above) is frequently useful where the Greek text is in doubt, especially where the question of interpolations arises. The summary in the text is based on Istrin's edition.

21. Pseudo-Methodius' interpretation of II Thess. 2 and I Cor. 15:24, pp. 23–25 Istrin.

22. Pseudo-Methodius' interpretation of Psalms 68:31, p. 22 Istrin.

23. See, for example, G. Moravcsik, *Byzantino Turcica*, 2nd ed., vol. I, Berliner Byzantinistische Arbeiten, X (1958), 426. For some remarks about the purpose of this work see my article "Medieval Apocalypses as Historical Sources," *American Historical Review*, LXXIII (1968) 997–1018.

24. *Vom Römischen Kaisertum*, p. 50 and passim.

25. On the Byzantine view of God as the source of imperial power see, for example, W. Ensslin, in *Cambridge Medieval History*, IV, Part II (Cambridge, 1967), p. 6 f.

26. Zezschwitz, *Vom Römischen Kaisertum*, p. 50.

27. "Das Rätsel des Pseudo-Methodius," *Byzantion*, VI (1931), 273–96; see also V (1929–30), 422–24. The manuscript referred to in the text is the *cod. Vat. Syrus* 58, fol. 118–36. Sackur, *Sibyllinische Texte*, pp. 53–55, had shown from internal evidence that the author of the Greek text had been a Syrian, but had been of the opinion that this Syrian author had written in the Greek language (p. 55).

28. *Cod. Vat. Syrus*, fol. 118 verso: "And the Lord sent to him [Methodius] one from among his hosts to the mountain of Shenāgar and he showed him all the generations. . . ."

29. *Terminus post*: allusion to an Arab navy, which was created between 644 and 649. *Terminus ante*: no reference to the Arab civil war (661–65) and particularly to the unsuccessful Arab siege of Constantinople (674–78). The author's silence on the latter event is all the more remarkable inasmuch as in connection with his general thesis that the Byzantine Empire is superior to all its enemies and will last to the end of the world he mentions several Roman-Byzantine victories down to the Persian-Avar siege

of Constantinople in 626, but fails to mention the Arab failure before Constantinople in 678.

30. *Cod. Vat. Syrus* 58, fol. 135 recto: "And immediately the Son of Perdition [= Antichrist] is revealed. Then the king of the Greeks will go up and stand on Golgotha and the Holy Cross will be set in that place in which it was set up when it carried the Christ. And the king of the Greeks will place his diadem on top of the Holy Cross, and will stretch out his two hands to heaven and will hand over the kingship to God the Father."

31. *Cod. Vat. Syrus* 58, fol. 126 recto: "However, many brethren of the clergy suppose that the blessed David spoke this word [Psalms 68:31] concerning the kingdom of the Ethiopians. And those who thought this erred concerning this, for it is the kingdom of Greece which is from the seed of Chuseth. . . ."

32. On the history of Ethiopia to the seventh century see Carlo Conti Rossini, *Storia d'Etiopia*, I (Bergamo,1928). On religious developments in particular: G. Lanczkowski, "Aethiopia," *Jahrbuch für Antike und Christentum*, I (1958), 134–53, esp. 143–45 (with bibliography).

33. Denha of Tagrit, *Biography of Marutha*, ed. and trans. F. Nau, *Patrologia Orientalis*, III (Paris, 1909), pp. 81–83: "Quand je considère tous les biens que possèdent maintenant les fils de Tagrit (la ville) bénite, c'est à dire: leur foi orthodoxe, leur zèle pour elle et l'accomplissement des bonnes oeuvres qui lui conviennent; leurs offices spirituels et la célébration des divins mystères: le bel ordre des clercs; les rangs disciplinés des prêtres qui sont à leur tête, le beau maintien et la belle tenue des diacres au milieu d'eux dans le sanctuaire; leur station autour l'autel; le service des sous-diacres, des lecteurs et des chantres; les continuelles, louangeuses et louables psalmodies de l'esprit et d'intelligence; et tout le clergé, et les beaux vêtements qui les ornent ainsi que toute l'église et l'autel; le voile (du calice), les tentures, les patènes, les calices, les encensoirs, les tabernacles et leurs richesses avec le reste des ornements sacrés; de plus leur exultation et leur joie dans les fêtes du Seigneur et les mémoires des saints qu'ils fêtent et célèbrent joyeusement et ardemment avec attention et sans négligence; en même temps que leur amour et leur soumission les uns vers les autres et surtout envers leurs chefs et leurs gouverneurs ecclésiastiques et séculiers (litéralement: dans l'Eglise et dans la ville et le monde); quand je vois ce consentiment et cette adhésion unanime au bien, je comprends que notre saint père a été pour eux la racine, la cause et le fondement de tout cela. . . . (il fut cause) aussi qu'avec amour (les habitants de Tagrit) honorèrent les Pères, les reçurent avec joie, participèrent à leurs honneurs et à leurs bénédictions, s'occupèrent des besoins des solitaires et des moines et de la construction des églises, des monastères et des saints couvents; répandirent des aumônes sur les pauvres; délivrèrent les captifs et les prisonniers. . . . En un mot Tagrit grandit tellement et acquit un si bon renom et une (telle) efflorescence de biens à son époque. . . ."

34. *Cod Vat. Syrus* 58, fol. 131 recto.

35. Wilhelm Bousset, *Der Antichrist* . . . (Göttingen, 1895), p. 82, was of the opinion that probably the voluntary surrender by a Last Roman Emperor of his empire to God is implied in an apocalypse preserved in Latin

and attributed variously to St. Ephraem or St. Isidore. The relevant passage reads as follows: ". . . iam regnum Romanorum tollitur de medio, et Christianorum imperium traditur Deo et Patri; et tunc venit consummatio, cum coeperit consummari Romanorum regnum . . ." (ed. C. P. Caspari, *Briefe, Abhandlungen und Predigten aus den zwei letzten Jahrhunderten des kirchlichen Altertums und dem Anfang des Mittelalters* [Christiania, 1890], pp. 208–20, esp. 213 f.). In all probability the work dates from the late fourth century. The passage has indeed many similarities with the *Apocalypse* of Pseudo-Methodius. In particular it contains the same references to II Thess. 2:7 and I Cor. 15:24 and is immediately followed by a reference to the appearance of the Antichrist. It is noteworthy, however, that it lacks the most characteristic Biblical citation of Pseudo-Methodius, Psalms 68:31, and fails to mention the Last Roman Emperor as agent of the surrender, which is put in the passive voice (*traditur*). The most natural interpretation of the passage of Pseudo-Ephraem, therefore, is that the author is here simply following I Cor. 15:24 and thinking of Christ himself as surrendering the kingdom to God. In other words, Pseudo-Ephraem seems to be lacking precisely that element which is important in the present context, the figure of the Last Roman Emperor. Pseudo-Ephraem's work originated, however, within the Syrian church (Johannes Dräseke, "Zu der eschatologischen Predigt Pseudo-Ephräms," *Zeitschrift für Wissenschaftliche Theologie*, XXXV (1892), 177–84), and very probably represents a stage of Christian eschatology from which the legend of the Last Roman Emperor developed organically. Sackur, *Sibyllinische Texte*, 164–70, also was of the opinion that the legend of the *Last Roman Emperor* surrendering his power at Jerusalem originated in the fourth century. It is indeed mentioned in the Latin translation of the apocalypse attributed to the Tiburtine Sibyl (Sackur, p. 186, lines 7 ff.), but not in the Greek version of the same text (see my *Oracle of Baalbek*, Dumbarton Oaks Studies X [Washington, D.C. 1967], p. 116). Consequently it is unlikely to have formed part of the original (Theodosian) version of the Sibyl's apocalypse (*Oracle of Baalbek*, p. 136). Its presence in the Latin translation probably represents a borrowing from Pseudo-Methodius.

36. Sackur, *Sibyllinische Texte*, p. 55 f. Four of the Latin manuscripts are no later than the eighth century.
37. Ibid., p. 59 f.: ". . . quoniam nostris sunt aptius prophetata temporibus. . . . ut iam per ipsa que nostris cernimus oculis vera esset credamus ea quae praedicta sunt a patribus nostris."
38. Ibid., p. 89 f.: ". . . et exiliet super eos rex Gregorum siue Romanorum in furore magna et expergiscitur tamquam homo a somno vini, quem extimabant homines tamquam mortuum esse et in nihilo utilem profecisse. hic exiet super eos a mare Aethiopiae et mittit gladium et desolationem in Ethribum. . . ." P. 93: ". . . ascendit rex Romanorum sursum in Golgotha, in quo confixum est lignum sanctae crucis . . . et tollit rex coronam de capite suo et ponet eam super crucem, et expandit manus suas in caelum et tradit regnum christianorum Deo et patri. . . ."
39. See notes 15 and 17, above.
40. Peter Munz, *Frederick Barbarossa*, p. 376.
41. *Ludus de Antichristo*, ed. K. Langosch, *Geistliche Spiele* (Berlin, 1957),

p. 206: "Imperator cum suis intret templum et, postquam ibi adora-
verit, tollens coronam de capite et tenens eam cum sceptro et imperio ante
altare cantet:

> Suscipe, quod offero!   nam corde benigno
> Tibi regi regum   imperium resigno
> Per quem reges regnant,   qui solus imperator
> Dici potes et es   cunctorum gubernator."

Cf. Munz, *Frederick Barbarossa*, p. 377.

42. Munz, *Frederick Barbarossa*, p. 8 f. See, for example, in the mid-fourteenth
century the chronicler John of Winterthur's sceptical report on rumors
concerning a return of Frederick II from the dead: "Post resumptum imperium iustius et gloriosius gubernatum quam ante cum exercitu copioso
transfretabit et in monte Oliveti vel apud arborem aridam imperium re-
signabit" (ed. F. Baethgen and C. Brun, in *Monumenta Germaniae Historica, Scriptores Rerum Germanicarum*, N.S. 3 [Berlin, 1924], p. 280 f.,
sub anno 1348).
43. Munz, p. 14.
44. See also Munz, esp. pp. 19–21.

The Addressee and Interpretation
of
Walahfrid's "Metrum Saphicum"

David A. Traill

IN HIS *Introduction to Medieval Latin Studies*, Martin R. P. McGuire describes Walahfrid as "the most gifted poet of the age."[1] Walahfrid's appeal to the modern reader, however, rests mainly on his achievements in what he probably regarded as his slighter works. Of his longer poems only the *De Cultura Hortorum*, now generally known as his *Hortulus*, is really free from the leaden atmosphere so prevalent in Carolingian poetry.[2] There are besides a few short personal poems which are remarkable for their freshness and vigor. One of these is the famous Sapphic ode, in which he celebrates his beloved island monastery and home — Reichenau. For the reader's convenience the text of this poem is given below.

"METRUM SAPHICUM"[3]

1. Musa, nostrum plange, soror, dolorem,
   pande de nostro miserum recessum
   heu solo, quem continuo pudenda
       pressit egestas.

2. Nam miser pectus sapiens habere   5
   quaero; quam ob causam patriam relinquo
   et malis tactus variis perosus
       plango colonus.

3. Nulla solatur pietas docentum,
   nec bonus quisquam refovet magister: 10
   sola sustentant alimenta corpus
       vile ciborum.

4. Frigus invadit grave nuditatem,
   non calent palmae, pedibus retracta

69

        stat cutis, vultus hiemem pavescit   15
          valde severam.

5. In domo frigus patior nivale,
     non iuvat cerni gelidum cubile,
     nec foris lectove calens repertam
        prendo quietem.   20

6. Si tamen nostram veneranda mentem
     possidens prudentia contineret
     parte vel parva, ingenii calore
        tutior essem.

7. Heu pater, si solus adesse posses,   25
     quem sequens terrae petii remota,
     credo nil laesisse tui misellum
        pectus alumni.

8. Ecce prorumpunt lacrimae, recordor
     quam bona dudum fruerer quiete,   30
     cum daret felix mihimet pusillum
        Augia tectum.

9. Sancta sis semper nimiumque cara
     mater, ex sanctis cuneis dicta,
     laude, profectu, meritis, honore,   35
        insula felix.

10. Nunc item sanctam liceat vocare,
      qua dei matris colitur patenter
      cultus, ut laeti merito sonemus:
         insula felix.   40

11. Tu licet cingaris aquis profundis,
      es tamen firmissima caritate,
      quae sacra in cunctos documenta spargis,
         insula felix.

12. Te quidem semper cupiens videre,   45
      per dies noctesque tui recordor,
      cuncta quae nobis bona ferre gestis,
         insula felix.

13. Nunc valens crescas, valeas vigendo,
      ut voluntatem domini sequendo   50
      cum tuis natis pariter voceris
         Augia felix.

14. Donet hoc Christi pietas tonantis,
      ut locis gaudere tuis reductus
      ordiar, dicens: vale, gloriosa   55
        mater, in aevum.

15. Christe, rex regum, dominus potentum,
    qui patris prudentia nominaris,
    nostra digneris refovere corda
        dogmate vitae.   60

16. Da, precor, vitae spatium, redemptor,
    donec optatos patriae regressus
    in sinus, Christi celebrare laudis
        munera possim.

17. Gratias summo canimus parenti,   65
    prole coniuncta patulo favore,
    spiritu virtute pari regente
        tempora saecli. Amen.

Not the least of this poem's charm lies in the immediacy of its appeal. Serious problems of interpretation are not apparent on first or even second reading. The identity of the addressee — indicated only by "pater" in line 25 — would appear to be a minor problem. In fact our understanding of the whole poem revolves around it. It is the purpose of this paper to examine this question, and to put forward an interpretation of the ode as a whole, which will, I hope, make some contribution towards a deeper appreciation of Walahfrid as a lyric poet.

Two candidates for addressee have been put forward: Hrabanus Maurus — proposed by Ebert with the *editio princeps* of the text and followed by most editors and translators;[4] and Grimald, later abbot of St. Gall — proposed by Miss Waddell.[5] I can find no clear marshaling of the arguments for the opposing views. Accordingly, in this paper I will indicate what I take to be the line of reasoning that led to the adoption of Ebert's interpretation. Then I will show why I believe Miss Waddell's view is to be preferred. Throughout this paper I will assume that the poem is biographically valid.

From the first stanza we see that this poem was written (or purports to have been written) when the poet was away from his homeland and feeling homesick. His unhappiness is enhanced by his humiliating poverty. The second stanza shows that he left home to further his education. From these two stanzas it is reasonable to infer that the poem was written during Walahfrid's stay at Fulda. In 827 Walahfrid, aged eighteen, left Reichenau to continue his studies at Fulda under Hrabanus Maurus. Two years later we find him in Aachen at the court of Louis the Pious as tutor to his youngest son, Charles the Bald.[6] Lines 5 and 6 strongly suggest that the poem belongs to this period at Fulda, and that the poem is therefore to be dated between 827 and 829. All scholars are agreed thus far.

The third stanza raises difficulties. How can Walahfrid say that no "pietas docentum" brings him solace or that there is no good teacher to comfort him? What about Hrabanus Maurus, the foremost scholar in Europe? Stanzas 4 and 5 provide a vivid description of Walahfrid's intense physical discomfort in the bitter cold of a Hessian winter. His monk's habit is no protection against the frosts; his hands are numb and the skin on his feet has drawn tight as a drum. Even indoors he finds no relief from the "frigus nivale;" it gives him no joy, he observes wryly, to contemplate his "gelidum cubile."

In the sixth stanza he seems to suggest, half-jokingly, that if only he could acquire some wisdom, the heat of his brain would provide him with a little warmth. In the seventh stanza Walahfrid appeals to the addressee, whose company he so acutely misses. "Quem sequens," which Winterfeld renders as "zu dem ich kam," [7] suggests that Hrabanus himself is the addressee. "Tui/alumni" in the next lines seems to confirm this. If Hrabanus is the addressee, the difficulty of the third stanza is resolved. But if Walahfrid is not with Hrabanus in Fulda, and yet clearly not at Reichenau, where is he?

Ebert looked around for an explanation. He found one in a theory first put forward by P. T. Neugart in 1803 and subsequently taken up by J. Koenig in 1868.[8] Neugart had, of course, not seen this poem. However, to explain poems IX.2 and 3,[9] addressed by an apparently impoverished Walahfrid to his "Magister Hrabanus," Neugart supposes that either because of the military unrest or out of a wish to be alone Walahfrid spent an indefinite period in a cell in the neighborhood of Fulda. He suggests, in fact, the cell of St. Sola in the diocese of Eichstädt, where Gundram, nephew and pupil of Hrabanus, was "custos" about this time. Ebert seized on this theory to provide a solution for the major difficulty — how Walahfrid could be a student of Hrabanus and yet apparently not at Fulda itself. This theory is deemed probable by Dümmler in a footnote to his edition of the poem [10] and is implicit in Winterfeld's translation. It is accepted by K. Beyerle in his outline of Walahfrid's life in *Die Kultur der Abtei Reichenau* and by A. Bergmann in his discussion of the poem in the same work.[11] Miss Waddell seems to be alone in rejecting it. However, she offers no explanation for the awkward third stanza, as it is one of the four omitted from her edition.

The principal objections to Ebert's views are as follows:

(1) The poem as a whole is indisputably about the poet's separation from Reichenau, not Fulda.[12]

(2) In particular, if the addressee of the sixth stanza is Hrabanus, the emotional outburst "ecce prorumpunt lacrimae, recordor . . ." is absurd, not to say downright rude. For in that case we are supposing Walahfrid to be saying, "If only you were here, Hrabanus. . . . See! the tears come to my eyes when I remember how happy I was at Reichenau [i.e., before I met you]." Consideration for the sequence of thought and respect for the poet's sense of tact require us to identify the addressee as someone either at Reichenau, or at least closely associated in the poet's mind with it. The "tui/alumni" indicates that he stands in the relation of teacher or mentor to Walahfrid. After the death of Wettinus in 824, Walahfrid's teacher was Tatto. But Walahfrid does not seem to have been very happy under his tutelage.[13] Though one cannot therefore rule out Tatto as a possible candidate for the addressee, it is perhaps preferable to give the honor to Grimald, with whom Walahfrid appears to have been on consistently good terms.[14]

I can find three passages in the poem where one might see difficulties for identifying the addressee as Grimald. The first of these occurs in lines 9 and 10. These lines are ambiguous and capable of bearing three interpretations:

(1) There are no teachers here. So I have no one to comfort me.

(2) There are no *sympathetic* teachers here.

(3) There is no teacher here kind enough to give me the wherewithal to keep me warm.

Both the second and third interpretations imply that Walahfrid was not entirely happy under Hrabanus. Ebert balked at this and opted for the first in conjunction with the cell theory. But as Professor Bischoff points out,[15] we should not be surprised at a certain amount of friction between the two in view of Walahfrid's friendship for Gottschalk. Moreover, it could be said that Walahfrid was quite adept at quarreling with his elders. The year 827 alone shows him on decidedly bad terms with his abbot, Erlebald, and, as we have noted, unhappy with Tatto. Even to his friend Adalgisus we find him offering to let bygones be bygones![16] There is nothing, then, inherently implausible in an interpretation that assumes a lack of sympathy between Hrabanus and Walahfrid.

Of the second and third interpretations the second, perhaps, is the one that most readily occurs to the reader, but there are a few pointers to the third. First, the structure of the third stanza — "no X gives solace, no Y gives comfort, only Z sustains my body" — suggests that in the first two lines as well as the third Walahfrid is concerned with bodily comfort, and that the third interpretation is therefore correct. Secondly, in the following two stanzas the development of the coldness theme is concerned purely with the effects of physical coldness, not social rejection. Finally, the theme of poverty begun by "egestas" in the first stanza is picked up by "nuditatem" in the fourth. Interpretation (3) would thus link stanzas 1, 3, and 4. It is perhaps not too fanciful to see in "nuditatem" a reference to the same "vilissimae vestes" that he is complaining about in his letter to Adalgisus in 826/7.[17] A complaint in the third stanza that his teachers were not keeping him warmly enough clothed would be an appropriate preparation for the "nuditatem" in the fourth.

However, the overriding objection to understanding line 9 in sense (3) is that it immediately follows "perosus plango colonus." This makes the interpretation of line 9 in the moral sense (2) inevitable. Perhaps the best solution then is to understand line 10 in both interpretations (2) and (3) — (2) because it follows line 9, and (3) in retrospect, as it were, to effect an appropriate transition to lines 11 and 12.

The second difficulty occurs in the sixth stanza, and hinges on the interpretation of "prudentia." This word seems usually to have been understood in the sense of academic enlightenment,[18] thus providing a cue for Hrabanus in the next stanza. But the language is strange. Why "veneranda"? Why, too, does Walahfrid depict himself in such a passive role with regard to this "prudentia," being possessed and contained by it rather than actively acquiring it? A clue is provided in the fifteenth stanza, where Walahfrid is attempting to sum up the first half of the poem. He refers to Christ as "qui patris prudentia nominaris." This, I believe, is a reference to I Corinthians 1:24, where Paul calls Christ "Dei sapientia." "Sapientia" is hard to fit into a Sapphic line, and in any case "prudentia" is frequently used as a synonym for it.[19] Whether or not Walahfrid is thinking of this passage in particular, he is clearly referring to the doctrine that Christ is the embodiment of Divine Wisdom. Accordingly, in the sixth stanza as well — for stanza 15 is merely recapitulating, as I shall show later — "prudentia" means spiritual, not academic, enlightenment. Hence, the "veneranda" and the mystical use of "possidens." This interpretation rescues "ingenii calore" from the shallow and unsatisfactory significance "by the heat of the brain" imposed on it by the former interpretation. It can now be rendered "by an inner fervor."

The third passage is "quem sequens" in line 26. Any possible difficulty here is eliminated by Miss Waddell's translation "at whose behest." For "sequi" with a personal object in the sense of "obey" cf. Prudentius, *Contra Symmachum*, II, 392, "quem [sc. orbis auctorem] rerum summa sequatur."

Consequently, I can find nothing in the poem that is inconsistent with Miss Waddell's view regarding the addressee. Since I have already indicated the serious objections to Ebert's view, I conclude that the addressee is a friend at Reichenau, probably Grimald.

There are some remarkable similarities between this poem and Gottschalk's "Ut quid iubes, pusiole," (the text of which is printed in full at the end of this article). Vielhaber has shown that Gottschalk's poem was written at Reichenau ca. 825.[20] When he refers to himself as an "exile" this is to be understood in the sense merely that he is away from home, as indeed is the case with Walahfrid in his poem. With the publication in 1960 by Professor Bischoff[21] of the three new stanzas he discovered in an Angers manuscript, we can see the similarities, both in structure and content, even more clearly. To underline these similarities I offer the following résumé, which applies equally to either poem.

The poem falls into two nearly equal parts linked by a transitional passage (in Gottschalk stanza 7, in Walahfrid stanzas 7–8) and ends with a brief coda (in Gottschalk stanza 13, in Walahfrid stanzas 15–17). The first part (in both, 1–6) deals with the poet's unhappiness in exile; in sharp contrast the second part (in Gottschalk stanzas 7–12, in Walahfrid stanzas 9–14) breaks out into a jubilant hymn of praise culminating in the prayer that the poet may be permitted to return home. The cue for the transition is provided by the poet's relationship to the addressee. Throughout one part of the poem (in Gottschalk the first, in Walahfrid the second) all the stanzas close with the same refrain.

Some of the differences are more superficial than substantial, and reflect differences in the two poets' techniques rather than in overall intentions. For instance, in Gottschalk's poem the exile theme is used *formally* in the first part. It provides the motive for the *recusatio* that forms the framework for the first part of the poem. The *recusatio* structure is used in its customary role of preparing the audience for the main statement of the poem. In Walahfrid the exile theme has no such formal application. How then is it used? Before we attempt to answer that, let us first reconsider the significance of the first part of this poem.

If we leave aside the awkwardly ambiguous third stanza, we see that most of what Walahfrid has to tell us about his exile concerns the physical effects of the bitter cold on his body. However, from its position just before the transition we would expect the sixth stanza to be the climax of the first part of the poem. This expectation finds confirmation in stanza 15, which is clearly intended to summarize the first half of the poem, just as stanza 16 does for the second; here it is stanza 6, not 4 or 5, that is restated. Consequently, while stanzas 4 and 5 are by their stark realism perhaps the most memorable of the whole ode, we are probably right to regard them as a foil for the crucial sixth stanza. But they are more than a foil. Walahfrid's frozen limbs and face are an externalized prefiguration of his frozen soul. It is this spiritual stagnation, not the bitter cold, that is his real danger at Fulda, and it is the realization of this that makes him turn to Grimald with the avowal that if only *he* were with him, Walahfrid's "pectus" (not his *corpus*) could come to no harm.

Walahfrid has used the exile theme to depict a spiritual nadir from which release is necessary. He finds that release in the praise of Reichenau, the memory that unites him with his far-off confidant. Thus, while in Gottschalk's poem the exile theme has a formal function within a well-known convention, Walahfrid uses the theme *dynamically*. In both the same end is achieved — an entirely negative situation from which a positive release is required. The second part of the poem in both cases represents the achievement of this release.

If we turn now to the second part of the two poems we see that the content here is quite different. After a rather peremptory praise of the Holy Trinity (stanza 10) Gottschalk makes an avowal of penitence. This leads to the hope that Christ will take pity on him (stanza 11) and allow him to return home very soon (stanza 12). Mr. Dronke's assessment of Gottschalk's prayer [22] that "it is too selfish to be holy" reflects, I think, the sense of anticlimax that the reader experiences in this part of the poem. After all the fuss Gottschalk has created about his exile making him too unhappy to sing, it is a little disappointing to find that all he really has to say is that he hopes he can get home soon. Although Walahfrid's sentiments expressed in the culminating fourteenth stanza are essentially the same as those in Gottschalk's parallel twelfth, the reader's reaction, I think, is much more favorable. One reason for this is that with his generous hymn of praise and prayer for Reichenau, Walahfrid avoids the danger of overloading the poem with brooding self-pity. So when he returns to a prayer on his own behalf, the reader is more inclined to be sympathetic. Again, by identifying and describing his homeland, and in particular by demonstrating to the reader his deep love for it, he succeeds in communicating something of that love to him. He wins the reader's sympathy by involving him emotionally in his plight.

In Walahfrid's poem, stanza 14 performs the same function for the second part as stanza 6 does for the first. It contains the essence of its half of the poem, making explicit what was implied or pre-figured in the preceding stanzas. Just as stanza 6 is echoed in stanza 15, so stanza 14 is taken up in stanza 16. The structure of the whole poem is thus seen to be highly symmetrical:

1–5	Misery of exile	
6	Spiritual nadir	} 1st PART
7–8	Transition via addressee	
9–13	Praise of Reichenau (spiritual release)	
14	Prayer for return	} 2nd PART
15	Restatement of 6	
16	Restatement of 14	
17	Concluding "Trinity" formula.	

This is similar to but more elaborate than the structure of Gottschalk's poem:

1–6	Refusal to sing because unhappy in exile
7	Transition via addressee
7–12	Hymn (praise of Godhead, penitence, plea for pity, prayer for return)
13	Promise to continue singing.

As in Walahfrid's poem the final stanzas of each half contain the essence of the preceding, though they are less clearly marked off from the other stanzas in this respect.

I do not think that these remarkable similarities of theme and structure can be explained away. I have found nothing in earlier poetry that much resembles either of these poems. Yet each resembles the other very closely indeed. The conclusion that one was inspired by the other seems the most obvious explanation. Such literary imitation between Walahfrid and Gottschalk would not be surprising even if we had no evidence for it elsewhere. But there exists an interesting parallel in the case of Gottschalk's poem "Ad Rathramnum,"[23] which, as Traube points out, is clearly modeled on Walahfrid's "Ad Gottschalk" (*MGH*, *PLAC*, II, 362). In the present instance it would appear that Walahfrid was imitating Gottschalk, since the evidence suggests the date of ca. 825 for Gottschalk's poem and, as we have seen, 827–29 for Walahfrid's. We should not be surprised at this conclusion. Much of Walahfrid's work is firmly based on earlier models, witness his rewriting of the lives of St. Gall and St. Otmar and his versification of Heito's prose version of the *Visio Wettini* (which he had just completed in 827).[24] His achievement in this case is, in my opinion, remarkable.

It would be foolish to attempt to disparage the obvious excellence of Gottschalk's poem. But few would deny, I think, that the primary merits of the poem derive from the virtuosity of his verbal skill — the flawless and captivating rhythm, the endless facility for rhyme, the charming, playful diminutives, and the haunting refrains. Walahfrid's verbal skill is less spectacular. However, he has devoted more care to the emotional development of the poem, as I have attempted to show, and in this respect is more successful than Gottschalk. He has retained the addressee as the essential pivot of the poem, but abandoned Gottschalk's purely formal method of preparing for the second part. This is one of the most successful features of Walahfrid's poem. The cue for the second part arises naturally from the subject-matter itself. The structure is thus dynamic rather than formally imposed. I think, too, that Walahfrid is more successful than Gottschalk in achieving his overall purpose, which I conceive to be the same for both poems — namely, to demonstrate the poet's will and ability to break through the depression caused by his exile and become spiritually renewed. I agree with Mr. Dronke's judgment that in the last stanza of Gottschalk's poem he achieves "a measure of serenity." I think though that this serenity owes less to the spiritual than the formal development of the poem. The structure is intrinsically satisfying — (1) I can't sing because I'm an unhappy exile, (2) But just for you I will sing, (3) (Sings), (4) I will go on singing. In his closing stanzas Walahfrid too conveys a feeling of serenity. This is partly due to the satisfying symmetrical structure of the poem, but much more to the emotional development I have outlined above. The reader has an unconscious conviction, I think, that since the prayer of stanza 15 has been implicitly fulfilled by the spiritual growth of the second part of the poem, so too the prayer of stanzas 14 and 16 will be fulfilled, and Walahfrid will indeed return to Reichenau.

GOTTSCHALK'S "UT QUID IUBES"[25]

1. Ut quid iubes,   pusiole,
  quare mandas,   filiole,
      carmen dulce   me cantare,
      cum sim longe   exul valde
         intra mare?
      O cur iubes canere?

2. Magis mihi,   miserule,
  flere libet,   puerule,
      plus plorare   quam cantare
      carmen tale,   iubes quale,
         amor care.
      O cur iubes canere?

3. Mallem scias,   pusillule,
  ut velles tu,   fratercule,
      pio corde   condolere
      mihi atque   prona mente
         conlugere.
      O cur iubes canere?

4. Scis, divine   tyruncule,
  scis, superne   clientule,
      hi diu me   exulare,
      multa die   sive nocte
         tolerare.
      O cur iubes canere?

5. Scis captivae   plebiculae
  Israheli   cognomine
      praeceptum in   Babilone
      decantare   extra longe
         fines Iudae.
      O cur iubes canere?

6. Non potuerunt   utique,
  nec debuerunt   itaque

carmen dulce   coram gente
alienae   nostri terrae
     resonare.
   O cur iubes canere?

7.   Sed quia vis   omnimode,
o sodalis   egregie,
     canam patri   filioque
     simul atque   procedente
       ex utroque.
   Hoc cano ultronee.

8.   "Benedictus   es, domine,
pater, nate,   paraclite,
     deus trine,   deus une,
     deus summe,   deus pie,
       deus iuste."
   Hoc cano spontanee.

9.   "Exul ego   diuscule
hoc in mari   sum, domine,
     annos nempe   duos fere
     nosti fore,   sed iam iamque
       miserere."
   Hoc rogo humillime.

10.   Plenus enim   facinore
ego sum, o   rex optime,
     pleniorem   sectae verae
     pietatem   novi esse
       fateorque.
   Hoc credo firmissime.

11.   "Propterea,   piissime,
miserere   iam, domine,
     pietatis,   rector clare,
     famulique,   rex aeterne,
       memorare,"
   prono posco pectore.

12.   "Reduc me ve-   locissime,
o ductor cle-   mentissime!
     Nolo hic me   magis esse,
     pater sancte,   flatus alme
       veridice."
   Hoc rogo praecipue.

13.   Interim cum   pusione
situs hac in   regione
     psallam ore,   psallam corde,

psallam die,   psallam nocte
carmen dulce,
tibi, rex piissime.

NOTES

1. (Washington, 1964), p. 54.
2. Ed. E. Dümmler, *MGH, PLAC*, II (1884), 335–50. Best edition: Werner Näf and Matthäus Gabathuler, *Walahfrid Strabo: Hortulus* (St. Gall, 1942/1957).
3. Ed. E. Dümmler, *MGH, PLAC*, II, 412–13, except for a few minor changes in punctuation.
4. A. Ebert, "Zu der Lebensgeschichte Walafried Strabo," *Sächs. Akad. Wiss. Philo-Hist. Kl. Ber. Verh.*, XXX (1878), 100–12.
5. Helen Waddell, *Medieval Latin Lyrics* (London, 1929). Text (omitting four stanzas) and trans. pp. 122–25; notes, pp. 322–24.
6. The best accounts of Walahfrid's life are Dümmler's introduction in *MGH, PLAC*, II, 259–63, and the chapter on Walahfrid in Eleanor S. Duckett's *Carolingian Portraits* (Ann Arbor, 1962), pp. 121–60.
7. Paul von Winterfeld, *Deutsche Dichter des Lateinischen Mittelalters in deutschen Versen*, ed. Hermann Reich (Munich, 1922), p. 167.
8. P.T. Neugart, *Episcopatus Constantiensis* (St. Blase, 1803), I, 154 f.; Ebert, p. 102 f.
9. *MGH, PLAC*, II, 358.
10. Ibid., 412, note 4.
11. *Die Kultur der Abtei Reichenau*, ed. K. Beyerle et al. (Munich, 1925), I, 96; Bergmann, II, 726.
12. Cf. stanza 2 and stanzas 8–16.
13. Cf. Walahfrid's letter to Grimald prefacing his *Visio Wettini* (*MGH, PLAC*, II, 302 *fin.*–303), and the implications of his earlier letter to Grimald (ibid., 334, esp. lines 18–28).
14. Cf. the two letters mentioned in the preceding footnote, the inclusion of Grimald in the description of the royal procession at Aachen in 829 (*MGH, PLAC*, II, 377, lines 227–32), and the dedicatory epilogue of the *De Cultura Hortorum* (*MGH, PLAC*, II, 349 f.).
15. B. Bischoff, "Eine Sammelhandschrift Walahfrid Strabos," *Zentralblatt für Bibliothekswesen*, Beiheft 75 (1950), p. 41, collected in his *Mittelalterliche Studien* II (Stuttgart, 1967), 45.
16. See *MGH, Formulae* (= *Legum Sectio V*) (1886), 376, lines 18–24 (Erlebald), and 24–26 (Adalgisus). Regarding authorship and addressee of this letter see K. Plath, "Zur Entstehungsgeschichte der Visio Wettini des Walahfrid," *Neues Archiv*, XVII (1892), 261 ff.
17. *MGH, Formulae*, 376, line 16.
18. Miss Waddell translates the sixth stanza as follows:

I think perhaps if I had any sense,
Even a little smattering pretence
Of wisdom, I could put up some defence,
Warmed by my wits.

81

Winterfeld (see n. 7), who by rendering "quem sequens" (line 26) as "zu dem ich kam" indicates he regarded the addressee as Hrabanus, presumably also understood "prudentia" in this sense, though his translation ("hohe Weisheit") is ambiguous.

19. E.g., see Romans 8:6–7.
20. K. Vielhaber, "Gottschalk der Sachse," *Bonner Historische Forschungen*, V (1956), 14 and 86.
21. B. Bischoff, "Gottschalks Lied für den Reichenauer Freund," *Medium Aevum Vivum*, ed. D. Schaller and H. R. Jauss (Heidelberg, 1960), pp. 61–68; collected in his *Mittelalterliche Studien*, II, 26–34.
22. Peter Dronke, *The Medieval Lyric* (London, 1968). He discusses the poem on pp. 34–36. His dating of the poem (p. 231) to ca. 850 seems not to take Vielhaber's work into account.
23. Ed. L. Traube, *MGH, PLAC*, III (1896), 733–37.
24. *Vita Beati Galli*, in *MGH, SS. Rer. Mer.*, IV (1902), 280–337. *Vita S. Otmari*, in *MGH, SS*, II (1829), 41–47. *Visio Wettini*, in *MGH, PLAC*, II, 301–33.
25. For stanzas 1–6, I have followed the edition of L. Traube in *MGH, PLAC*, III (1896), 731 f. For stanzas 7–13, I have followed Bernhard Bischoff, *Mittelalterliche Studien*, II (Stuttgart, 1967), 29–31.

Representations of Charles V of France (1338-1380) as a Wise Ruler

Claire Richter Sherman

THE IDEAL OF THE WISE RULER, which is customarily associated with the humanistic orientation of the Renaissance, was in fact well developed in the later Middle Ages.[1] The reign of Charles V affords an excellent example of how the king's reputation for wisdom, reflected in his epithet, *le sage*, and justified by his personality, was reinforced by a conscious cultural program that embraced both literature and the visual arts. These concerted efforts to emphasize Charles V's wisdom did not have a humanistic motivation but instead were directed toward the practical goal of reviving the power and prestige of the monarchy after the disastrous first phase of the Hundred Years' War.[2]

The *sagesse* of Charles V appears prominently in his iconography. The surprisingly large number of his extant portraits, mainly confined to miniatures and sculpture, show a clear, if gradual, shift away from the purely conventional images characteristic of the medieval period to works that record the king's own physical appearance (Figure 1).[3] Charles V's personal characteristics, such as his long nose, thin face, and high cheekbones, which literary descriptions and more advanced portraits confirm, occur even in illuminations of a notably non-naturalistic style (Figure 2). Although many portraits show only simplified reductions of these identifying characteristics, others — particularly in the more advanced medium of sculpture — are well-modeled and lively likenesses, which reveal the king's personality (Figure 3).

The king's long-established reputation both for the wise conduct of public affairs and for his scholarly, intellectual tastes is founded on the biography written by the famous poetess Christine de Pisan. Born in Venice in 1364, Christine grew up at Charles V's court, since her father, a distinguished physician and astrologer, had been summoned to Paris by the king. Christine's work *Le Livre des fais et bonnes meurs du sage roy Charles V*, composed in 1403 at the request of Philip, Duke of Burgundy, is in several respects a typical medieval biography.[4] First, its panegyric tone and catalogue of virtues recall the traditional saint's life. Secondly, its point of view and tripartite organization — based on Charles V's *noblesse de coeur, chevalerie*, and *sagesse* — are derived from Aegidius Romanus' manual for the ideal ruler, *De regimine principum*.[5] This manual, an example of a large and constantly evolving genre of medieval literature, offered advice on social forms, moral and religious principles, and ideal modes of conduct appropriate for a model ruler. In Christine's biography of Charles V, the first two sections do not, apart from isolated descriptions of the king's appearance and retinue, accurately reflect his historical personality, for poor health and individual predilection led him to abandon in practice the chivalric ideal which governed his predecessors' behavior. But the *sagesse* section, while still based on a virtue long considered desirable in the ideal ruler, does describe certain individual characteristics and actions of Charles V that are corroborated in other contemporary sources. Indeed, as in the illuminated and sculptured portraits, there seems to be a conscious effort to identify Charles V's *sagesse* as both an ideal and an individual feature of his personality.

Christine's definition of the components of *sagesse — sapience, science, entendement, prudence*, and *art —* come indirectly from Aristotle's *Ethics*. But her immediate source and authority for the changes from the original, antique meaning of these terms is Thomas Aquinas' *Commentary on the Metaphysics of Aristotle*.[6] Thus, when Christine calls Charles V an *ameur de sapience, sapience —* the equivalent of the highest speculative wisdom — denotes "a knowledge of first causes and principles" based on a study of theology and on metaphysics as well.[7] While Christine's definition of *sapience* is therefore both orthodox in meaning and conventional as a virtue associated with the ideal ruler, her account of its manifestation in Charles V reveals her own individual knowledge and observation of the king:

> En ce le demoustra nostre bon roy, car il voult en ycelle par
> sages maistres estre instruit et apris, et, pour ce que peut-estre
> n'avoit le latin, pour la force des termes soubtilz, si en usage
> comme la lengue françoise, fist de theologie translater plu-
> sieurs livres de saint Augustin et aultres docteurs par sages

84

Figure 1. *Charles V Receives the Book from Jean de Vaudetar*, by Jean Bondol. *Bible historiale*, The Hague, Museum Meermanno-Westreenianum, MS 10 B 23, fol. 2 (photo: Museum Meermanno-Westreenianum)

Figure 2. *Charles V Discusses the Translation with Jean Golein. Rational des divins offices*, Paris, Bibl. Nat., MS fr. 437, fol. 1. (photo: Archives photographiques)

Figure 3. *Donor Statue of Charles V*. Paris, Musée du Louvre. (photo: Archives photographiques)

Figure 4. *A King in His Study (Charles V?).* Traité *sur la sphère,* Oxford, St. John's College MS 164, fol. 1. (photo: Bodleian Library, courtesy of St. John's College)

Figure 5. *The Future Charles V (?) Receives the Book from Pélerin de Prusse.* Traité *sur la sphère*, Oxford, St. John's College MS 164, fol. 33. (photo: Bodleian Library, courtesy of St. John's College)

Figure 6. *Charles V Receives the Translation from Jean Golein.* Opuscules *de Bernard Gui*, Rome, Vatican Library, MS reg. latin 697, fol. 1. (photo: Vatican Library)

Figure 7. *The Future Charles V Disputes with the Nine Judges of Astrology. Le Livre des neuf anciens juges d'astrologie,* Brussels, Bibl. Royale, MS 10319, fol. 3. (photo: Bibliothèque Royale)

Figure 8. *Charles V in His Study. Le Policratique de Jean de Salisbury,*
Paris, Bibl. Nat., MS fr. 24287, fol. 1. (photo: Archives photographiques)

Figure 9. *Charles V*, u. l.; *Fathers of the Church, Pagan Philosophers, and Solomon*, u. rt.; *Courtiers*, l. l.; *Hunters*, l. rt. *Le Policratique de Jean de Salisbury*, Paris, Bibl. Nat., MS fr. 24287, fol. 12. (photo: Bibliothèque Nationale)

Figure 10. *Charles V Receives the Translation from Nicole Oresme*, above; *Félicité humaine*, below. *Les Éthiques d'Aristote*, The Hague, Museum Meermanno-Westreenianum, MS 10 D 1, fol. 5. (photo: Museum Meermanno-Westreenianum)

Figure 11. *Charles V Receives the Translation from Nicole Oresme*, u. l.; *A King (Charles V) and His Family*, u. rt.; *A King and His Counsellors Attend a Lecture*, l. l.; *The Expulsion of a Youth from a Lecture*, l. rt. *Les Éthiques d'Aristote*, Brussels, Bibl. Royale, MS 9505–6, fol. 2 v. (photo: Bibliothèque Royale)

Figure 12. *Charles V Receives the Translation from Raoul de Presles. La Cité de Dieu.* Paris, Bibl. Nat., MS fr. 22912, fol. 3. (photo: Bibliothèque Nationale)

Figure 13. *Charles V Receives the Book from an Unknown Author.*
Le Songe du verger, London, Br. Museum, Royal MS 19 C. IV, fol. 2.
(photo: British Museum, by gracious permission of the Trustees)

Figure 14. *Charles V Receives
the Translation from Nicole
Oresme. Les Éthiques d'Aristote,*
Brussels, Bibl. Royale, MS 9505–
6, fol. 1. (photo: Bibliothèque
Royale)

theologiens, si comme sera cy après declairié, ou chapitre de
ses translacions; et de theologie souvent vouloit ouir, enten-
doit les poins de la science, en sçavoit parler, sentoit par raison
et estude ce que theologie demoustre, laquelle chose est vraye
sapience. . . .[8]

The king's desire to receive instruction from learned masters is confirmed by Charles V's employment of the outstanding intellects of his
time. Men like Nicole Oresme, who made original contributions in
economics and science, formed a kind of propaganda bureau to
re-establish the power of the monarchy.[9] One part of this program
called for the recovery and translation into French of texts favorable
to royal power. Among the works which Christine mentions are Saint
Augustine's *City of God*, John of Salisbury's *Policraticus*, and Aristotle's *Politics* and *Ethics*.[10]

The second component of *sagesse* which Christine discusses is
science, "habit des conclusions par les causes plus basses."[11] Although
still in the realm of speculative wisdom, *science* is concerned with less
elevated matters than theology. If we are somewhat surprised that
Christine singles out the king's lifelong interest in astrology, which
we view as a pseudoscience, Thorndike explains that: "Indeed at this
period wisdom and astrology were considered almost synonymous."[12]
In his enthusiasm for the subject, Charles V commissioned new treatises on astrology as well as translations of older works. Furthermore,
the king established and equipped a college at the University of Paris
for the study of astrology.[13] Apparently Charles V frequently consulted the astrologers at his court and used their predictions as guides
to political decisions.[14]

Christine goes on to speak of the king's *entendement*, or understanding, "le concept des choses veues, sceues, et opinées par vraies
raisons."[15] Gifted with great eloquence of speech, Charles V was able
to address the most learned men of his time on equal terms.[16] His
rhetorical abilities, conspicuous at an early age, were noted by no less
an authority than Petrarch.[17] On state occasions, such as an assembly
during the visit of the emperor Charles IV, the king could expound
the justice of the French cause against the English.[18] Christine, in a
later passage of the *sagesse* section, elaborates on the king's fondness
for discussions with the clerics in his entourage:

La congregacion des clers et de l'estude avoit en grant reverence;
le recteur, les maistres et les clers solempnelz, dont y a maint,
mandoit souvent pour ouir la dottrine de leur science, usoit

de leurs conseilz de ce qui apertenoit à l'esperituaulté, moult
les honnoroit et portoit en toutes choses, tenoit benivolens et
en paix. . . .[19]

Raoul de Presles, in the prologue to his translation of the *City of God*,
also wrote in this vein: ". . . vous avez tousjours aimé science et
honoré les bons clers, et etudié continuellement en divers livres et
sciences, se vous n'avez eu autre occupacion. . . ."[20]

When Christine turns to practical wisdom, the primary meaning of
sagesse in modern French, she dwells on Charles V's *prudence*.[21] As
an example of his wise conduct, she cites his ordinance fixing fourteen
years as the age at which kings could rule alone.[22] This law was just
one instance of Charles V's rational and discreet conduct of public
affairs during his reign. The king's characteristic qualities of prudence,
patience, and willingness to negotiate have been considered by both
contemporary and modern historians as sources of his success in
reversing the French defeats suffered during the first phase of the
Hundred Years' War.[23]

Also part of Christine's definition of *sagesse* was the term *art*, which
dealt with the theory of painting and architecture and not just their
execution. To prove that the king was a *droit artiste*, Christine first
cites his expertise in the seven liberal arts.[24] But she devotes more
attention to the king's extensive patronage of art, particularly the
rebuilding of palaces and walls, his construction of chapels, and his
generosity to religious foundations.[25] Again, her list of works is well
documented in other contemporary sources. Moreover, it is now
recognized that Charles V's patronage of art, in the fields of manuscript
illumination, sculpture, and architecture, set the pattern for both the
artists and the types of programs which would characterize the mature
International Gothic style.[26]

After citing examples of Charles V's competence in the five components of *sagesse*, Christine's biography continues on the general
topic without further classification of the king's activities. She mentions the king's love of books and his huge library housed in a tower
of the Louvre especially furnished for research purposes.[27] Charles V
provided his library not only with luxurious physical facilities but
also with a highly respected and competent *gardien des livres*, Gilles
Malet, who kept careful track of the collection.[28] The king's accounts
also record expenses for purchasing parchment and rich fabrics for
the bindings of the manuscripts.[29] And Charles V's enthusiasm for

learning extended to the encouragement of libraries other than his own by donating books to them.[30]

From Delisle we learn that Charles V's great collection of more than nine hundred manuscripts, unequaled in Europe at that time, contained many volumes designed for study.[31] Works on theology, law, science, history, and literature aided scholars intent on re-affirming the power of the crown.[32] A concrete example of the library's practical purpose was the group of eight coronation *Ordines,* two foreign and six French, which the authors of the 1365 *Ordo,* modeled on Charles V's coronation, seem to have consulted carefully.[33]

Thus, Christine's account of Charles V's *sagesse* has, within its conventional framework, cited particular examples of the king's conduct of public affairs, his love of learning, and his enthusiasm for the company of the intellectuals in his entourage. Indeed, these scholars — especially in the prologues of their translations commissioned by the king — clearly associate Charles V's wisdom with that of the ideal ruler. Philippe de Mézières, both man of action and man of letters, whom the king made the Dauphin's tutor, wrote of Charles V as a close personal friend.[34] In his *Songe du vieil pélerin,* de Mézières describes the king's piety and his concern for his children's education, and refers to *la sapience et prudence* of Charles V, the *saige Salomon.*[35] Nicole Oresme, whom the king warmly thanked for his translation of Aristotle's *Ethics* and *Politics,* praised God for granting France such a wise king.[36] Drawing on Ecclesiasticus, Denis de Foulechat voiced a similar tribute in the prologue of his translation of John of Salisbury's *Policraticus.*[37]

Charles V's *sagesse* is also celebrated in a number of portraits contained in manuscripts which he commissioned. Our first two examples, dating from 1361, are found in two astrological treatises. Of these, the manuscript of the *Traité sur la sphère* and other writings by Pélerin de Prusse, now in the library of St. John's College, Oxford, offers two images of a king. In the first scene (Figure 4), the king is alone; in the second scene (Figure 5), he receives the book from the author. These portraits, although completely conventional, probably are intended as allusions to Charles V. If the manuscript is the original copy made in 1361–62, it is difficult to account for the presence of the crown which Charles wears, since the book antedates the Dauphin's coronation by several years.[38] It is possible, however, that the crown was painted in at the same time as the horoscopes of the royal family were added.

Despite these problems concerning the Oxford miniatures, it is important to note the illuminator's desire to stress the prince's reputation as a scholar. To this end he adapted the iconography of an author seated in his study rather than the usual, formal dedication where the king was represented as a remote figure in ceremonial dress, separated from the author or scribe by both physical distance and hieratic scale (Figure 6). The illuminator's substitution in Figures 4 and 5 of the more intimate study, furnished with lectern and books, for the customary throne room implies a closer relationship between the king and the author. Both a clear exchange of glance and an oral dialogue are suggested. Perhaps the illuminator is trying to illustrate the Dauphin's interest in the text, a fact the author mentions in his prologue. Despite the crudity of the portrait and the style of these Oxford miniatures, the representation of a king in a scholarly setting is an important innovation.

In a more formal manner, the dedication page of the second astrological treatise dated 1361 also reveals the Dauphin's intellectual interests. The first illumination of *Le Livre des neuf anciens juges d'astrologie* (Figure 7) is a variation of a proper presentation scene, for the future Charles V hypothetically addresses Aristotle, one of the nine judges who will answer his questions. The poses of the Dauphin and the philosopher duplicate those of recipient and author, while the banderole is a substitute for the book.[39]

This portrait (Figure 7) is the first recognizable likeness of the future Charles V, with the typical features confirmed by later images and described by Christine. Also characteristic of the period before the accession is the short, forked beard and the mantle with three strips of ermine at the shoulder.[40] Despite the extremely linear style and the lack of modeling, the representation of the king's individual appearance is convincing. Again, the illumination depicts a direct exchange between the Dauphin and an intellectual personage. Although this representation is more imaginary in character and placed in a more formal setting than that shown in the Oxford manuscript (Figure 5), both emphasize the prince's *ameur de sapience*.[41]

The frontispiece of de Foulechat's translation of the *Policraticus* (Figure 8) extensively develops the scholarly, informal setting of the Oxford miniatures. Dated 1372, the translation of this work was part of the king's program to make available in French classics favorable to monarchical power.[42] The large size of the miniature and the bold treatment of the chair and lectern contribute to the clarity and simplicity of the composition. And instead of depicting the fuzzy, generalized features in the Oxford miniatures, this portrait clearly represents the king's individual appearance as it occurs in the Louvre donor portrait (Figure 3).[10] The glove on Charles V's right hand, worn to allay the effects of gout, is probably another personal reference.[44] Thus, Charles V dominates the center of a strongly organized and plainly identifiable portrait.

Despite the fleur-de-lis mantle and crown, the king is represented primarily as a scholar. Under God's blessing hand, he points to a book (the *Policraticus*, the present volume itself) open to a quotation from Ecclesiasticus: "Beatus vir qui in sapientia morabitur et qui in iustitia. . . ."[45] The translator, de Foulechat, adds to his praise of wisdom as an attribute of the ideal ruler these words: "[Le] vray roy . . . [c'est] le roy garni de sapience. . . ."[46] The *Policraticus* frontispiece is significant because it offers a specific image of Charles V as an incarnation of the wise king who rules with a divine blessing. Of paramount importance is the transfer of an iconographic type, previously reserved for authors and scholars, to the representation of a specific historical personality.

Another illumination from this *Policraticus* manuscript (Figure 9) carries on the same theme. This image of Charles V, by a lesser hand, is one of four small panels inserted in the text. The illuminated letter *T* in the column below is also part of the ensemble. Christ, in a mandorla, blesses the king and the neighboring group of sages. The sages, who are shown drawing books and scrolls from a large straw basket, represent antiquity, the Old Testament, and the Latin church fathers.[47] Contrasting with these austere figures, worldly personages in the bright costumes of courtiers stand in the lower panels. In the crossbar of the *T*, above a crowd kneeling in prayer, an inscription reads: "Benedicta terra cujus rex sapiens."[48]

Even in this small and sketchy miniature, an attempt to render the king's typical features is apparent. Thus, Charles V is designated as the *rex sapiens* to whom the people pay tribute. And as a wise and virtuous ruler, the king belongs on the same level as wise men of the past.

The organization of the illumination corresponds to the contrast between virtue and folly which is a central theme of the *Policraticus*. The upper portion reveals the positive message, while the lower part describes and admonishes against "the vices and follies which are apt to prevail among princes and their entourage."[49] Charles V plays the part of the wise ruler who continues the tradition of Solomon, the only king included in the distinguished gathering of sages represented in this illustration. As in the frontispiece, the ideal of the wise, virtuous ruler and his historical incarnation in Charles V coexist. The flattering comparison of the king's wisdom to that of such famous sages suggests again a conscious effort to increase Charles V's prestige.

It is interesting that Nicole Oresme's translation of Aristotle's *Ethics* contains several dedication pages which pay further tribute to Charles V's wisdom. In the Hague copy of Oresme's work, a rather complex, two-part illumination (Figure 10) carries on the translator's praise of his patron's interest in the text. In the upper half of the illustration, the king receives the book as messages written on scrolls specify his motives. A personification of *Félicité humaine* (Human Happiness) fills the lower half. The portrait type of Charles V, although youthful and idealized, is recognizable by the long nose and high cheekbones.[50]

The inscriptions on the scrolls provide the key to the moral message. Charles V says, "Dedi cor meum ut scirem disciplinam atque doctrinam," and Nicole Oresme states, "Accipite disciplinam magis quam pecuniam, et doctrinam magis quam thesaurum eligite." The king's words, which derive from a passage in Ecclesiastes, mean roughly: "I gave my heart [I devoted myself] to learning discipline and doctrine." The writer, replying also in Biblical terms, counsels: "Accept learning [discipline] rather than money and choose instruction, more valuable than treasure."[51] These sentiments echo the theme of Oresme's prologue, which stresses the importance to both the individual and the wise ruler of practicing high moral standards,[52] for the knowledge of virtuous conduct and adherence to these standards discussed in the *Ethics* are the foundation of Human Happiness, personified by the figure seated below the king. Thus, Charles V's *sagesse* is equated with his motive for commissioning the translation.

The second, or text dedication, page in the Brussels copy of Oresme's translation of the *Nicomachean Ethics* (Figure 11) combines four scenes which again explain the king's interest in this work of Aristotle. The presentation ceremony shown in the upper left scene shows Charles V's initial act in diffusing knowledge by his commission of the translation. Below this, on the lower left, the scene of a king and his counsellors attending a lecture enlarges on the value of studying the right methods of government.[53] The miniature on the upper right depicts the king's responsibility for his children's education, as it involved the future welfare of the state.[54] The fourth scene, on the lower right, very probably illustrates the passage which claims that young people are not good listeners to political science lectures, owing to their lack of experience and good sense.[55] Although less explicitly than the dedication page of The Hague manuscript (Figure 10), the Brussels miniature (Figure 11) shows that the translation was motivated by the king's responsibility to extend knowledge of both ethical standards and the science of government. Again, the tribute to Charles V's wisdom, while unspoken, is clearly evident.

Thus far, the miniatures have illustrated a correspondence between the *sagesse* of the ideal ruler and Charles V's historical character. Many of the same scenes also reveal the king's friendship with the writers in his entourage. The king's warm reception of the works presented by Raoul de Presles (Figure 12), Nicole Oresme (Figure 11), and the unknown author of *Le Songe du verger* (Figure 13) also reveal an important change in royal dedication iconography. The still generalized portraits of the *Traité sur la sphère* (Figures 4 and 5) broke from previous tradition in representing the king as a scholar rather than as a remote ceremonial figure separated from the author by physical distance and hieratic scale (Figure 6). In a group of dedication scenes from the 1370's a greater informality accompanies the specific portraits of the patron. A charming example of this development is the scene of Raoul de Presles' presentation to Charles V of his translation of the *City of God* (Figure 12). Despite the presence of a saint and two angels, a relaxed and informal mood prevails. Hieratic scale is absent, and the differences in level and distance between the two major figures are diminished. Unlike the representations in the more formal tradition (Figure 6), the king here wears a simple mantle, and Raoul de Presles' posture is less humble. With keen interest, the king bends over to examine the open page of the book. Raoul de Presles anxiously peers over the top of the volume to catch sight of Charles V's face. Although their glances do not meet, they share an area of common interest. The artist is trying to express the king's interest in the book and his friendship for the translator.[56]

The first or prologue dedication page in the Brussels copy of Aristotle's *Ethics* (Figure 14) surpasses even the humanized character of the *Cité de Dieu* miniature. The warm exchange and direct confrontation of glance between Charles V and Nicole Oresme, as well as the king's smile and welcoming pose, give the impression of an informal relationship. Furthermore the distance between the two men has almost vanished: Oresme's hands and knees cross the king's area of the picture space indicated by the gold curtain.

In the second or text dedication scene from this manuscript (Figure 11), the king does not wear a crown, but a simple cap or bonnet called the *béguin*. The model for this detail, as well as for the king's general type and posture, is Jean Bondol's famous miniature in The Hague (Figure 1). Here even more than in the Brussels prologue dedication scene (Figure 14) the king and Oresme draw closer together. The translator bends forward and moves even more emphatically into Charles V's sphere.[57] The warm relationship between the king and Oresme confirms the evidence of Christine, Raoul de Presles, and Pélerin de Prusse that Charles V respected and admired the scholars and intellectuals in his employ.

Charles V's *sagesse* was described fully by Christine de Pisan following Aristotle's definition and its reformulation by St. Thomas Aquinas. Christine attempted to fit Charles V's historical character into an ideal framework combining the features of the saints' lives and the manuals for the conduct of the perfect ruler. There was a merging of Christine's ideal standards and the king's personal character. His prudence in public affairs and his abilities as a speaker joined with a scholarly nature and personal predilection for the company of the clerics in his employ. The library of Charles V, his literary program, and his "propaganda bureau" also reveal an interplay between policy and personal taste.

The various illuminations described here show a similar relationship between the ideal and historical character of Charles V's *sagesse*. Verbal references and representations of Charles V as a scholar in his study show the king as an incarnation of the wise ruler as well as patron of literature and friend of men of letters. The individual character of the portraits strengthens the theme of a careful identification of Charles V with the ideal of the wise ruler.

Tempting as it might be to place these representations of Charles V as a wise ruler within a protohumanistic framework, it is more accurate to view them as deriving from the medieval tradition of the "mirror of princes" literature and from the individual response of Charles V to the specific historical and political circumstances of his reign.[58]

NOTES

1. For a discussion of the development of the ideal of the learned king in the Middle Ages, see W. Berges, *Die Fürstenspiegel des hohen und späten*

Mittelalters, Schriften der Reichsinstituts für ältere deutsche Geschichts-kunde. Monumenta Germaniae historica, II (Leipzig, 1938), 66–71.

2. P. E. Schramm, *Der König von Frankreich: Das Wesen der Monarchie vom 9. zum 16. Jahrhundert, Ein Kapitel aus der Geschichte des abend-ländischen Staates*, 2d edn. (Weimar, 1960), I, 241. See also the excellent exhibition catalogue, *La Librairie de Charles V* (Bibliothèque Nationale, Paris, 1968), pp. 87–88.

3. For a recent study of the portraits of the king, see C. R. Sherman, *The Portraits of Charles V of France, 1338–1380*, Monographs on Archaeology and the Fine Arts Sponsored by The Archaeological Institute of America and The College Art Association of America, XX (New York, 1969).

4. Christine de Pisan, *Le Livre des fais et bonnes meurs du sage roy Charles V*, ed. S. Solente, 2 vols. (Paris, 1936–40). The book will henceforth be cited as Christine, *Fais et bonnes meurs*.

5. For the analogy of the biography to a saint's life, see Schramm, *Der König von Frankreich*, I, 246. For Christine's tripartite scheme, see Christine, *Fais et bonnes meurs*, I, Introd., xxx, lxii. For a full discussion of "the ideal ruler" literature, see Berges, *Die Fürstenspiegel*. For a survey of the contents of various French treatises, see D. Bell, *L'Idéal éthique de la royauté en France au moyen âge d'après quelques moralistes de ce temps* (Geneva, 1962).

6. Christine, *Fais et bonnes meurs*, II, 10, n. 3. For a discussion of the meaning of wisdom in the Middle Ages, see E. F. Rice, Jr., *The Renaissance Idea of Wisdom* (Cambridge, Mass., 1958), pp. 1–29.

7. Rice, *The Renaissance Idea of Wisdom*, pp. 15–16.

8. Christine, *Fais et bonnes meurs*, II, 13.

9. Berges, *Die Fürstenspiegel*, p. 267.

10. For Christine's list as well as Solente's comments, see *Fais et bonnes meurs*, II, 43–44, and 44–45, n. 3.

11. Ibid., p. 16; pp. 16–17, n. 5.

12. L. Thorndike, *A History of Magic and Experimental Science*, III (New York, 1934), p. 585.

13. Ibid., p. 589.

14. *La Librairie de Charles V*, p. 88.

15. See Christine, *Fais et bonnes meurs*, II, 19–20.

16. Christine de Pisan, *Le Livre du chemin de long estude*, ed. R. Püschel (Berlin, 1881), vss. 4997–5008; cited by Solente in *Fais et bonnes meurs*, II, 16, n. 5.

17. Letter of Francesco Petrarca to Pope Urban V, *Epistolae seniles*, IX, i, in *Francisci Petrarchae Florentini Opera omnia* (Basel, 1554), II, 937; quoted by R. Delachenal, *Histoire de Charles V*, II (Paris, 1909), 363, n. 3.

18. Christine, *Fais et bonnes meurs*, II, 116–21.

19. Ibid., pp. 46–47.

20. Paris, Bibl. Nat., MS fr. 22912, Prologue. See A. de Laborde, *Les Manu-scrits à peintures de la Cité de Dieu de Saint Augustin* (Paris, 1909), I, 66. Even as Dauphin the future king enjoyed the company of clerics, according to Pélerin de Prusse, who wrote the *Traité sur la sphère* and other astro-logical treatises for the prince in 1361: ". . . avec tout cela il aime clergie,

spécialement ceux qui usent des plus hautes sciences de Dieu et de la foi, et encore ceux qui usent de vraies et subtiles sciences naturelles et juridiques. . . ." Oxford, St. John's College MS 164, fol. 33 v.; quoted by Delachenal, *Histoire de Charles V*, II, 368. For the portraits in this manuscript, see my Figs. 4 and 5.

21. The first meaning of *sagesse* in E. Littré, *Dictionnaire de la langue française*, VI (Paris, 1958), 1824, is: "Juste connaissance, naturelle ou acquise, des choses."

22. Christine, *Fais et bonnes meurs*, II, 22, and 22, n. 2.

23. An adequate summary of Charles V's accomplishments is found in J. Calmette, *Charles V* (Paris, 1945). Calmette follows the estimate by Delachenal, Charles V's definitive biographer, of the king's character; see *Histoire de Charles V*, II, 366 ff.

24. Christine, *Fais et bonnes meurs*, II, 33–34.

25. Ibid., pp. 37–41.

26. Sherman, *Portraits of Charles V*, p. 16.

27. Christine, *Fais et bonnes meurs*, II, 42. For details of the furnishings of the king's library, see L. Delisle, *Recherches sur la librairie de Charles V* (Paris, 1907), I, 7–8; see also *La Librairie de Charles V*, p. 45. For the royal collection of books prior to Charles V, see *La Librairie de Charles V*, pp. 55–57, and M. Meiss, *French Painting in the Time of Jean de Berry, the Late Fourteenth Century and the Patronage of the Duke* (London, 1967), I, 287.

28. For a biography of Gilles Malet, see Delisle, *Recherches*, I, 10–22. See also *La Librairie de Charles V*, pp. 45–46, 87.

29. *La Librairie de Charles V*, p. 46.

30. Ibid., p. 46.

31. Delisle, *Recherches*, I, 1–2. If the manuscripts belonging to the king in his other residences are added to those kept in the Louvre, the total is more than a thousand books. See *La Librairie de Charles V*, p. 46. For the fate of Charles V's library under Charles VI and its eventual dispersal, see Delisle, *Recherches*, I, 125–41.

32. Schramm, *Der König von Frankreich*, I, 241.

33. Ibid., p. 237.

34. P. de Mézières, *Le Songe du vieil pélerin*, ed. G. W. Coopland (Cambridge, 1969), II, 214.

35. Ibid., p. 296.

36. "Si me semble que nous devons beneïr et loer le Roy du ciel qui a son pueple pourveü de tel Roy terrien plain de si grant sagesce." N. Oresme, *Le Livre de Ethiques d'Aristote, published from the text of MS 2902, Bibliothèque Royale de Belgique with a Critical Introduction and Notes by A. D. Menut* (New York, 1940), p. 98. In the prologue of Oresme's translation of the *De Caelo* of Aristotle, the former refers to Charles V as "desirant et amant toutes nobles sciences." N. Oresme, *Le Livre du ciel et du monde*, ed. A. D. Menut and A. J. Denomy (Madison, 1968), p. 38.

37. See note 48. For two additional references to Charles V's wisdom by contemporary men of letters, see Sherman, *Portraits of Charles V*, p. 82, n. 5.

38. The presence of the crown has been explained by a later dating of the manuscript. See *La Librairie de Charles V*, p. 115, no. 199.

39. The inscription on the banderole reads: "Chier sire de vos questions verres cy nos ententions."

40. For an early example of the three bands of ermine as an identifying attribute of the royal family, see P. Pradel, "Monuments funéraires de deux fils de Saint Louis," *Bulletin de la Société nationale des Antiquaires de France* (1962), pp. 76–78. For another example of the future Charles V wearing this costume, see *La Librairie de Charles V*, no. 167, Plate 3.

41. In another astrological treatise commissioned by the future Charles V, a translation of Ptolemy's *Quadripertitum* by Nicole Oresme (Bibl. Nat., MS fr. 1348), an image on fol. 1 shows the Dauphin receiving the book from the translator. The work, which may be Oresme's first translation for his royal patron, is dated about 1362–63; see *La Librairie de Charles V*, pp. 114–15, no. 198, and Plate 3. The style is very crude and the portrait conventional. The hairstyle, beard, and the strips on the mantle (see above, n. 40) are, however, consistent with the early iconography of the prince. The informal relationship of the Dauphin and Oresme, enhanced by the absence of an architectural setting or onlookers, prefigures later dedication portraits involving the two men. (See Figs. 11 and 14, and below, n. 57.)

42. Because this copy of the manuscript is absent from inventories of the king's library after 1380, Delisle is not certain whether it is the original presented to the king. He states, however, that it is at least a replica and a contemporary of the original; see *Recherches*, I, 263–64.

43. C. Maumené and L. d'Harcourt, *Iconographie des rois de France*, I. Archives de l'art français, XV (Paris, 1928), 48.

44. Delachenal, *Histoire de Charles V*, V, 390. In Fig. 1 Charles V was also wearing a glove on his right hand, though he had removed it, perhaps in order to examine the book.

45. The passage comes from Ecclesiasticus 14:20: "Happy is the man who meditates on wisdom, and who reasons with his understanding."

46. The passage is quoted by G. Dodu, "Les Idées de Charles V en matière de gouvernement," *Revue des questions historiques*, 110–11 (1929), p. 18.

47. The personages are Saint Jerome, Aristotle, Saints Ambrose, Gregory, and Augustine, Solomon, Plato, and Thales. Only six are actually shown.

48. The inscription is a reformulation of Ecclesiastes 10:17: "Beata terra cuius rex nobilis est." It is significant that *nobilis* has been changed to *sapiens* to reinforce the idea of the wise king.

49. John Dickinson, "Foreword," to *Frivolities of Courtiers and Footprints of Philosophers, Being a Translation of the First, Second, and Third Books and Selections from the Seventh and Eighth Books of the Policraticus of John of Salisbury*, trans. J. B. Pike (Minneapolis, 1938), p. vi.

50. Other examples of the same physical portrait type are shown in Figs. 12 and 14.

51. The passage is from Ecclesiastes 1:13: "And I gave my heart to seek and search out by wisdom concerning all things that are done under heaven. . . ." Oresme's words come from Proverbs 8:10–11.

52. Another miniature which I believe contains a portrait of Charles V and an allusion to his wisdom is the frontispiece of a *Bible historiale*, Bibl. de l'Arsenal, MS 5212. Placed in the central part of the miniature, a king kneels before and prays to the Trinity with the words: "Bonitatem et dis-

ciplinam et scientiam doce me." The message is related to the inscriptions in Aristotle's *Ethics* in The Hague (see above, n. 51, and Fig. 10). The association between wisdom and the Trinity, which long ago had been made by St. Augustine, further strengthens the allusion to Charles V, who seeks *sapientia*, thus fulfilling his obligation as a wise ruler (Rice, *The Renaissance Idea of Wisdom*, pp. 11–13). The costume, pose, and features of the king are close to those of Charles V in the *Parement de Narbonne*. (See *La Librairie de Charles V*, Plate 2. For the full history of the Arsenal MS and for a similar (but independently reached) identification of the king in the frontispiece with Charles V, see F. Avril, "Une *Bible historiale* de Charles V," *Jahrbuch der Hamburger Kunstsammlurgen*, 14–15 (1970), pp. 45–53, 72–73, and Plates 1 and 3.

53. See Oresme, *Le Livre de Ethiques d'Aristote*, pp. 99–100.

54. For a discussion of the similarity between the roles of a king and of a father, see Ibid., p. 438.

55. "Et pour ce un joenne homme n'est pas convenable auditeur de politiques, car il n'est pas expert des faiz qui aviennent a vie humainne" (Oresme, *Le Livre de Ethiques d'Aristote*, p. 107).

56. See above, n. 20.

57. Another dedication page which shows Charles V receiving the book from Nicole Oresme is found in Oresme's translation of Aristotle's *Politics and Economics* into French, dated after 1372. (Private collection, fol. 4. See *La Librairie de Charles V*, Plate 3, no. 203, and p. 118.) The portrait is a closely related, if less accomplished version of the dedication miniature shown in Fig. 11.

58. For a previous example of a miniature celebrating the wisdom of a living ruler, see the Neapolitan *Bible of Robert of Anjou* (Malines, Grand Séminaire, MS 1, fol. 3 v.), dated about 1340. The enthroned king, Robert of Anjou, surrounded by eight Virtues, is described in an inscription on the canopy above his head as "Rex Robertus, res expertus in omni scientia." See F. Avril, "Trois manuscrits napolitains des collections de Charles V et de Jean de Berry," *Bibliothèque de l'École des Chartes*, 127 (1969), pp. 324–26, and Plate XI.

The Praise of Folly *and* *Its* Parerga

Genevieve Stenger

Pointing to the significance of the *PARERGA* in the course of an article on More's *Utopia*, R. S. Sylvester remarked that "before the Yale edition of 1965 appeared no printing of *Utopia* preserved all of this introductory and supplementary material."[1] Unfortunately such an inclusive edition of *The Praise of Folly* has not yet appeared, so that few readers have viewed Folly in her original milieu. Yet the *parerga* of the *Folly*, large and small, trivial and grave, do throw some new light on Folly herself.

The first Latin edition (issued in Paris by two different publishers, Gilles de Gourmont and Jean Petit, 1511)[2] contained, in addition to the *Folly*, only the prefatory letter to Thomas More. This, at least, appeared in all the Latin editions published in the lifetime of Erasmus, though a number of editions added other items. The first Strasburg edition (E840) published by Matthew Schürer in August 1511, included at the end a letter from James Wimpfeling to Erasmus, a six-line poem by Sebastian Brant, a letter from Wimpfeling to all poets and cultivators of poetry, and two distichs, the first from Martial and the second a modernization or application of it. When the first Froben edition (E846) appeared in 1515, it had none of Schürer's additions,[3] but carried the Listrius commentary and Listrius' dedicatory letter to Paludanus. Later, bound at the head of the same edition[4] were Seneca's "ludus" on the death of the Emperor Claudius and John Free's Latin translation of Synesius' encomium on baldness; each of these had its own introductory letter and commentary by Beatus Rhenanus, and the Synesius had also a quotation from Suetonius on the author and a prefatory letter by the translator. In 1516 (E848) Froben added Erasmus' letter to Dorp. The 1519 Paris edition (E852) published by Badius van Assche was apparently based on the most recent Froben edition (E849) but added the letter from Dorp to Erasmus. The 1521 Froben edition (E860) did not insert the Dorp letter but it did add pagination and an index.[5] No one edition then or since has brought together all of the *parerga*.

An examination of Erasmus' prefatory letter shows, for one thing, that publication of the work was deliberate from the very first, Erasmus' own protestations to the contrary notwithstanding. Though addressed to Thomas More, the prefatory letter is directed as well toward a reading audience. Erasmus asks More to accept "this little declamation" and requests that he "also undertake to defend it," but what follows is a defense that anticipates attacks against both method and content. Certainly More is not among the "contentious fellows," the "any . . . who are offended by the lightness and foolery," those who make "bristling and pompous arguments," or the "some . . . perversely religious." Or even among those who needed reminding that there were precedents among the works of great authors of the past that could be marshalled forth in defense of the *Folly*. And Erasmus shows in the conclusion of his letter that he is aware not only that he has written defensively but also that he has not written this for More's benefit:

> Yet why do I say these things to you, an advocate so distinguished that you can defend in the best way even causes not the best? Farewell, learned More, and doughtily defend your Moria.[6]

More significantly, Erasmus' prefatory letter tries to prepare his reader for an intelligent reading of the book. His method, he warns, is that of the *persona*. "Since I have feigned her [Folly] speaking, it was of course necessary to preserve decorum in her character." Once he has passed those words "Stultitia loquitur," the reader is to be left to deal with Folly according to his own devices. Erasmus likewise warns that there is a serious center in the work: ". . . I have praised folly in a way not wholly foolish" (p. 3). What the reader is to find at that serious center he also hints. He reminds his reader that men of wit have a license to poke fun at the general manners of men, and he implies that the main thing that causes him to wonder at men "in these times" is their eccentric sense of humor:

> . . . I wonder a little at the tenderness of ears in these times, which can tolerate nothing, almost, but solemn forms of address. Yes, you will see some so perversely religious that they can endure the broadest scoffs against Christ Himself sooner than hear a pope or a prince glanced at in the most casual sort of jest. . . . [p. 3]

This seems to be his clue as to the standard for his satire. It glances at his method, and it indicates that the focus of the work, the point from which the true humor of things may be seen, is to be ultimately Christian.

Among the first to respond to *The Praise of Folly* was James Wimpfeling, a theologian and, according to Allen, "the type of serious German humanism." He was a teacher, polemicist, and founder of literary societies wherever he lived. Engaged in a controversy with Philomusus (James Locher, Lector in Poesy at Ingolstadt, poet laureate, and supposed defender of the humanist cause), Wimpfeling had in 1510 published his *Contra turpem libellum Philomusi Defensio theologiae scholasticae et neotericorum.*[7] In a sense, the Wimpfeling letters published with the *Folly* are a defense or clarification of his own position.

Wimpfeling begins the letter to Erasmus by asking him not to think of the *Defensio* as an attack on the *Folly*. And he goes on to distinguish the relative merits of scholastic philosophy, on the one hand, and what might be called scriptural theology, on the other. Scholastic philosophy, he argues, has its values, first as a mental discipline for young minds, and then as a preparation for drawing up civil and ecclesiastical contracts and prebends, guiding souls, and handling cases in general councils. But it also has its limitations and should not become so dominant as to exclude study of the Gospels. Nor should it take up the study of modern theologians to the neglect of Augustine, Gregory, Leo, William of Paris, and Jean Gerson. In this he sees agreement between his *Defensio* and Erasmus' *Folly*. And he has persuaded his fellow citizen and relative Matthew Schürer to print the *Folly*. To this extent, then, it would seem that he draws Erasmus into his camp in the controversy.

Erasmus, of course, is not the only one he adduces in his favor. One of the others, who "agrees with us somewhat," is Aulus Gellius, a Latin writer of the second century whom Erasmus quoted several times in his *Adages.*[8] Taking a knowledge of Gellius for granted, Wimpfeling merely cites the place at which Gellius quotes Plato's *Gorgias.*[9] The passage quoted by Gellius is a reproof of philosophers made by Callicles, a character "ignorant of true philosophy" but "possessing a reputation for common sense and understanding and a kind of uncompromising frankness." Gellius thinks that although Callicles

heaps dishonourable and undeserved abuse upon philosophers, yet what he says is to be taken in such a way that we may gradually come to understand it as a warning to ourselves not to

99

deserve such reproofs, and not by idle and foolish sloth to feign the pursuit and cultivation of philosophy. [*Attic Nights*, p. 273.]

The quotation from Plato begins, "Philosophy, Socrates, is indeed a nice thing, if one pursue it in youth with moderation; but if one occupy oneself with it longer than is proper, it is a corrupter of men." The passage quoted from Plato is, as Wimpfeling says, a long and elegant one, but Wimpfeling's emphasis is on Gellius, and it is significant to note that the import of the quotation is somewhat modified by Gellius' conclusion:

> He [Plato or perhaps Callicles] does not, of course, refer to that philosophy which is the teacher of all the virtues, which excels in the discharge of public and private duties alike, and which, if nothing prevents, governs cities and the State with firmness, courage and wisdom; but rather to that futile and childish attention to trifles which contributes nothing to the conduct and guidance of life, but in which people of that kind grow old in "ill-timed play-making," regarded as philosophers by the vulgar, as they were by him from whose lips the words that I have quoted come [i.e., specifically Callicles]. [p. 277]

Gellius is concerned not only with the proper function of philosophy but also with the interpretation of what seems to be a general rebuke. By citing Gellius quoting Plato, Wimpfeling opens up a long vista of human history in which past and present thought about the moral value of philosophy form parts of a continuing dialogue.

Another that Wimpfeling names as "agreeing with us" is Oecolampadius; in the same breath he mentions for the second time Gerson. Oecolampadius (John Hussgen, 1482–1531), a parish priest at the time of this letter, had once been a student of Wimpfeling. He was to meet Erasmus in 1515 through another friend of Wimpfeling, Joannes Sapidus, who recommended him for his knowledge of theology, Greek, and Hebrew.[10] As proofreader for Froben from 1515 to 1518, he was to work on Erasmus' editions of the New Testament and St. Jerome, and to prepare numerous editions and translations of the Greek fathers. Later, he was to become one of the leading Protestants in the struggle of the Reformation. Gerson (Jean Charlier of Gerson, 1363–1429) was an earlier reformer. More than a century before, as chancellor of the University of Paris, he had written a number of epistles and treatises advocating reforms at the university, notably his *Mémoire sur la réforme de l'enseignement théologique* (1400),[11] in which he rejected scientific theology as cut off from the spiritual concerns which should prepare students for the pastoral life. According to Gerson, a theologian was "a good man, versed in the Scriptures, — not simply with a learning of the intellect, but rather, and much more, of the heart, so that once he understood a truth he could translate it into his own life."[12] In his letter to Erasmus, Wimpfeling says that Oecolampadius

> is disgusted by those who reduce theology to a verbal loquacity and, as Gerson says, to a kind of chimerical mathematics, who continuously bring forward the approved opinions of Aristotle, Averroes, and Avicenna, and adduce nothing from the law, from the prophets, from the Gospel, from the Apostles, who raise up a fragile reed to defend their sayings and keep hidden in its scabbard that sword sent from heaven which can never be conquered, in which they might place their trust.[13]

"That sword sent from heaven," here symbolizing Biblical theology, recalls the "sword of the spirit" in Erasmus' interpretation of Luke 22:35 36.[14]

Wimpfeling's letter to poets and cultivators of poetry[15] is an assurance that his *Defensio* was not an attack on all poets and all poems. He says that for enjoyment he reads Prudentius or Baptista Mantuan, and that he is still angry about the substitution of Vincensius for Iuventus in a decretal listing approved writers, especially as he lived much later than the decretal. He pleads in conclusion that poets and cultivators of poetry transfer their study to the understanding of higher letters, to the praise of God, to the welfare of the republic. This letter does not so much as mention Erasmus or *The Praise of Folly*, and, for a modern reader, an oblique reading of it as relating to the *Folly* makes it seem rather personally defensive on Wimpfeling's part. Certainly the letter betrays a limited view of poetry. Perhaps it should be thought of as one more manifesto in the humanist cause, which at the moment of publication was probably understood as part of an ongoing dialogue that comprehended many authors and lecturers all over the continent.[16] But Wimpfeling's efforts to mediate between the humanists and the scholastic theologians in the letters he printed with the *Folly* seem rather ineffectual. His conciliatory view hardly seems based on a deep understanding of the issues at stake.

At the foot of Wimpfeling's letter to poets are two distichs, which together might be thought of as exhibiting a characteristic effort of the Renaissance to update the works of classical writers. Except that it shows a somewhat similar mettle, Martial's couplet itself seems to have nothing to do with *The Praise of Folly*.

> If you are poor, you'll always be that way;
> Only the rich get richer in our day.[17]

But the application of it to the granting of benefices, in the second distich,[18] recalls Erasmus' remark in his prefatory letter concerning those whose ears are offended at jests about a pope or prince, "especially if something touching revenues is involved" (pp. 3–4). In *The Praise of Folly* itself, the idea gets a much wider application:

> Wherever you circulate, in short, among popes, princes, judges, magistrates, friends, enemies, the great, or the humble, everything is done by cash in hand; and as the wise have contempt for cash, it carefully maintains the custom of avoiding them. [p. 104]

A colleague of Wimpfeling in the Strasburg literary society, Sebastian Brant, wrote a six-line poem on the *Folly* for the 1511 Schürer edition (sig. [H.v]). In 1494, while he was still on the faculty at Basle University and correcting proofs for Froben, Brant had published his *Narrenschiff*. It was natural that he think of the *Folly* as another Ship of Fools. "Content to jostle low-class fools in our ship," his poem says, "we left untouched the toga. Now comes the *Moria*, which, taxing the hooded cloak, the long trailing robe, the fasces, conveys philosophers and druids. O me, what uproars, what bloody blots will she call forth, stirring up bile with anger."[19] Here we see ecclesiastical, academic, and civic emblems of the higher classes that are objects of reproach in the *Folly*, as opposed to or as complementing the *Narrenschiff*. "Druidas" seems a deliberately dissonant kind of word, suggesting "perversely religious," essentially pagan practices which are a focal point of satire in the *Folly*.[20] The uproars Brant predicted were not long in coming.

The commotion stirred up by the *Folly* is recorded in a letter addressed to Erasmus by Martin Dorp. He writes him that "your Moria has excited a great disturbance even among those who were formerly your most devoted admirers."[21] He thinks that there must be very few who approve it and asks if it is not madness to go to a lot of trouble to seek nothing other than hatred. Wouldn't even the best fable be foolish if no one could read it unhurt and most were exceedingly offended? (ll. 19–24 in Allen).

Dorp objects to several things especially. He questions the benefit of the sharpness of the attacks against theologians, even though they sometimes strike at truths regarding certain ones (ll. 24–27). He questions whether pious ears should hear folly attributed to Christ, and no other future promised for the blessed than a kind of madness; he asserts that most councils — the Council of Constance, for one, as affirmed by the distinguished doctor Jean Gerson — have condemned things that, though true, would occasion the ruin of weak ones, for whom Christ as freely expended his life as for great and wise men (ll. 28–35). Finally, he says that the rough jokes, even when they contain a good deal of truth, leave behind them a bitter taste. Heretofore, all have admired Erasmus and read his works avidly, and the most distinguished theologians and lawyers have desired his presence, but behold suddenly the unfortunate *Folly*, like Davus, confuses everything. The style, indeed, and the invention and erudition they approve. The jokes they do not approve, not even the literati (ll. 50–55).

Dorp seems to have feared that even worse would follow, a public renunciation of Erasmus (ll. 47–50). The implication is that his other works, the *Adagia*, the *Enchiridion*, *De Copia,* and *De Ratione Studii*, for which he had won wide fame, would suffer too. What was done was done, but there was hope that something might yet be salvaged of his good reputation if only he would follow Dorp's advice: write and publish a praise of Wisdom. This, Dorp pleads, would be worthy of his talent and his studies, and would deserve the thanks of posterity, on which account it would bring him favor, friendship, celebrity, and, he adds, what Erasmus may contemn: profit.

At the end of his comments on the *Folly*, Dorp seems to be concluding his letter,[22] but in the next sentence he announces that the argument of the letter remains to be said. He leads into it with a compliment on Erasmus' work on the Epistles of St. Jerome, a task he thinks worthy of Erasmus.

The second major topic and focus of attack is Erasmus' work on the New Testament, but the force of the argument is not constant. In the first place, Dorp maintains absolutely the truth and integrity of the Vulgate and protests against correcting the Latin codices by collation with the Greek. He points out on the one hand the Vulgate's long acceptance by the universal church and its use in canonical decisions; on the other hand he argues against the notion that the

103

Greeks could be trusted to have taken the better care in preserving the sacred books. But in the course of his shifting arguments Dorp's attack seems to lose focus and weaken: he questions the possibility of determining which of many codices might be correct; he asserts that Erasmus' work will undoubtedly surpass those of his contemporaries Lorenzo Valla and Jacques Lefèvre; at the same time, still insisting upon "saying good-bye to the Greeks" whenever there is a difference of any significance, he would seem to limit the possibility of a valid contribution to a matter of more elegant translation; he cites St. Augustine's recommendation "that Latin rivulets be irrigated from Greek springs"[23] (but answers that Augustine predated the Vulgate as well as the corruption of the Greek fountain, presumably the schism); he sees in the mere pointing-out of differences in the Latin and Greek New Testament the equivalent of an attack upon the faith, yet what he finally advises Erasmus is, in the case that significant changes are to be made, to respond to his objections in a prefatory letter.

Dorp's letter itself stirred up some commotion, for several reasons. Not the least of these was the manner of its publication. Though it was written probably in September or October of 1514,[24] Erasmus did not see it until he was again in the Netherlands in March, 1515. There he found that copies of the letter had been circulating, and a friend showed it to him. No doubt, Erasmus was shocked. Dorp was a man to reckon with, a professor of philosophy and a member of the council of the University at Louvain. He had published several orations and a dialogue. He also worked with the publisher Thierry Martens, correcting proofs for the press and writing verses or prefaces for many books. One of the works he saw through the press was Erasmus' *Opuscula*.[25]

Erasmus' immediate reply to Dorp's letter is lost. And Dorp's letter was not printed with the *Folly* until 1519 (E852), but it is possible that Dorp's objections had something to do with succeeding changes in plan for the publication of the *Folly*. Beatus Rhenanus wrote to Erasmus from Basle on April 17, 1515:

> Of the thousand and eight hundred copies [of Froben's first printing] of the Moria only sixty [in Allen, sexingenta: 600] remain. It is therefore to be reprinted at once; and if you like the volume may include the *Scarabeus*, *Sileni*, Plutarch's *Gryllus*, and the *Encomium Muscae* of Lucian.[26]

Then on April 30, 1515, he wrote:

> To the *Moria* we shall add Plutarch's *Gryllus*, the *Parasitica* and *Musca* of Lucian, and also the *Scarabeus* and the *Sileni Alcibiades*.
>
> Seneca is being printed at two presses. . . . We have sent the *Claudius* of Seneca.[27]

The Plutarch and the Lucian had been mentioned in Erasmus' prefatory letter as examples of "the same thing" as the *Folly* (p. 2). The *Scarabeus* and the *Sileni Alcibiades* had been among Erasmus' *Adages*.[28] To judge from Van der Haeghen's descriptions of the 1515 Froben editions of the *Folly*, however, it seems that, instead of these works, the remaining copies (of E846) and the new printing (E847) added only Seneca's *In Mortem Claudii Caesaris* and Synesius' *De Laudibus Calvicii*. But Beatus Rhenanus' letters, coming as they do in the wake of Dorp's expostulation, suggest that bringing Folly forth in the company of antique paradoxes was more than a convenient device of the printer to fatten up a volume.

By including these two works with the *Folly*, Erasmus was asking for direct comparison with respected moral writers, one of them a bishop. Both had already been listed in the prefatory letter as examples of "the same thing" as the *Folly*. The two works are satires, much shorter than his and somewhat less ambitious. Both of them, however, share a tendency to proverbial expression, and, what is more significant, both of them view their subjects from worldly and otherworldly points of view.

In form Seneca's work bears little resemblance to the *Folly*. It is a narrative interspersed with passages of poetry, the mixed form characteristic of Menippean satire. At the outset the narrator establishes himself as a historian who wishes "to record an occurrence which took place in heaven on the third day before the Ides of October in the new year which began our fortunate era."[29] In fact, however, the narrative proceeds from heaven to earth to the underworld; and the narrator is by turns a historian and a poet. His history is without affidavit: "Who ever demanded affidavits from an historian?" (p. 132, sig. [a2ᵛ]). But those who insist upon an authority he advises to "apply to the man who saw Drusilla going heavenward," an allusion to the Roman senator who testified that he saw Caligula's sister Julia Drusilla taken up to heaven.[30] Like Folly, the narrator does and does not take his task seriously.

The poetry is used as an ironic method of diminution. Seneca effects this with the first appearance of poetry, a description of the season in mythological terms (Cynthia triumphing over Phoebus, and Bacchus aging) followed by the deliberately deflating prose statement, "I presume I shall be better understood if I say that the month was October and the day October thirteenth . . ." (p. 133, sig. [a3ᵛ]). Then he announces the time of day and gives another such passage of poetry. By the time he gets to the third and longest passage of poetry, in which he pictures Clotho [31] "breaking off the royal days of his [Claudius'] stupid existence" and, at much greater length, Lachesis spinning a golden age for Nero (pp. 135–37, sigs. [b1ᵛ]–b2), the use of poetry is itself suspect. Such a notion Erasmus must have had in mind when he had Folly name Seneca among the "men who are too clever," saying that "Nero was suspicious of Seneca" (Hudson translation, p. 115). Erasmus' Folly has no original poetry for her oration (though she rewrites some), but her frequent quotations of Latin and Greek poetry remind us of Seneca's mock-heroic manner of applying lofty verse to sordid facts (e.g. pp. 137, 139, 140–41; sigs. b2, [b2ᵛ]– [b3], [b4]–[b4ᵛ]).

The chief object of Seneca's satire, the deification of the emperor Claudius, gets only a passing mention as "most arrant folly" in Erasmus, and in characteristically general terms: "the deification, at great public ceremonies, of criminal tyrants" (pp. 34–35). Seneca shows Claudius' entrance into heaven, where he is not expected and not known, where his speech is unintelligible, his quotation of Homer without regard to meaning is called "nonsense," and his gesture of command goes unheeded. By flattering Hercules, Claudius gets help to storm the senate house of the gods and force the proposal for his deification. Of course, the proposal fails and Claudius is banished. One of the grounds proposed for his deification is his blood relationship to Augustus, and it is Augustus, portrayed as eloquent and virtuous, who expresses shame at his murders and injustice, at his appearance and his language, and who formulates the resolution that carries. In Augustus, Seneca provides a noble protagonist to contrast with the villainous Claudius. Thus his satiric method is simpler than Erasmus'. For in the *Folly* a single persona says what Erasmus believes and what he does not believe, and usually both at the same time. This dramatic duality, which delights and dumbfounds Erasmus' readers, goes far beyond Seneca's method of ironic contrast.

The journey back through Rome toward the lower regions gives Seneca the opportunity to show the funeral ceremonies in progress, another minor object of Erasmus' satire (p. 59). Mercury conducts

Claudius down the Via Sacra, where a crowd of people is engaged in "a most elegant and elaborate display, so that you would easily recognize that a god was being carried off to burial" (pp. 147–48, [d1ᵛ]). The funeral scene is an ironic contrast and is full of ironic contrasts. The chant, announced as "a dirge in anapests," is characterized mainly by the rhythm of alternating dactyls and spondees. Conventional expressions of sorrow ("tears . . . woeful voices . . . sorrowful cries . . . Mourn . . . forsaken . . . despair . . . bewail") are undermined by the "high spirits" of the crowd. The dirge laments that "nobly has fallen a man most sagacious," but Seneca has earlier attributed Claudius' death to straining himself "while listening to comic actors" (pp. 137–38, b2–[b2ᵛ]) and to fever, which was the official cause given (see p. 139, sig. [b3]). The dirge lauds him for two military victories, both of them open to question: the "rebellious" Parthians had not been subjected to Rome, and in the last fight against the Roman allies during the reign of Claudius the Parthians had won; and the conquest of the Britons took place without any battle or bloodshed. The dirge also praises Claudius for quickly deciding law cases, "Only at hearing one side of the quarrel, — Often not either," but, as Seneca has shown in the scene in heaven, that was the source of the greatest sense of shame to the divine Augustus.[32] The final lines associate Claudius with frauds, half-fledged poets, and gamblers. Claudius, however, is "delighted with his praises" (p. 149, sig. [d2ᵛ]).

The scene in the lower regions completes the reversal of his deification and shows him to be a fool as well as a "criminal tyrant." At the announcement of his name, a crowd of officials, relatives, and friends (many of them named) come forward "with clapping of hands and chanting: 'We have got him: let us rejoice!' " (p. 150, sig. [d3], *n.*). He seems to think this is a triumphal procession. Before the tribunal, the charges are made: "Senators killed . . . Roman knights . . . other persons. . . ." Defense is not heard: as the judge explains, "right will be done him if he be treated as he treated others." Seneca explains that "to Claudius it seemed more unjust than new" (pp. 151–52, sig. [d3ᵛ]).

On the whole, Seneca's *Claudius* is, like Erasmus' *Folly*, indeed a bold attack, but it has little of *Folly's* mercurial and elusive wit. What light-heartedness it has is attached to relatively minor points of satire: remarks such as "it's easier to get philosophers to agree than timepieces"; or his fancying that the reader would prefer his poetry to his "clumsily put" prose; or Clotho's intention to give Claudius a little more time "till he should make citizens out of the few that are left outside — for he had made up his mind to see everybody, Greeks, Gauls, Spaniards, Britons, wearing togas"; Fever's declaration that "as a Gaul ought to do, he captured Rome"; the narrator's profession of fear of comic actors; or Hercules striking the pose of a tragedian to be more terrifying.

Synesius' *De Laudibus Calvicii* resembles *The Praise of Folly* more closely in that it takes the form of an oration, and it treats a light subject in a manner that is not altogether trifling. On the other hand, Synesius' work, occasioned by the reading of another work, Dio Chrysostom's encomium on hair,[33] appears to consist mainly in the presentation of and refutation of Dio's arguments. Whereas Folly begins by boasting of her power as an orator and then mockingly violates oratorical conventions, Synesius begins in mock humility with protestations of the worth of Dio's book, of his own country background, his lack of rhetorical training, the difficulty of the subject, and then displays a virtuoso's ability in definition, analogy, enthymeme, and attack on his opponent's character and oratorical practices.

As in the *Folly*, many of the arguments are facetious. Synesius argues, for instance, that Achilles tore out his hair to be buried with his friend Patrocles because the hair was a dead thing, devoid of life. He argues that the senses are precious things by which all living creatures have life and feeling, that the eyes are the liveliest of all the senses and that they are bald; hence he concludes that baldness deserves honor and that the very best things are bald. He suggests a substitution in the fact that Ceres festivals, called Anacalypteria because people were bald and bare-headed for the celebration, were also known by the name Epibateria, meaning the ascending of the mind to the contemplation of heavenly things. He argues that baldness assures one's health because the bald man bears on his person the image of bald Aesculapius, father of medicine.

Synesius, like Erasmus, is fond of executing a turn in an argument or proverb so as to arrive at an unexpected conclusion. He asserts that beasts devoid of reason have hair all over, whereas men, having a higher estate, have less hair. "Wherby it commeth to passe, that howe much the lesse haire any one hath about his bodie: so much the more doeth he excell other, even as farre as a man is to be preferred before a beast."[34] Then he turns his conclusion to the effect that as man is the smoothest and wisest, so the sheep, completely covered with hair, is the most foolish. Again, sleek dogs serve better in the hunt than

108

shaggy dogs. With that we are brought almost full circle to man the wily beast.

De Laudibus Calvicii, like *The Praise of Folly*, has a serious underlying argument. For if Nature supports Dio's praise of hair, as Synesius asks, where is the place for Divine Providence in the scheme of things? At the beginning he assumes the position of Epicurus, who denied God's providence, for he observes that things do not turn out as men deserve. His mother and his sisters are on the side of Dio, as is the example of Queen Parysatis, who of two sons preferred the one having more hair. Synesius' own affections are on the side of Dio. He tells us that he put his mind to work but that he was more set upon revenging than upon reasoning; however, he soon began to feel somewhat appeased. He calls to mind that Diogenes, Socrates, Plato, and wise men "ex seculo" have been depicted bald; that Jupiter assigned the charge of Bacchanalian celebrations to bald Silenus to keep them in check; that Socrates rejoiced in his likeness to bald Silenus, and yet the comparison between them was not perceptible to the foolish multitude; apparently identifying baldness with the tonsure, he says that he who is beginning to be bald "has entred holy orders, and is instructed and taught from above the mysteries of the highest God" (sigs. [b.vij^v]–[b.viij]).[35] The question here becomes one of the relation between nature and grace. Does grace build on nature? And what is meant by nature? By the ignorant ("imperitis") the gifts of Nature and Fortune (among them, hair, of course) are believed to bring blessedness. Thus it is that writers and speakers, who must have the good opinion of the people or drink poison, treat of such matters as people like, and thus it is that Egyptians, noted for their wisdom, keep the multitude at the church porch and offer their sacrifices in secrecy. But Synesius, in opposition to the common opinion, maintains that the hair falls out as naturally as leaves fall from the tree when the fruit matures, and that any man who lives out his full age becomes bald. "Baldnesse therefore is the end of nature, which end every one hath not the gift to attaine" (sig. [c.vj]; E847, sig. [g4]). Finally, he grants that common consent may rest with Dio, yet he claims that the most praiseworthy are ranged on his side: officers in the temples of the Gods, teachers and instructors, army officers, and others believed to excel (sig. [D.v]; cp. E847, [h2^v]–[h3]).

Synesius belittles Dio's encomium on hair for wanting pith and substance. He had merely taken up an apparent good and illustrated its apparent goodness. "If he had undertaken to commend baldness, as he hath attempted the contrarie, he had (no doubt) gotten him selfe greater credite, and purchased more praise" (sig. b.ij; E847, [f1ᵛ]);[36] for, as Synesius might have added, he would not have been able to rest with an apparent good. In this lies the value of the paradox. And in this Synesius' work is closer to the *Folly*. Yet there is a great difference. For Synesius attaches his praise to one term and his dispraise to another. In the *Folly*, the praise and dispraise are attached to the same term, which comes to mean ignorance, carelessness, madness, but also mirth, faith, ecstasy. Not only that, but the dispraise is subsumed ironically under the guise of praise.

Although Erasmus wrote Dorp that he had written into the work safeguards for its interpretation, "so that no man, however simple, would be led astray" by his words, the first Froben edition (referred to in the April letters of Beatus Rhenanus), with Listrius' commentary, was already in print. In his dedicatory letter to John Paludanus, Listrius says that he wrote the commentary because there are many things in the book which cannot be understood except by very learned and attentive persons: partly because of the Greek which is mixed in everywhere, partly because of the frequent and unidentified allusions, partly because of Erasmus' clever jokes, which cannot easily be understood except by somebody who has a very good nose at smelling out such things.[37] Thus Listrius frequently identifies allusions. For such a phrase as αὐτὴ ἑαυτὴν αὐλῇ he gives the translation in Latin ("Id est, Ipsa sui tibicina sit") and then explains that the proverb applies when someone commends himself by his deeds, although here Folly distorts it to mean that she is boasting.[38] Indeed, some of the more interesting notes are those which call attention to Folly's twisted quotations and allusions. The commentary does much more than this, however, keeping in mind the method by reminding the reader at strategic points that Erasmus is making Folly speak, pointing out parodies, indicating rhetorical gestures, often defensively modifying Folly's remarks or reinforcing and elaborating upon them, sometimes indulging in a short essay on some part of the humanist program, and illustrating in its own tone and content the progression in Folly's moods as she approaches the serious climax.[39]

In the corresponding dedicatory letters for the Seneca and the Synesius,[40] Beatus Rhenanus makes several statements that have some bearing on the *Folly* or on the controversy over it. In his letter on Seneca, addressed to Thomas Rapp of Durlach, a professor of liberal arts, he says that he will easily see that among the ancients it was permissible to fix criticism upon wicked princes by way of some fiction or story, which though it may not always be advisable is nevertheless not always to be reprehended.[41] The defensive note of this remark would seem to indicate that the letter was written with certain reactions to the satire of the *Folly* in view. His apologies — for the manner in which the Seneca commentary was drawn up, "tumultuanter," for the conjectures that it was necessary to make in preparing the text, for not being able to translate the Synesius afresh or at least correct the translation of John Free [42] on account of not having the Greek manuscript available — suggest hasty preparation for printing and glance at the larger controversy over Greek and Latin texts. Rhenanus jests with Martin Ergerinus,[43] to whom he has addressed his dedicatory letter for the Synesius, about the usefulness of that satire for him: it will help him the better to bear his baldness if he has up to now followed the common opinion, or it will make him all the happier in his advantage by giving him a better understanding of it. But if not, certainly, he adds, he will take delight in the "festiuissima doctrina, simul & doctissima festiuitate" (p. 56), a simultaneous reversal of opposites that is quite characteristic of Erasmus' *Folly*, a book termed "nec minus eruditus, & salutaris, quam festiuus" on the title pages of early editions. Synesius was both a philosopher and a bishop, Rhenanus notes, commenting that the joke is indeed worthy of a learned and serious man. He concludes his letter with remarks on the humor of the age.[44]

Most important for the interpretation of the *Folly* is Erasmus' letter to Dorp.[45] This letter, probably an enlarged version of the immediate reply that is now lost, graciously thanks Dorp for his criticism as worth more than all the daily received letters of praise. In it Erasmus takes up the discussion of the three works Dorp mentioned in his letter (the *Folly*, the Jerome, and the Greek New Testament) and, like More in his long reply to Dorp's letter, touches powerfully and swiftly almost the whole gamut of the humanist program.

With regard to the *Folly*, he defends his purpose and his method by citing predecessors, ancient and modern, classical and Christian, by way of comparison or contrast. In content and purpose, as he explains, the *Folly* is related to other works of his. Just as, in his *Panegyric*, he tried to do in an oblique manner what he had done openly and directly in *The Education of a Prince*, so in the *Folly* he was trying to do under the semblance of a jest what he had done openly and directly in the *Enchiridion*. He professes not to believe that theologians should take offense any more than another group of people "for no species of the human race did Folly neglect." (Yet it should perhaps be noted that his additions of 1514, so lengthy as to create an imbalance in his book, mainly concerned theologians.) Finally, to the charges that he attributes folly to Christ and that for the blessed life he appoints no other future than a kind of madness, Erasmus answers with guidelines for an analysis of the passage that amounts to the climax of his book. He emphasizes the importance of context (the section on the blessed life, he points out, he was careful to preface with Plato's three forms of madness and to follow with a distinction between types of folly and insanity), of examining the very words of key sentences (the two sentences introducing the passage on the blessed life, in the Hudson translation the opening of the first paragraph beginning on p. 119), and of tracing the steps in the argumentation.

> Indeed, while Folly was attempting to fix upon every class of being the label of foolishness and was teaching that the greatest human happiness depended on foolishness, every class of being was touched upon, right up to kings and supreme pontiffs. From these we came to the Apostles themselves and even to Christ, to whom we find attributed a folly of a sort in Sacred Scripture. [Olin, pp. 74–75]

Erasmus thinks there is no danger that anyone should think Christ and the Apostles were really foolish, but they were human and often appear lacking in wisdom: "But this very foolishness conquers all worldly wisdom . . ." The implication is that his *Praise of Folly* is, ironically, his *Praise of Wisdom*.

The remainder of the letter, responding to Dorp's compliment on Erasmus' restoring of Jerome and his strictures on the projected edition of the New Testament, shows Erasmus' work to be of a piece. For it shows the same attitude toward languages that we find in the *Folly*, where he counts it to Jerome's credit that he is "master of five languages" (p. 110); in the *Adages*, where he calls it "not only stupid, but impious, to take on oneself to treat the mysteries of Theology" without a knowledge of Greek, Latin, and Hebrew, and of the whole of antiquity;[46] and in the *Colloquies*, where Peter, the doorkeeper of "The Godly Feast," greets the caller in three languages.[47] It shows the same predilection for Jerome, Origen, and Augustine that occurs in the *Folly* (pp. 84, 114), in some of the *Adages*,[48] and in the *Enchiridion*.[49] It presents the attitude toward scriptural theology that is expressed in the *Folly* — particularly in the long passage added in 1514 to the section on theology [50] — and in the *Adages*,[51] and that informs both "The Godly Feast" and the *Enchiridion*.[52] Finally, it shows his explicit desire to extend these interests to others in the European community of scholars.

Though Erasmus, in this letter to Dorp, says that his prefatory letter to Thomas More should have sufficed for sincere men, the various introductory and supplementary material published with the *Folly* betrays the continuing concern with the religious dimensions of the work and the difficulties involved in the satiric method. Much of the material comes to the defense of the work, directly or indirectly, so that even Rhenanus' introduction to the Synesius, for example, becomes a reminder of the playful sense of humor that animates satire. The Brant, the Martial, the Seneca, the Synesius — these supply a gradually broadening context in which the work can be placed as part of a literary and philosophic tradition and understood by reason of the parallels and differences in method and content. The Listrius commentary and Erasmus' letter to Dorp provide direct aids to understanding: Listrius with explanations for definitions and allusions, translations of Greek quotations, and interpretation of difficult passages; Erasmus with an analytic approach to the central paradox of the work. The *parerga* thus furnish early and no doubt representative reactions to the *Folly* and, thanks to them, Erasmus' attempts to respond to the need for various approaches to a complex and controversial literary work.

NOTES

1. " '*Si Hythlodaeo Credimus*': Vision and Revision in Thomas More's *Utopia*," *Soundings*, LI (1968), 278.
2. Listed as E838 and E839 in Ferdinand Van der Haeghen, ed., *Bibliotheca Belgica: Bibliographie Générale des Pays-Bas*, rev. ed. Marie-Thérèse Langer (Bruxelles: Culture et Civilisation, 1965), II, 867, 870. Van der Haeghen's numbers for identifying editions are used throughout.
3. After his first edition, Schürer himself dropped the poetry and Wimpfeling's letter to poets and cultivators of poetry (E842); after the second, he dropped also Wimpfeling's letter to Erasmus (E843); in his fourth and fifth editions (E850, E853) he included Erasmus' letter to Dorp.
4. With a page showing the contents, but otherwise the same. In Van der Haeghen, given a new listing as E847.
5. The index refers not so much to the text itself as to topics dealt with in the commentaries. Thus it functions somewhat in the manner of the *Adagia*.
6. Hoyt Hopewell Hudson, tr., *The Praise of Folly* (New York: The Modern Library, 1941), p. 4. This edition is used throughout for passages translated from Erasmus' prefatory letter and the *Folly*.

7. For Wimpfeling's letter to Erasmus and its factual background, see Epistle 224 in P. S. Allen, ed., *Opvs Epistolarvm Des. Erasmi Roterodami*, I (Oxford: Clarendon Press, 1906), 462–65. In the 1511 Schürer edition of the *Moriae Encomivm*, the letter appears at sig. H.iiij–[H.iiij^v]. I have devoted a somewhat disproportionate space to the letter because it is not available in English translation.

8. See, for instance, "Frons occipitio prior," "Festina lente," and "Ollas ostentare," in Margaret Mann Phillips, *Erasmus on His Times: A Shortened Version of the "Adages" of Erasmus* (Cambridge: University Press, 1967), pp. 1, 5, 142.

9. See *The Attic Nights of Aulus Gellius*, tr. John C. Rolfe, II (Cambridge: Harvard University Press, 1927), 273–77. Wimpfeling cites Book IX, chap. 22, but the opinion to which he refers is in Book X, chap. 22.

10. See Francis Morgan Nichols, tr., *The Epistles of Erasmus* (New York: Longmans, Green and Co., 1904), Ep. 341, II, 217; Allen, Ep. 354, II, 143.

11. Jean Gerson, *L'Oeuvre Epistolaire*, Vol. II of *Oeuvres Complètes*, ed. Mgr. Glorieux (Tournai: Désclée & Cie., 1960), pp. 26–28.

12. Quoted in James L. Connolly, *John Gerson: Reformer and Mystic* (Louvain: Librairie Universitaire, 1928), p. 81.

13. "Sic et noster Icolampadius nobis consentiens abhorret ab eis theologis qui theologiam ad verbosam loquacitatem et (vt Gerson ait) ad chymerinam mathematicam redigunt, qui Aristotelis, Auerrois, et Auicennae probatiores sententias creberrime proferunt, ex lege, ex prophetis, ex Euangelio et Apostolis adducunt nihil, fragilemque harundinem pro defensandis dictis suis leuant, et coelitus missum ensem nunquam superabilem, in quo fidere possent, vagina reconditum seruant" (Allen, I, 464).

14. See pp. 111–12 of the *Folly*; also, "Sileni Alcibiadis," in Phillips, p. 87, where it seems to mean detachment. Similarly, it suggests the central metaphor of the *Enchiridion*, "a kind of hand dagger, which you should never put aside"; see Raymond Himelick, tr., *The Enchiridion of Erasmus* (Bloomington: Indiana University Press, 1963), p. 58.

15. In the 1511 Schürer edition, sig. [H.v^v].

16. See Peter R. Allen, "*Utopia* and European Humanism: the Function of the Prefatory Letters and Verses," *Studies in the Renaissance*, X (1963), 91–107.

17. For this translation of V, lxxxi, see Martial, *Selected Epigrams*, tr. Rolfe Humphries (Bloomington: Indiana University Press, 1963), p. 64.

18.   Mos est praelatis praebendas non dare gratis
      Ast bene nummatis, vel eorum sanguine natis.
"It is not the custom to bestow benefices on deserving prelates but rather on the wealthy, or their offspring." The final phrase, directed as it is at a celibate clergy, probably contains a barb which Folly herself might have admired.

19.   Vulgares nostra stultos vexisse carina
        Contenta, intactam liquimus ire togam
      Moria nunc prodit, que byrrhum, syrmata, fasces
        Taxans, philosophos conuehit & druidas
      Heu mihi, quas turbas, quas sanguinis illa lituras
        Eliciet, biles, cum stomachisque ciens.

20. See for examples pp. 56–58 in the Hudson translation.
21. Nichols, Ep. 304, II, 168–69; Allen, Ep. 304, II, 12. The complete letter is not available in English.
22. "Hoc consilii siue probes siue non probes, ego certe tuus sum eroque semper" (Allen, II, 14, lines 79–80).
23. Charles Béné, *Érasme et Saint Augustin ou Influence de Saint Augustin sur l'humanisme d'Érasme* (Geneva: Librairie Droz, 1969), in Ch. V, "Première défense de la nouvelle exégèse: Érasme et Martin Dorp," pp. 207–13, shows how St. Augustine, and especially his *De Doctrina Christiana*, figures in the argumentation on both sides of the controversy.
24. The introduction and the conclusion give clues as to its date. It was written not long after Erasmus' stay at Louvain in late July and early August, 1514, yet after the printing of the Cato. Allen says "c. September" (II, 10); Nichols says in or about the month of October (II, 167).
25. See Allen, II, 11; Elizabeth Frances Rogers, ed., *St. Thomas More: Selected Letters* (New Haven: Yale University Press, 1961), p. 7. The Rogers volume contains More's letter to Dorp in defense of Erasmus.
26. Nichols, Ep. 321, II, 196–97; Allen, Ep. 328, II, 62–65.
27. Nichols, Ep. 324, II, 204–5. In a note Nichols says, "I do not know whether any edition of the *Moria* accompanied with these extracts exists." It is possible, but it seems unlikely that there would have been three Froben editions in 1515. Allen, Ep. 330, II, 65–66.
28. Erasmus used the Silenus in the *Folly* (p. 36) to illustrate the apparent and hidden aspects of "all human affairs," and in the *Enchiridion* (p. 105) to figure the surface and hidden meanings to be observed in all reading, but especially of the Holy Scriptures. The Silenus figure also appears in Synesius' encomium on baldness.
29. Allan Perley Ball, *The Satire of Seneca on the Apotheosis of Claudius* (New York: The Columbia University Press, 1902), p. 132. (Passages from Seneca are taken from this translation.) In the 1515 Froben edition of the *Folly* (E847), sig. a2: "Quid actuum sit in coelo, ante diem tertius Eidus Octobris, Asinio Marcello, Acilio Auiola Coss. Anno nouo, inicio seculi felicissimi, uolo memoriae tradere."
30. Livius Geminius. He was rewarded with 250,000 denarii. See Ball's note, pp. 157–58.
31. The Fates seem to be confused. Clotho should be spinning, Lachesis measuring, and Atropos cutting off the thread.
32. Beatus Rhenanus points out the humor in carrying off a god dead (E847, sig. [d1ʳ] and in Claudius' ability to judge "more quickly" (sig. [d2ʳ]). He also notes the irregularity of the versification and calls attention to accounts of Claudius' military endeavors in Tacitus and Suetonius (sigs. d2–[d2ʳ]).
33. Dio Chrysostom's encomium on hair survives only as Synesius presents it in his work. See *Dio Chrysostom*, V, tr. H. Lamar Crosby (Cambridge: Harvard University Press, 1951).
34. Synesius, *A Paradoxe, Proving by reason and example, that Baldnesse is much better than bushie haire, &c.*, tr. Abraham Fleming ([London:] H. Denham, 1579), sig. b.iiij–[b.iiijʳ]. In E847, sigs f2–[f2ʳ]. According to the *DNB*, Fleming based his translation on Free's Latin version as it was pub-

lished with the *Folly*. In his introduction, Fleming mentions the *Folly* among the works comparable to Synesius' satire, and in one of his marginal notes he credits Beatus Rhenanus for supplying the rest of a proverb only given in part in the text.

35. Though the Latin version is not so direct, it suggests the same association: "Nam qui caluus esse coepit, is initiatus est, & apparentis dei sacra edoctus." E847, sig. [f4ʳ].

36. It should perhaps be noted that the metaphor is not in the Latin version, which says simply that "maiorem utique de se expectationem fecisset."

37. "Verum sunt in eo permulta, quae non nisi ab eruditis & attentis possint intelligi: partim ob Graecitatem passim admixtam, partim ob allusiones & crebras & tacitas, partim ob argutiam in iocando, quam non facile sentiat, nisi qui naris sit emunctissimae." E847, sig. [A1ʳ].

38. E847, sig. B2. Hudson translates the proverb, "She is her own flute-player" (p. 8). Today we generally understand Folly's twisted meaning.

39. For a full analysis of the Listrius commentary, see the article by J. Austin Gavin and Thomas M. Walsh, "*The Praise of Folly* in Context: The Commentary of Girardus Listrius," *Renaissance Quarterly*, XXIV (1971), 193–209.

40. In the Froben editions of 1515, 1516, 1517, 1519, 1521, 1522, and in the Paris editions of Badius van Assche published in 1519 and 1524 — that is, E847, E848, E849, E852, E854, E860, E862, and E866.

41. "Quem libellum cum leges, facile intueberis, apud priscos etiam licuisse, malis principibus, genuinum, iuxta paraemia, infigere, quod ut non semper consultum, sic nec ubique reprehendum iudicamus." See E847, sig. [a1ʳ].

42. Free, one of the early English humanists to go to Italy to study, had translated Synesius' *Laus Calvicii* during his stay there (1456–65) and dedicated it to another Englishman who studied there from 1459 to 1461, John Tiptoft, Earl of Worcester. R. Weiss, in *Humanism in England During the Fifteenth Century* (Oxford: Basil Blackwell, 1957), p. 111, ranks Free "beyond all doubt above every fifteenth century English humanist before the time of Grocin and Linacre." In his dedication, Free defends beginning his translating with this work by Synesius as "from this one speech alone you might declare him both a great philosopher and a most grave orator" (E847, sig. c2).

43. Purchasing agent of Schlettstadt. See sigs. c1–[c1ʳ] of E847.

44. "Nunc ridiculi sumus, etiam cum seria scribimus. Faceti non sumus. Quod si quando iocari uolumus, Camelum saltare dices, ut est in prouerbio. Et aut obscoena producimus, quod genus sunt infacetissimae Pogij Facetiae, aut stulta" (E847, sig [c1ʳ]).

45. Allen, Ep. 337, II, 90–114. First published with the *Folly* in Froben's 1516 edition (E848, so dated by Van der Haeghen, II, 875) and after that included in most of the early Latin editions (E849, E850, E852, E853, E854, E855, E858, E860, E862, E866, E870). This letter is available in translation in John C. Olin, ed. and tr., *Christian Humanism and the Reformation: Desiderius Erasmus* (New York: Harper and Row, 1965), pp. 55–91. In "Humanism et Théologie dans la Controverse entre Erasme et Dorpius," *Filosofía*, XIV (1963), 886, Pierre Mesnard insists that the Erasmus-Dorp

letters should be considered as a unit apart from the *Folly*, belonging to a different genre — debate — and coming "six" years after the publication of the Folly, during which period Erasmus had time to become more definite about his vocation and, as Mesnard maintains despite Erasmus' long defense, to repent of having written the *Folly*.

46. See "Illotis manibus," in Phillips, p. 75.
47. See Craig R. Thompson, tr., *Ten Colloquies* (Indianapolis: The Bobbs-Merrill Company, Inc., 1957), pp. 133–34.
48. In Phillips, "Festina lente," p. 12; "Herculei labores," p. 31; "Sileni Alcibiadis," p. 91; "Ne bos quidem pereat," p. 159.
49. See Himelick translation, pp. 53, 107.
50. In Hudson, p. 79, "These finespun trifles . . . " to p. 83, ". . . silly, sordid terms and sentiments."
51. See, for instance, Phillips, "Dulce bellum inexpertis," p. 124.
52. A mere paging-through the text or a glance at the notes in the Himelick edition will suffice to give this impression; but see especially pp. 49–54 and 105–8.

Lord Berners

A SURVEY

N. F. Blake

ALTHOUGH IN THE OPINION of C. S. Lewis, "no prose writer of that period has deserved nearly so well of posterity as Sir John Bourchier, Lord Berners," [1] the work of Lord Berners has never been studied in depth. His excellence and importance are suggested by his appearance in most histories of English literature and by the fact that most of his translations have been re-edited with introductions in the nineteenth and twentieth centuries, but no attempt has been made to evaluate his work as a whole or to consider the problems which it presents. This article is therefore a preliminary survey of what is known about Berners' literary activity, with some suggestions as to possible solutions for the many problems connected with his career, presented in the hope that it may encourage more research on the subject. It is simplest to commence with a brief review of Berners' biography and then to proceed by considering each book and its attendant problems in turn. A final statement of the present state of knowledge may then be attempted.

The broad outlines of Berners' life are known, but much remains obscure. He was born about 1467 as a member of that influential and aristocratic family, the Bourchiers. His father was killed fighting for Edward IV at the Battle of Barnet in 1471, and he himself succeeded his grandfather as Baron Berners in 1474. On Henry VII's accession he entered into a long period of service with the Tudor monarchy. He married at some stage Catherine Howard, whose father had died fighting for Richard III at the Battle of Bosworth and had been a man of considerable importance and influence under the Yorkist kings. When Henry VIII came to the throne, Berners acquired high office and joined that circle of young men who surrounded the king, though there is nothing to suggest that he enjoyed any particular favour. He became Chancellor of the Exchequer in 1516, went on an embassy to Spain in 1518, and was in attendance on Henry VIII at the Field of the Cloth of Gold. However, he became embroiled in lawsuits over property and was forced to borrow money from the king. He was Deputy of Calais from 1520 to 1526, and again from 1531 till his death on 16 March 1533. His effects were seized by the crown in settlement of his debts, and the inventory made of them recorded that he had eighty books in his possession at his death. In his will he left his goods in Calais to Francis Hastings, the future second Earl of Huntingdon, who was in Calais with him, and his English estates were inherited by his only child, a daughter.

Of the translations made by Berners only that of Froissart's *Chronicle*, the text by which he is most widely remembered, is definitely known to have been printed in his own lifetime. It appeared in two volumes printed separately by Richard Pynson in 1523 and 1525. The colophon to the second volume states that the translation was finished on 16 March 1525 and printed on 31 August 1525. The first volume was printed on 28 January 1523, so it would be reasonable to assume that the translation was started in the early part of 1521 when Berners was in Calais, and finished about June 1522. How Berners came to translate this work and whether it is his first translation are more difficult questions to answer.

The prologue records that the book was translated "at the highe comaundement of my moost redoubted soverayne lorde kynge Henry the viii." Modern commentators have taken this statement at its face value and have understood that Henry VIII ordered the translation. Not only does this ignore the workings of Tudor patronage and the traditional phraseology of many prologues, but it also raises further problems which have to be answered. If Berners began his translation about 1521 in Calais, Henry would presumably have asked him to make it some years earlier, before Berners left for Calais. And if the Froissart is Berners' first translation, as is widely assumed though definite proof is lacking, why should Henry have asked Berners to make it? Berners' interest in books was shared by many courtiers and would not necessarily imply an ability to translate or any intention to do so. Although translations had been made by noblemen in the fifteenth century — Malory and Rivers spring immediately to mind — the translations made under the early Tudors were more usually undertaken by humanist scholars or hacks attached to the printing houses. It is thus difficult to think why Henry would have asked Berners to make the translation. It would seem more probable that Berners started the translation on his own initiative and then presented it to the king in order to win favour or even some financial remuneration. After all, at an earlier stage in the prologue, Berners had written:

> Whan I advertysed and remembred the manyfolde comody-
> ties of hystorie, . . . [I] fixed my mynde to do some thyng
> therin; and ever whan this ymaginacyon came to me, I volved,
> tourned, and redde many volumes and bokes, conteyning fa-
> mouse histories. And amonge all other, I redde dilygently the
> four volumes or bokes of sir Johan Froyssart . . . whiche I
> judged comodyous, necessarie, and profytable to be hadde in
> Englysshe.[2]

This seems to imply that Berners made the decision himself after extensive reading. Furthermore, in the second volume of 1525 there is far more fulsome praise of Henry VIII in the prologue than that found in the first volume's prologue. This could mean that the translation had found favour with Henry when it first appeared and that Berners wished to gain all possible advantage from its reception. We do not know why Berners was sent to Calais, but it is always possible that he left under a cloud because of his financial embarrassments. If so, having left the busy life at court he may have used the relative leisure of his life at Calais to make his translation and thus win back his position. While the reasons for his undertaking the translation remain dubious, it seems probable that Berners himself is responsible for the idea of the translation. Whether he came back to England to persuade Pynson to print the work or whether his friends in England attended to this matter will probably never be known.

The choice of Froissart may be explained by that late flowering of chivalry investigated by A. B. Ferguson.[3] Caxton had translated many chivalric works, and in his epilogue to the *Order of Chivalry* he encouraged the nobility of England to read Froissart, the chronicler of the Hundred Years' War, who had been as interested in the deeds of Englishmen as much as those of Frenchmen. Apart from this common interest in Froissart and chivalry there are several points of contact between Berners' translation and Caxton's work. Berners included a prologue in his translation which is an adaptation of that in the *Historical Library* of Diodorus Siculus,[4] except that the conclusion has been modified to make it suitable for his Froissart. Caxton had used the same prologue, adapted in a similar way, for his edition of Trevisa's translation of Higden's *Polychronicon*. While it is probable that Berners followed a Latin version of Diodorus rather than Caxton's, there are some correspondences which could possibly indicate that he also had access to Caxton's text.[5] There are also verbal similarities, in the two texts, in their additions to these prologues modelled upon Diodorus Siculus.[6] Berners may have been using Caxton as a model, though many of the phrases common to both authors had become traditional by now. It would, however, be natural to assume that if the Froissart is one of Berners' first translations he looked to Caxton for a suggestion as to what to translate and how to translate it.

It is difficult to assess the popularity of the translation. It seems to have been reprinted only once (in 1545) before modern times. Yet historical works were popular, and histories continued to be written during the sixteenth century. Indeed Lee has suggested, perhaps too boldly, that Berners' translation "inaugurated the taste for historical reading and composition by which the later literature of the century is characterised. Fabian, Hall, and Holinshed were all indebted to it."[7] But this is a point which further research will have to confirm. The absence of reprints is noteworthy, since French editions appeared regularly in the fifteenth century: in Berners' own lifetime there were editions by Verard in c. 1498, by Michel le noir in 1505, and two further editions in 1517 and 1518. These normally appeared in four volumes, and Berners no doubt used one of these editions, since he refers to the reduction of the original four volumes of the French text to his own two.

Two of the books Berners translated are chivalric romances, and hence are closely associated with Froissart in tone and background. The first of these is *Huon of Bordeux*. Two editions of the work are extant: the earlier is undated, the later was printed in 1601. The sole surviving copy of the first edition has lost possibly a leaf and a half at the end; at the beginning it opens immediately with the heading for Chapter One. That the translation is by Berners is accepted from the preface and colophon of the 1601 edition, which is in itself a corrected reprint. Whether there was a corresponding prologue or colophon in the first edition is uncertain; but Lee, the book's modern editor, has assumed that both were present.[8] I find his reasons for assuming this uncompelling, since books were frequently issued without prologue or colophon at that time. The typography is said to be characteristic of Wynkyn de Worde's books, and so Lee has dated its appearance c. 1534, the date then accepted for de Worde's death. But de Worde issued fewer books late in life, and the book, if it came from his press, may precede 1534, possibly by several years. A more exact typographical investigation is required to place the appearance of the book more accurately, for it is a point of some consequence. If de Worde printed the book, it may have appeared before Berners' death in 1533, and this could affect our evaluation of why it was printed.

The problem of the first edition is complicated by the printer's preface and colophon attached to the 1601 edition. They deserve quotation in full: [9]

[Preface] The foundation of all true fame and repute, which in this world is most to be reckoned of and esteemed (according to the opinion of all writers both ancient & moderne), consisteth in bold, honourable, and heroycall resolution which enflames the soule with a continuall thirsting desire of pursuing braue and generous purposes, perfourming of high and aduenturous actions which, when their bodies are mantled vp in the obscure moulde of the earth, leaueth their names cannonized in fame's æternall calender and renownes them as rare presidents to all following posterities. And from so perfect ground of good and laudable example, the young infant spirits of latter growth, taking vp the embers of their worthy proceedings, the sparke of glorious imitation catcheth hold of their warme and forward desires and, so enkindling further till it breake foorth into a flame, burnes vp and consumes all conceits of cowardise, and as an enlightned beacon on a promontorie toppe calles & inuites them to the like honourable atchieuements. Hence ensured that desertfull and wellworthy to bee remembred purpose of Sir Iohn Bourchier knight, Lord Berners, when not onely in this woorke of *Huon of Bordeaux* but many other famous translations of like consequence by him perfourmed, he gaue witnesse to the world of so labourious an endeauour and, as it were, squared out an excellent platfourme for generous imitation. But let me not herewithall forget that the right noble Earl of Huntingdon, Lord Hastings, was a continuall spurre to him in the pursuite of such paines and likewise a cheerefull encourager of me in the imprinting, assisting euer both with his purse and honourable countenance the trauaile that sorted to so good example. Which being now finished and made compleat with better abilitie of will then other perfourmance, we leaue to the gentle acceptance of such as knowe how rightly to iudge and kindly to entertaine; to others our paines are not imparted.

[Colophon] Thus endeth the ancient, honourable, famous and
   delightfull historie of Huon of Bordeaux, one of the
   peeres of Fraunce and Duke of Guyenne, and of diuers
   princes liuing in his time; translated out of French into
   English by Sir Iohn Bourchier knight, Lord Berners,
   at the request of the Lord Hastings, Earle of Huntington, in the yeare of our lord God one thousand, five
   hundred, threescore and ten; and now newly reuised
   and corrected, this present yeare, 1601.

Lee assumed from these remarks that the first edition which he dated
to 1534 was published at Lord Hastings' request after Berners' death
and that there was a second edition, which had not survived, from
1570. While, because of the 1601 colophon, one may accept the
possibility of a 1570 edition, the first edition, as we have just seen,
may have appeared during Berners' lifetime. Which Lord Hastings is
meant is uncertain, though there would appear to be three possibilities.
George Hastings was created first Earl of Huntingdon in 1529 and
died in 1545. Francis Hastings, his son, who was born in the early
part of the sixteenth century, succeeded to the title in 1545 and died in
1561. His son Henry, born in 1535, became the third earl in 1561.
Lee understood that George, the first earl, was meant. This is acceptable only if one assumes that the prologue of the 1601 edition also
appeared in the first edition, for Lee had accepted that the prologue
was originally written by Berners and was modified by the printer
after Berners' death and before printing. The second earl, on the
other hand, is known to have been friendly with Berners, who attended
his marriage and gave him several presents. Francis Hastings was
present in Calais when Berners died, inherited his goods there, and
was executor of his will. But Francis died in 1561 and cannot have
been responsible for the assumed 1570 edition. If he was the Earl of
Huntingdon referred to, we would have to assume that there was
another lost edition between the first edition and the hypothetical 1570
edition, and that the preface and colophon stem from this edition. The
third earl, Henry, was born after Berners' death and would therefore
not seem to be a serious contender unless one assumes that the preface
came into existence only with the 1570 edition. All three earls present
certain difficulties in the identification with the one mentioned in the
1601 preface and colophon. However, in the light of our present
knowledge Francis Hastings appears the most suitable candidate. This
identification would imply that the first edition was printed in Berners'
lifetime with no prologue, that there was a lost second edition printed

for Hastings between 1545 and 1561 when the 1601 preface and colophon first appeared, that there was a possible 1570 edition, and that the 1601 edition is the fourth edition.

The original French prose version was made in 1454 for three nobles at the court of Charles VII. The French text was printed by Michel le noir in 1513 and 1516 and was frequently reprinted. *Huon of Bordeux* belongs to the so-called group of Charlemagne romances. Apart from *Huon* itself there are only two other English prose texts in this group, *Charles the Great* and the *Four Sons of Aymon*. These were both translated from French and printed by Caxton. Berners' translation therefore carries on the Caxtonian tradition. Several poetic versions belonging to the Charlemagne group also exist in English, though they are all much earlier than the prose versions.

There are fewer problems connected with *Arthur of Litell Brytayne*. Two editions are extant; neither is dated. The first was printed by Robert Redborne about 1555; the second appeared about 1582. The two editions differ little from each other. There is no evidence that the book was ever printed in Berners' lifetime, though it does contain a prologue he wrote for it [10] which may indicate an intention to print. This prologue contains many echoes to prologues by Caxton, particularly those to the *History of Troy* and *Morte d'Arthur*. According to his prologue, after he had decided to attempt the translation Berners translated a page or two and then decided to give it up because he thought the work was too full of the supernatural and hence was incredible. Later he persuaded himself that, while the work was fictitious, it was no doubt written for the inculcation of virtue, and so he completed the translation. Caxton, in his prologue to the *History of Troy*, mentions how he had translated a few pages of that work and then fell into despair because of his inferior style and abandoned the project. It was only after Margaret of Burgundy had corrected his style and ordered him to continue that he completed it. In the *Morte d'Arthur* Caxton reports a conversation supposed to have taken place between himself and some of his noble customers. He mentions that he was hesitant about printing the life of King Arthur because it was widely considered to be fictitious. The customers provided him with many proofs of the historical existence of Arthur, and while Caxton's scepticism was not entirely allayed he nevertheless felt that the work was written for our benefit in that it taught how to practise virtue and avoid sin. It is almost as though Berners' prologue is an amalgam of the two Caxton ones. However, the similarities are interesting, for

125

whereas the two themes seem natural in the Caxton prologues, Berners' handling of them is unconvincing. There is far less credibility in his starting, stopping, and continuing again, partly because he has internalized the discussion within himself. Set against Caxton's prologues, Berners' remarks appear forced: he obviously felt that a writer should express his hesitations and doubts, but he was unable to find a suitable framework within which to place them. This weakness in itself indicates that he was copying a tradition rather than relating his own experience — and as I have suggested it was the tradition represented by Caxton that he followed.

That Berners knew some of Caxton's prologues is supported by the many verbal parallels between the two writers. The sentence in Berners, "and also bycause that ydelnesse is reputed to be the moder of al vices; wherfore somwhat in eschewynge thereof," echoes Caxton's "In eschewyng of ydlenes moder of all vices" in the *History of Troy*.[11] The way in which Berners announces himself as the translator is typically Caxtonian, and the expression "our maternall tongue" for English was one that Caxton used many times. When Berners is in some doubt about whether to continue the translation, he remembers "that I had redde and seen many a sondrye volume of dyverse noble hystoryes." In much the same way Caxton had recalled that "many noble volumes be made of hym [Arthur] and of his noble knyghtes in frensshe which I have seen and redde beyonde the see," when debating whether to print the story of Arthur. Finally Berners' comments upon his insufficient command of French and of rhetorical terms could be paralleled from many Caxtonian prologues: Berners has also, like Caxton, followed his original as closely as possible; he wishes that his readers might take the translation "in gre"; they are to lay the blame for any faults on his "rude unconnynge and derke ignoraunce"; they are to "mynysshe, adde or augment" as they find need; and Berners for his part will pray to God that he give them "the perdurable joye of heven." All these are commonplaces in Caxton's translations, where they are expressed in identical or very similar words. It is also true that such expressions are found in other texts as well, but there are so many correspondences between Caxton's and Berners' words that it is probable that Berners was to some extent following Caxton in his choice of both material and its expression.

The French version of *Arthur of Lytell Brytayne* was printed at Paris by Michel le noir in 1514, and it seems probable that Berners used this edition, though the matter has not been investigated.

The other two translations made by Berners, the *Castell of Love* and the *Golden Boke of Marcus Aurelius*, are of Spanish texts, though in both cases Berners made use of a French translation. However, Berners had visited Spain in 1518 and he may have known some Spanish. The *Castell of Love* is ascribed to Diego de San Pedro and was first published in Seville in 1492. It was reprinted at Burgos in 1496, and a continuation by Nicolas Nunes was added to the 1508 edition printed in Logroño. It soon achieved international popularity: the first Italian translation appeared in Venice in 1515, the first French one in Paris in 1525. Other French editions appeared in 1526 and 1533. The 1526 edition includes a preface, not found in the Spanish texts, which agrees closely with Berners' prologue. But Berners' translation also includes the continuation by Nunes, which is not found in any of the extant early Italian or French editions. Crane concluded from this evidence that Berners had both a French and a Spanish edition of the *Castell of Love* and that he may have learned his Spanish from using the French translation. Gradually, as he became more proficient in Spanish, he relied less upon his French version.[12] This is quite feasible, but the possibility should not be overlooked that a French edition with the continuation may now be lost. It may also be added that Berners' translation dates from after 1526.

There are three extant editions of Berners' *Castell of Love*, but the order in which they were printed is disputed. The one printed by John Turke and usually dated to 1549 is probably the earliest extant. A second edition by Robert Wyer appeared soon afterwards.[13] A third edition was printed in 1560. There is no evidence that the book was printed during Berners' lifetime. According to the title page the translation was made at the request of "Lady Elizabeth Carew, late wyfe to Syr Nicholas." Nicholas Carew died in 1539; I have not discovered the date of his wife's death. Elizabeth Carew was the sister of Sir Francis Bryan and the niece of Lord Berners, though little else is known about her. Carew was one of the young men who surrounded Henry VIII. He fell from favour in 1519 and was sent to Calais as lieutenant of the tower of Ruysbanke. He later regained the royal favour and spent much of his time trying to arrange a lasting settlement between Henry VIII and Francis I of France. He made the preparations for a meeting in Calais in 1531. Carew was held in esteem by the French king, upon whose recommendation he was made a Knight of the Garter in 1536; but he was beheaded for treason in 1539. An inventory of goods made at his death includes a list of books; among others he possessed the works of Gower, Froissart, and Monstrelet.

The *Castell of Love*, like another work attributed to Diego de San Pedro, the *Tractado de Analte y Lucenda*, has been called a sentimental novel because it is a short work devoted to the expression of tender feelings rather than to the narration of heroic adventures. The popularity of the *Castell of Love*, however, is attributable as much to its style as to its matter, for the author used many rhetorical devices and expressions. The resultant style is not heavy, since an excessive use of synonyms or exotic vocabulary is not present, as it so commonly is in late fifteenth-century works. The style tends towards balance and rhythm.

According to the colophon, Berners' translation of the *Golden Boke* was finished on 10 March 1532 (23 Henry VIII).[14] It was thus finished almost exactly a year before he died and was probably Berners' last translation, since he was ill during the final months of his life. The earliest known edition is that by Berthelet of 1535. The book was extremely popular and was constantly reprinted — a further ten editions having appeared by 1586. This popularity could mean that some editions have not survived, although it does not seem likely that the translation appeared in print before Berners' death. The colophon of the 1535 edition states that the book was translated by Berners from French at the request of Sir Francis Bryan. Sir Francis was Berners' nephew, for he was the son of Sir Thomas Bryan and Margaret Bourchier, Berners' sister. He was another of the courtiers who surrounded Henry VIII. He was honoured with gifts at court entertainments, he was the king's cupbearer in 1516 and master of toyles in 1518, and attended the Field of the Cloth of Gold in 1520. He may have been related to Anne Boleyn, and he helped to arrange the king's first divorce. But he seems to have been unaffected by Anne's subsequent death, possibly because he put his loyalty to the king and his own survival before all else. Sir Francis was interested in literary affairs: he is referred to in the works of Erasmus and Ascham, he wrote poetry (most of which has not survived), and he translated Guevara's *A Dispraise of the Life of a Courtier and a Commendation of the Life of a Labouring Man*, which was printed by Berthelet in 1545. It fits in with what we know of him that he should have urged his uncle to translate Guevara's *Golden Boke*. We may also assume that he was responsible for the book's publication in 1535.

Guevara's *Golden Boke* was published in Spanish in 1529 in Antwerp and Paris; though it may have appeared earlier in lost Spanish editions. It was translated into Castilian, and from Castilian into French by R. Berthault. The French translation was printed in 1531 and reprinted in 1533. Berners' translation was made from the 1531 edition, and it can thus be fairly accurately dated between 1531 and 10 March 1532.[15] Guevara's book is traditional in that it is one of the collections of wise sayings and aphorisms that had been so popular throughout the Middle Ages. But it was written in the new style, which no doubt contributed to its great success. This style is sometimes referred to as an early form of euphuism. It is now generally held that Berners' translation was not an important element in the development of the euphuistic style in England,[16] though it does share with euphuism the continual use of parallelism and balance.

A tabulation of the main facts about Berners' translations produces the following results:

Huon of Bordeux after 1513, from the French edition of Michel le noir.

Arthur of Litell Brytayne after 1514, from the French edition of Michel le noir.

Froissart's Chronicle c. 1521–25 (March), probably from the French edition by Michel le noir.

Castell of Love after 1526, probably from the French edition only, but possibly from a Spanish edition as well.

Golden Boke 1531–32 (March), from the French translation by Berthault.

Since it is probable that the *Golden Boke* is Berners' last translation, the *Castell of Love* can be dated between 1526 and 1531. It would also seem likely that these two are the last translations made by Berners. The major problem in the chronology of Berners' work is the dating of *Huon of Bordeux* and *Arthur of Litell Brytayne*. It has usually been assumed that these two are later than his Froissart, though no evidence of weight has been brought forward in support of this hypothesis. Two reasons are usually adduced. The first is stylistic, in that some scholars feel that the style of the Froissart suggests an early translation.[17] But such views are largely subjective, since

129

these three texts have never been submitted to stylistic analysis and we are ignorant of the way in which Berners' style may have developed. The second is the assumption that all Berners' literary activity was confined to his stay in Calais and, since his Froissart was made shortly after his appointment there, it must be his earliest translation. It was easier to accept this view when it was thought that Berners had been in Calais from 1520 till his death in 1533. But J. H. McDill proved that his stay in Calais was broken by a period in England; he was in Calais from 1520 to 1526 and again from 1531 till his death.[18] It is unlikely that all his translations could be crammed into these two periods abroad, and there is after all no very great reason why we should think that his translations were all made there anyway. Since some of Berners' translations were made in England, it is quite likely that *Huon of Bordeux* and *Arthur of Litell Brytayne* were made in England before Berners left for Calais the first time. At all events there is no compelling reason to put them after the translation of Froissart.

Of the texts translated by Berners, *Arthur of Litell Brytayne* is the one which shows the greatest similarity in its prologue with Caxton's works. Possibly this was Berners' first translation, and it may have been made in imitation of or following the example of Caxton. It is interesting to speculate whether Caxton was the model who inspired Berners to start translating. We know that Berners owned many books, and among them are likely to have been texts printed by Caxton. It is natural that Berners should have looked to the earlier courtly translator when embarking on his own work, so it is quite possible that the Froissart, far from being the original translation, may in fact have benefited from Berners' experience, gained from *Arthur of Litell Brytayne* and *Huon of Bordeux*. Though if we accept that Froissart is not his first translation, it may be necessary to modify some of the statements made earlier about the relationship between it and Henry VIII.

Further research may help to clear up the dates of the various translations, for I cannot agree with Lewis that the dating is unimportant.[19] If we accept tentatively an order of translation something like *Arthur of Litell Brytayne, Huon of Bordeux, Froissart's Chronicle, Castell of Love,* and *Golden Boke,* it could be accepted that there is a very distinct difference between the first three and the last two, not only in style but also in subject matter. The first three are all translations of French texts and carry on the Caxtonian tradition of translation of chivalric works of martial prowess. They are all of a historical nature, and attempt to relate their events to real people and places. They are all to some extent influenced by the aureate stylistic tradition. The last two, however, introduce the English public to sentimental literature about fictitious characters or to humanistic moralizing. More importantly, they are written in the new style, which puts balance and parallelism before an extravagant and labored vocabulary. Is it possible, then, to assume that these translations reflect a change in the taste of the court that took place in the 1520's? Possibly during his stay in England from 1526 to 1531 Berners became aware of a new literary fashion. In this respect the genesis of the two latest translations may be important. Each was asked for by a nephew or niece, and both these relatives were of course members of the younger generation. Was there a group of younger people, possibly related, who were increasingly turning to Spain rather than to France for their literary example, and had they managed to recruit Berners to their position? Without further work such ideas must remain speculative, but they are certainly worth pursuing.

These are among the interesting possibilities opened up by even such a brief survey of Berners' literary activity, although more definite proof must await detailed investigations. Particularly desirable would be stylistic analyses of each text, investigations into the actual French editions used for the translations, more detailed work on the biography, and further study of the literary taste within Berners' family circle, and more generally in the court at that time. I hope that this article has shown that such work would be worthwhile, and that Berners has been unjustly neglected.

NOTES

1. C. S. Lewis, *English Literature in the Sixteenth Century excluding Drama* (Oxford, 1954), p. 149.
2. W. P. Ker, *The Chronicle of Froissart*, 6 vols. (London, 1901–3), I, 5–6.
3. *The Indian Summer of Indian Chivalry* (Durham, N.C., 1960).
4. S. K. Workman, "Versions by Skelton, Caxton, and Berners of a Prologue by Diodorus Siculus," *Modern Language Notes*, 56 (1941), 252–58.
5. The development of Berners' prologue is more like Caxton's *Polychronicon* than Poggio's Latin, but this may be fortuitous.
6. Phrases which have a Caxtonian ring in Berners' prologue include: "Take this my rude translacion in gre"; "I remyt the correctyon therof to them that discretely shall fynde any reasonable defaute"; and the comments about the arrangement of the table of contents.
7. S. L. Lee, "Bourchier, John," in the *Dictionary of National Biography*.

8. S. L. Lee, *The Boke of Duke Huon of Burdeux*, EETS, e.s. 40, 41, 43, 50 (London, 1882–87), lii–liv.

9. I have modernized the punctuation, but not the spelling of the original.

10. Reprinted in Ker, I., xviii–xix.

11. Quotations from *Arthur of Litell Brytayne* are from Ker, *loc. cit.*, and those of Caxton from W. J. B. Crotch, *The Prologues and Epilogues of William Caxton*, EETS, o.s. 176 (London, 1928).

12. W. G. Crane, "Lord Berners's Translation of Diego de San Pedro's *Carcel de Amor*," *PLMA*, 39 (1934), 1032–35. See also Dale B. J. Randall, *The Golden Tapestry: A Critical Survey of Non-chivalric Spanish Fiction in English Translation, 1543–1657* (Durham, N.C., 1963), pp. 47–49, and passim.

13. See Crane, *op. cit.*, and the introduction to his facsimile reprint of the *Castell of Love* (Gainsville, Fla., 1950). The *Short Title Catalogue* dates this edition 1540.

14. Some editions read 24 Henry VIII, but this is probably a misprint.

15. See further J. M. Galvez, *On the Influence of Guevara on English Literature and on Lord Berners' Golden Boke* (Berlin, 1916).

16. Lewis, p. 150, and references in his bibliography.

17. E. V. Utterson, *The History of the Valiant Knight Arthur of Little Britain* (London, 1814): "This [i.e., *Arthur of Litell Brytayne*], from his prologue, would appear to be one of his first productions; but, on the other hand, it seems to indicate less adoption of French words, or rather a more full acquaintance with the English language, than his Froissart" (preface, pages unnumbered).

18. "The Life of Lord Berners," *Times Literary Supplement*, 17 April 1930, p. 336.

19. *Op. cit.* p. 151: "The chronology of his works is obscure and does not perhaps matter very much."

Kingship, Government, and Politics in the Middle Ages

SOME RECENT STUDIES

Michael Altschul

François Louis Ganshof. *Frankish Institutions under Charlemagne*, trans. Bryce and Mary Lyon. Providence: Brown University Press, 1968. Pp. xvi, 191.

Walter Ullmann. *The Carolingian Renaissance and the Idea of Kingship*. Birkbeck Lectures, 1968–69. London: Methuen, 1969. Pp. xiv, 201.

David C. Douglas. *The Norman Achievement, 1050–1100*. Berkeley and Los Angeles: University of California Press, 1969. Pp. xvi, 271, 14 plates, 4 maps, tables.

Peter Munz. *Frederick Barbarossa: A Study in Medieval Politics*. Ithaca: Cornell University Press, 1969. Pp. xxi, 422, 8 plates, 1 map, table.

DESPITE THE GROWING POPULARITY and innovative importance of social and economic history, most medieval historians continue to work in the still older tradition of political and constitutional development. The political historian, however, has much to gain by attention to these newer approaches and to innovations within the tradition itself. A number of recent studies tend, in fact, to reflect careful analyses of medieval notions of law, of the sources and nature of authority, and of political institutions in the context of social structures and change, rather than the old preoccupation with standard forms of narrative or of juridical anachronisms and abstractions. The purpose of this essay is to explore some recent works in light of these changes in the conventional political approach.

The books under consideration here form a recent, loosely connected representative sampling of important work on various aspects and periods of medieval politics. More specifically, they form two sets: Ullmann and Ganshof write on the theoretical and practical bases and operation of Carolingian kingship, and Douglas and Munz on innovations in political forces and organization in a new and more open eleventh- and twelfth-century setting. All are well-known scholars, and these works represent a continuation or culmination of previous con-

133

tributions. Ullmann has, in effect, detailed certain arguments adumbrated more generally elsewhere, especially in *Principles of Government and Politics in the Middle Ages* (1961; 2nd ed. 1966) and *The Growth of Papal Government in the Middle Ages* (1955; 3rd ed. 1970).[1] Ganshof's study was originally published in 1965 as part of a massive continental enterprise issued in commemoration of the 800th anniversary of the canonization of Charlemagne.[2] The gist of Douglas' book appeared in a short article in French in 1967, and puts in a broader comparative perspective his great work on Normandy and Norman England.[3] Munz' views are partially known through a series of articles which appeared in the 1960's.[4] These books are also connected in the sense that they are likely to develop a wide and rapid currency among English-speaking scholars, not least importantly for teaching purposes. All are, *mutatis mutandis*, major works; all are readily accessible to students; and all fill much-felt needs for up-to-date work on Carolingian political theory and practice, the remarkable Norman expansion of the eleventh century, and a modern re-assessment of the greatest of the Hohenstaufen emperors.

The medieval preference for the Carolingians over the Merovingians is an interesting and important question of medieval intellectual history, and its perpetuation by modern historians an equally interesting question of modern historiography.[5] The books by Ganshof and Ullmann shed light on this preference from the point of view of their contrasting interpretative and analytical frameworks. There has been much recent work on Charlemagne and the Carolingian period in general that has been subjected to an extensive and most valuable review and critique by D. A. Bullough, in which Ganshof's, but not Ullmann's, contributions are assessed.[6] The two are complementary in one important respect, in that they provide interpretations of the two basic dimensions of the same question, the nature and scope of Carolingian political authority. It is, however, worth pointing out that while Ganshof's book adds a very useful perspective and depth to Ullmann's, the reverse is not necessarily the case. To some extent this can be explained in that Ganshof strictly limits himself to the reign of Charlemagne, while Ullmann is only marginally concerned with him, devoting the bulk of his book to Louis the Pious and his successors. Of greater importance is the fact that Ganshof, unlike Ullmann, places his study in exact chronological perspectives, and in a precise social context. Ullmann's well-known tendency to take a more static approach, to view chronological development as largely the filling-out of preconceived ideological and programmatic principles, persists in his latest book. While both are concerned with legal definitions and content, their areas of concern rarely touch, and Ullmann's Carolingian ruler seems to inhabit a different historical world from Ganshof's.

Professor Ganshof's study is, as indicated, severely pragmatic and rigorously institutional in approach. For the English edition he has added a brief section on military organization and deployment, and has made small additions in other places. The result is all that one could ask for by way of a comprehensive and accurate depiction of the subject; historians have at last a succinct account of Carolingian government which they can use with complete confidence. Often the book takes on the characteristic of a reference work: each sentence a specific fact, with a note to the complete or representative sampling of relevant texts, established with as much geographical and chronological precision as possible. Yet Ganshof, abetted by his translators, avoids the massive heaviness of the *Verfassungsgeschichte* tradition; his account is not only definitive within its limits but also, gratifyingly, absorbing and almost "light" reading.

The most important conclusion to come from these pages is the sense of the limitations of power and institutional apparatus available to or devised by Charlemagne to fulfill his own programmatic intentions. It appears that his major contribution (this recalls the judgment of Professor Fichtenau on Charles' role as sponsor of the Carolingian Renaissance)[7] was the extension, elaboration, and standardization of institutions of his own or his ancestors' devising. The most important included the development of the *missi dominici*, the utilization of *scabini* as judgment-finders, the application of the *inquisitio* procedure, and the cultivation of royal vassalage. All are deftly defined and analyzed in masterly fashion.[8] All are of as great an importance as coronation ceremonials, Old Testament analogies, and Augustinian influences in forming the design which I would call "Christian mission" kingship. Charles was fully aware of the promise and responsibility of his consecrated position as king and emperor; but his awareness was informed, not by any implied superiority of the ecclesiastical orders to whom the tradition was indebted for articulation, but by his sense of responsibility to God. Ganshof points out how much of Charles' work, as reflected in the Capitularies and *notitiae*, suggests not pride but sorrow: a sense of unfulfillment, of guilt for the imperfect

135

realization of God's plans, most dramatically and urgently reflected (after the assumption of a by no means clear imperial designation) in his instructions to the *missi* and the new oath of fealty of 802. Charles was aware — and there is no reason to presume otherwise of his successors — of the real nature of the society which he felt God had set him to rule over, and of how far short of programmatic intent, of actual *renovatio*, he might actually fall. Frankish Christian society both prompted and defeated his efforts. The constructs of theory do not transform existing institutional and social patterns radically very often; rather, they reflect and rationalize them; and it is not difficult to move from the most favorable rationalization to the realm of mere wishful thinking. As Ganshof has occasion over and over again to emphasize, Charles' plans remained mere paper schemes as often as they were realized in institutional practice. It was his own personal capabilities, and the overwhelming majesty, awe, and fear that he aroused, that enabled him to translate as much theory into practice as he did. Historians persist in falling prey to the application of modern notions of government and state in writing of the Carolingian period, and to view Charles as a model or norm against which to posit the chimera of "feudal anarchy" overwhelming Carolingian central authority. It is not the least merit of Ganshof's work that it reminds us how primitive, how imperfectly centralized, and how morally preoccupied that government was.

One undeniable fact of the thought world of the ninth century was that Charles was indeed a model for his successors: a blessing under whose umbrella they could claim to repose, but also a curse, in whose shadow they labored in vain to emulate his image of purposeful achievement.[9] To recognize the fact, however, ought not to involve accepting its legitimacy as part of the intellectual assumptions of twentieth-century historians. The basic facts of society: economic autarky; the segmentation of political power; the externalized and ritualized formalism of ecclesiastical attitudes; the patterns of loyalty and behavior formed by the personal ties of kinship and lordship; the ubiquity of the vendetta — none of these were essentially altered by Charles, much less his successors. The Arnulfing family, dressed out as sacral kings and "Roman" emperors, accepted and fostered an ideology of Christian renewal and Christian mission, but their serious pursuit was not rewarded with many tangible results. They did impress on contemporaries a notion of positiveness, and one can point, for evidence, to Charles' unparalleled military successes, his assumption of emperorship, and the importance of his putting down on paper ideas, programmes, and codes of law (see Ganshof, pp. 53–55, 72–73). But it is naive to think that such actions were based on a wholly new concept of society that explicitly rejected every vestige of the old, or that they actually created a new order of society, or that they represented anything more than a partial, fitful, and ironically atypical record of centralized achievement.

It is precisely in this way that Professor Ullmann's book ultimately fails to convince. Here, no less than elsewhere, there is the unmistakable evidence, in the breathtaking vigor and challenge of the writing, of a great historian at work. The faults, however, are to be found as well. Some are terminological and stylistic: the old, imprecise words ("ascending," "descending," "totalitarian" — the more to be regretted in an historian who insists, rightly, on the precise definitions of texts), embedded in a style which, in my own experience, students find fascinating but extremely hard to follow, no less for its English than for its citation of Latin texts. More important is the propensity to a priori schemes. Ullmann regards the Renaissance as only superficially and marginally concerned with a revived cult of classicism and literary efflorescence;[10] but his own treatment seems unnecessarily strained. Basically he defines "renaissance" as the *de novo* birth of a Christian society, manifested in the speedy and universally accepted triumph of the papal monist-hierocratic doctrine of emperorship and paralleling the full acceptance of an episcopal view of the moral suitability of kings. Political authority, and society itself, are thus seen as the products of papal and episcopal programmes, quite overwhelming any independent lines of thought or action. The theocratic tradition spawned both royal and papal monism, but the latter won out, quickly and unequivocally, in ways which fixed the dimensions of thought and action for centuries to come.

Much of the argument is, to be sure, quite correct, and there are many excellent pages in the book, especially those on the coronation rites and *ordines* of the ninth century and those that contain remarks on writer-statesmen such as Hincmar of Rheims and lesser-known polemicists. Ullmann's book is a valuable addition to the works of such historians as Schramm, Kantorowicz, Bouman, and Morrison,[11] and is further enhanced by its admirable qualities of stimulating argument and by its wealth of references, especially to periodical literature not always easily accessible. But it suffers the faults of an idée fixe, in that it draws lines much too sharply and one-sidedly; it is not rooted in a sufficiently sensitive appreciation of the real Carolingian (or papal) world. The principles of kingship supposedly stem from the radical application of the *nova creatura*, a wholly new Christian society. Kingship, and then emperorship, far from being rooted in the context of Frankish society and history, are imposed upon, and are themselves part of, the *nova creatura*, taking their cue from the sacramental and symbolic elements of the liturgy and papal hegemonic programmes. The suspicion grows that it is Ullmann who is doing the imposing, in grand hierocratic fashion. He does not take into account (and believes that his theorists and propagandists did not take into account) the strength of Frankish customs and social-political organization, existing ideas regarding blood-right, election, and warrior abilities as criteria of eligibility to rule, or the previous identity of Frankish society and Roman Christianity in the Merovingian period. Charlemagne was, after all, as much a barbarian hero as a Christian ruler, and both on a magnificent scale. If his *epigonoi* suffer by comparison as Christian mission rulers, they also suffer as warrior leaders, and the problems they faced related more specifically to the circumscription of their zones of effective influence with the nobility (from whom the episcopacy was largely drawn) than to ecclesiastical programmes as such, although the latter received the literary and liturgical articulation.

There are many individual points that require comment. For example, Ullmann propounds (pp. 137–38) a static and ultimately pagan Byzantine tradition to compare, unfavorably, with a dynamic and socially regenerative papal theory, a position that the evidence does not warrant. More generally, he underestimates Merovingian precedent, in particular the cult of Constantine as Christian model, which arose with Clovis (Gregory of Tours, II, 31).[12] There was not a broadly new, much less brand-new, Christian society in 751, or in 800, but rather an explicit new emphasis on the awareness of a Christian mission as the predominant, but never exclusive, criterion of eligibility for rulership in a Christian society. The Carolingian kings, in their specific quasi-episcopal trappings, essentially represented the modernization, not the creation, of the image of the king as remote purveyor of divine mystery. The formula *dei gratia* is expressly Christian, but the idea behind it is not necessarily so. Surely it goes too far to claim that this kingship was devised wholly from Biblical cloth, decked out in liturgical symbolism; it is better history to see it as a western incorporation and liturgical articulation of older classical and Byzantine traditions, hitherto more dimly felt and expressed.

There was a substantial change, but it involved the intensification of Christian and the sublimation of non-Christian elements, not the elimination of a pagan past, as the *nova creatura* argument demands. The argument for creation *ex nihilo* is not a valid historical explanation of historical change.[13]

Ullmann argues that the *nova creatura* spawned theocratic kingship but simultaneously stunted it by the episcopal insistence of kingship under (divine) law and the papal monistic concept of the subordinate protectorship function of the Roman emperor. These lines continued unabated in later centuries and terminated in limited monarchy and an independent and superior ecclesiastical order. Just as papal ideas were fully worked out and required nothing more from the canonists than some terminological updating of hierocratic tradition, so also with rulership. Royal authority was delimited by episcopal criteria and the imperial office by the acceptance of the papal interpretation, so that the recovery of Roman law did not introduce substantive new elements with regard to utility, protection, community, or authority, but only a rather more precise juridical expression (and a certain secularization) of principles already formulated in liturgical and literary texts.

In truth, has not Ullmann elaborated another interesting, forceful, but untenable specimen of a static view of medieval history?[14] The Carolingian episcopacy simply cannot be regarded as prototypes of the Gregorian visionaries or the canonists. It is worthwhile to stress the innovative impact of Aristotelian naturalism and secularism (as in *Principles of Government and Politics* and, more recently, *The Individual and Society in the Middle Ages* [1966]), but in so doing it is not permissible to denigrate the force of Roman law or indeed to overlook the new social and political forces at work in later centuries. Romanists and canonists, theologians and propagandists did not conceive of themselves as applying mere icing on a Carolingian cake. This is as true of the papacy as of any other element of society. New papal ideas, and canonist and institutional development, marked a new path; but especially, there was an undeniably new spirit, an activist and militant vision, that informed the Gregorian and post-Gregorian epochs. Despite ideas rooted in the most ancient Christian traditions and in fundamental Biblical passages, it was the creative reinterpretation and application of these principles in concrete social terms that made them dynamic and respected. Not so the Carolingian royal and imperial traditions; they were truly archaic in twelfth-century terms.

Certain elements remained, most importantly the details of coronation ceremonial; certain were newly emphasized, such as thaumaturgy; and many received significant revival in the sixteenth- and seventeenth-century efflorescence of divine-right monarchy. All this is perfectly understandable, for society continued to view itself as a unified Christian commonwealth. But the thrust, from the twelfth century onwards, is also toward Roman law notions of corporation, status, inalienability, and the body politic, and toward bureaucratic-representative forms of political organization, with "absolutist" vs. "constitutionalist" interpretations of certain formulae an interesting but essentially secondary consideration. It is no denigration of Aristotelianism to say that the ground was prepared by a Roman legal emphasis on the naturalness of the state and of political behavior,[15] and that the most fruitful period of speculation was the fourteenth, fifteenth, and sixteenth centuries, when the complementary influences of Aristotle and Roman law were evident in theorists. Ullmann's arguments, that the essential features of all later (pre-Aristotelian) medieval political speculation on, and actual operation of, kingship were set down in the Carolingian age, have a certain pugnacious tone and are expressed in rather broad strokes. They seem to anticipate, not without a certain relish, criticisms and the joining of battle. This is all to the good. The historical profession can never have enough works of Ullmann's vigor, immense learning, and passionate interest in the issues and intellectual climate of the age. But has he fully entered it? Is he not in fact betraying an idée fixe, ultimately anti-historical? The term "Carolingian Renaissance" in the title has little to do with the term in any of the current usages; in his hands it becomes the functional equivalent of the triumph of a static papal hierocratic system in which Frankish kings, and Frankish society itself, are submerged. Ullmann has, as always, written an engrossing and forceful book, but in the end it fails to convince or to satisfy.

The new forces at work in the post-Carolingian centuries are matters that lie at the heart of the books by Douglas and Munz. Despite their obvious differences of subject matter, both share an acute awareness of the interplay of new institutions and attitudes in the eleventh and twelfth centuries and view their subjects, favorably in each instance, as both examples and catalysts of new ideas and organization.

Douglas confines his study to the last half of the eleventh century, and sees the Normans as promoters of and contributors to a new western militancy, expansionist energies, and papal and feudal aspirations. The book is marked by running comparisons between the Normans in England and in Sicily-South Italy. Feudalized and Christianized, Normandy brought England into a French orbit and thereby created, in a combined English-Norman state, the most powerful bloc in northwestern Europe. Simultaneously it made the Mediterranean a western, and western Christian, lake. All these groups of Normans were effectively detached from their Scandinavian homeland base, which went off on tangents all its own. Douglas is much fuller on Sicily and South Italy than on England, which has received magisterial treatment in his *William the Conqueror* (1964). This book is not Douglas' *magnum opus — William the Conqueror* is that — but a popular (in the best sense of that term) extension. Within the chronological limits it imposes, it supersedes Haskins' famous *The Normans in European History* (1915), and in particular makes excellent use of the scholarship of such writers as Erdmann, Chalandon, Cahen, and Gay. In limiting himself to a half-century, Douglas is able to provide a very full and solid narrative account; but it has inherent limitations. By not taking the story down to the mid-twelfth century, the age which witnessed the end of the Norman dynasty in England, the death of Roger II, first Norman king of Sicily, and the rise of new personalities elsewhere, such as Pope Alexander III and Frederick Barbarossa, Douglas has in effect written a general history of the later eleventh century and the place of the Normans within it. This treatment blurs the focus on the Normans per se, for whom a larger chronological perspective would have been more appropriate.

Douglas' theme is twofold: the dynamism of the later eleventh century, and the greatness of Norman achievement as both a reflection and a molder of this dynamism. The Norman conquests in England and the Mediterranean, and participation in the affairs of the papacy and the first Crusade, were all of a piece, prompting and exemplifying the first great age of western expansionism. Douglas extends his heroic vision of William the Conqueror to the other Norman leaders, notably the Guiscards, and has many good pages on their qualities of military command and organization, their support of clerical reform, and their creation of a Norman mystique. The later eleventh century witnessed the formation of a true Norman world, violent, often repellent, yet creative and purposeful. The enthusiasm for the Normans evident in the book is rooted in one overriding consideration: to demonstrate that the Norman world of the twelfth century, so finely and imagina-

141

tively articulated by Jamison and Haskins,[16] was in all essential respects foreshadowed in the late eleventh century (p. 110 and note). This is a very good point, well worth making, and well developed throughout the book. But its force is diluted by an overabundance of generalized political-diplomatic narrative (Douglas does not have the elegant stylistic knack of a Sir Steven Runciman, whose *Sicilian Vespers* [1958] automatically comes to mind in places). This enthusiasm, moreover, seems carried beyond permissible bounds at times. To be sure, the Normans thrust themselves into the cockpit of Mediterranean politics, and were not willing to settle for halfway measures or the mere appearance of success. But with recurrent frequency, papal fortunes (pragmatically conceived) are made to reside wholly in Norman hands. Military action for, or against, the later eleventh-century popes was obviously a critical factor, but Douglas tends to overlook other, more elusive and elastic, but nonetheless vital, sources of strength. The Norman determination of events is claimed, but not always proved.

Douglas has provided essentially a narrative and descriptive history, rather than one marked by close analysis. His intention is to emphasize the qualities of dynamism and forcefulness, for which an analytical, more static approach would have been inappropriate. As such, the book tends to be impressionistic, rather than exhaustive, on such vitally important comparative questions as the composition, size, and organization of the Norman nobilities in England and Italy. But it has suggestive and valuable remarks on the extent of Norman intercommunication, the place of the Duke of Normandy as something of a headman (cf. pp. 112, 171), and the Norman gravitation to the "holy war" mystique — and hence is a useful corrective to those, as for example Munz (p. 27), who see the Normans in purely empirical, secularized terms as inspired entrepreneurs and opportunists. Douglas has, in short, provided an informative survey of Mediterranean Norman history, with sufficient running comparisons with England, based on *William the Conqueror*, to satisfy an audience which is likely to be familiar with the latter. Within its limits, and for its purposes, he has written a book that teachers and students will be grateful for, a stimulating introduction to the wider Norman world of the eleventh century.

Munz is similarly attuned to the spiritual and psychological energies and social-economic changes of the twelfth century. The militancy that informed the Gregorian vision was giving way to a more legalistic and territorial orientation, rapidly and unintentionally disassociating itself from more popular religious aspirations. Munz provides an elaborate

and detailed examination of the political-diplomatic activity of Popes
Adrian IV and Alexander III, Barbarossa's great adversaries, who
figure as prominently in the middle sections of the book as does the
emperor himself. A special virtue of Munz' argument, one that lends
great credence to his entire treatment, is his fine appraisal of Otto of
Freising (see especially pp. 129–40), which satisfactorily resolves the
seeming historiographical and intellectual contradictions in the author
of the *Two Cities* and the *Gesta Friderici*. Like Otto, Munz takes a
favorable view of Frederick, not however as a pre-committed ideologue but as an astute and flexible statesman, who sensed the new
forces of his age and attempted to work with and shape them to his
own ends. Frederick, as Munz pointedly remarks, was no lawyer,
either of twelfth-century or twentieth-century stripe.[17] Neither was his
closest advisor, Rainald of Dassel, archbishop of Cologne, who was
an ideologue and upon whom Frederick relied too much for his own
good. Rainald receives a form of miniature biography in the book, one
that sheds a most useful light on twelfth-century Hohenstaufen imperial
ideology. Rainald championed the independence of Cologne from
Rome in an effort to preserve those elements of continuity of imperial-
episcopal relations which had not been violently altered by the Investiture struggle. In Munz' hands he appears as one of those resplendent,
formalistic prince-bishops, whose own nouveau-riche career strengthened aristocratic pretensions. As is well known, Rainald was chiefly
responsible for the grandiose pro-imperial, anti-papal rhetoric of the
mid-twelfth century. Munz places little importance on such Romanist-
universalist sentiments directed against the papacy, the Byzantines,
and the western monarchs, regarding them as ad hoc pronouncements
foisted on Frederick by Rainald and accepted unwisely, even unwit-
tingly at times, in the heat of the moment. They are not to be taken
seriously as conscious statements of policy. Yet Frederick stayed with
Rainald, for he relied heavily on his loyalty and his demonstrated military and administrative abilities, especially in northern Italy. This is
in itself a telling comment on the resources of personnel and patronage
available to the emperors. However, to Munz imperial aspirations and
sentiments, insofar as they reflected an "archaic" tradition, were out-
weighed by Barbarossa's modernity and astuteness: indeed, the most
important feature of the imperial mission was the assumption of the
crusader's role, and Frederick's entire reign was designed to provide
the proper circumstances and conditions for this task.

The basic argument of Munz' book is that Frederick's political career makes sense only when viewed in the light of three distinct "master plans," ultimately focussed on the crusading mission.

The first stage lasted from 1152 to 1156, and was characterized by attempted continuity with his predecessor, Conrad III. This involved the support of the papacy (and the acceptance of its ideas on emperorship) and a general rapport with the Italian towns and German clergy and nobility. At the outset, Frederick envisioned his position as essentially passive, seeking to capitalize on the general good will and desire for peace that surrounded his election after 75 years of civil war, bitter ideological recrimination, and massive social and political upheaval. Except, however, for his coronation in Rome in 1155, this first plan proved a fiasco. Attempted rapport with Lombardy provided only friction, and the German princes failed to back his intended Sicilian expedition. The papacy, as guided by Cardinal Roland (later Alexander III), subsequently sided with the Sicilian Norman monarchy, while Frederick simultaneously came under the influence of Rainald, whom he promoted to Cologne shortly thereafter.

Thus, by 1156 Frederick sensed the limitations of his first plan and sought a more activist and aggressive policy, along with firmer practical foundations. This issued in a second plan, which Munz terms the "Great Design." In Germany, Frederick washed his hands of the nobility by creating concrete territorial and juridical spheres for them; in this way he promoted the Babenbergers in Austria (the *Privilegium minus* of 1156) and left the way open for Henry the Lion in Saxony, the Zähringen family in parts of Burgundy, Albrecht the Bear in Brandenburg, and others to develop their own analogous princely sovereignties. At the same time, Frederick concentrated on the development of a European centralized "state" of his own by a concerted application of *Hausmacht* in Burgundy, Alsace, western Swabia, and Lombardy. In most regions he succeeded in territorial aggrandizement and the recruitment of *ministeriales*, and created a "state" which straddled the three component kingdoms, territorially conceived, of the empire. Not only does Munz credit Frederick with practical success, but also with daring and farsighted statesmanship. But the Great Design had one overwhelming weakness: Lombardy, and the unwanted but inextricable connections with a hostile papacy that ensued. The assumption of tangible authority in Italy demanded the violent reversal of communal particularism, but the Roncaglia decrees and poorly-mounted military campaigns merely served to unite the towns against him (no mean feat!). The coincidental split with the papacy, engineered by Rainald and Roland, resulted in the double election of 1159 and forced Frederick, at the Council of Pavia in 1160, to declare for Victor IV. Alexander cleverly exploited the emperor's commitment to a string of anti popes and to military action in Italy to saddle him with the appearance of a "tyrant," obsessed with a reactionary vision of imperial world domination. The result was devastating for Frederick's international stature and fatal to possible accommodations with the Italian towns. Indeed, according to Munz, the most successful result of the Great Design, outside of *Hausmacht* north of the Alps, was that it persuaded Otto of Freising and his continuator Rahewin to write (or rather, rewrite) the early history of the reign to make it appear that the Great Design came into being on the day of Frederick's election. Thus the *Gesta* treats the period 1152–60 as all of one piece, with the Council of Pavia as the logical termination. The intent was not to write a full-fledged biography, but a propaganda piece for the Great Design, with Frederick's choice of Victor IV as the fitting but unwanted culmination.[18]

By the mid-1160's, it was apparent that the Great Design was untenable. Frederick's support of Victor's successor Paschal III and the canonization of Charlemagne were grandiose but useless enterprises that underscored the extent to which the Great Design had unfortunately become mere anti-papalism. The creation of the Lombard League and the papal entanglement had defeated the original intent of the plan south of the Alps, and mere *Hausmacht* was an insufficient basis for royal authority in the north. With the death of Rainald, Frederick was freer to de-emphasize imperial rhetoric and seek to cut his losses in Italy. There followed a decade of indecisiveness, marked by inconsistent behavior towards the papacy, the towns, and the German nobility. The battle of Legnano did not mark the crushing defeat of the Great Design, but was a final proof that it was unworkable. Hence it was rapidly and firmly dropped in 1176. In its place Frederick devised a third plan, which proved successful, for it left him with the sufficient appearances of peace and concord to allow him the crusade as culmination of his spiritual and political aspirations.

The third plan, in a word, was feudalization. Frederick overcame Henry the Lion and created specific vassalic ties with the new *Reichsfürstenstand*, elaborated by the famous chivalric display of 1184 at which the emperor secured the hereditary succession for his son Henry. The struggle against Henry the Lion is not to be taken as a Staufen-Welf vendetta, or a contest between "imperial" and "German" aspirations of nineteenth-century nationalistic invention. Rather, Frederick felt that Henry was too powerful to allow feudalization to work. To insinuate himself as head of a discrete hierarchy, he enlisted the support of the other nobles, the condition of their support being the division of the spoils. They obtained what they wanted, and Frederick what he wanted — a limited estate of princes, clearly ranged below him as tenants-in-chief. Frederick had in effect improved upon the territorial and juridical objectives of the Great Design by placing the monarchy over all the princes in a feudal lordship sense, while in no way abandoning his own territorial acquisitions and organization in southwestern Germany.

Simultaneously Frederick achieved peace and a semblance of practical advantage in Italy. He dropped his support of Paschal's successor Calixtus and recognized Alexander III and his successors. At the suggestion of Lucius III, Frederick's son Henry was married to Constance, aunt of William II of Sicily, perhaps with the explicit hope of establishing a Hohenstaufen hereditary claim to the kingdom in the future. Frederick managed at last to establish normal relations with Lombardy; the towns were allowed the full enjoyment of their rights (most, of course, illegally asserted or usurped) in return for recognition of the emperor's suzerainty, with the understanding that his authority would remain respected as long as he made no effort to enforce it. To offset this loss, Frederick, with the papal approval already evident in the marriage alliance, acquired and exploited the Tuscan Matildan lands as a royal demesne. Even though they were not contiguous with his trans-Alpine possessions, they at least formed a specific territorial base in Italy.

In the 1180's, then, Frederick restored the respect and authority of his imperial status. He had no real government anywhere, no reliable or capable civil service, no permanent capital, no central institutional apparatus. Particularism was the legacy of the Investiture period, and the emperors had at least made peace with it, had ratified and legitimized it, in a feudal form in Germany and in a communal form in Italy. Frederick had reason, however, to be satisfied. As monarch in Germany, he reverted to the passive position characteristic of his first plan, but he still had the territorial nexus of the Great Design and an unquestioned feudal suzerainty. As emperor, free of pretension and ideological entanglement, he was able to undertake his crusading mission. Munz concludes by pointing out, briefly, how shallow were the foundations that he left, for within a generation his work was undone by disputed succession, an explicit Sicilian orientation, and the rise of papal and French antagonists far more devastating than anything Frederick himself had encountered in Alexander III or Henry the Lion.

Munz has written a splendid and spirited biography, one that demands a detailed summary because of the importance and wealth of his intricately connected arguments. But he is perhaps the victim of the overschematization he rightly criticizes in others. Were there really three distinct plans, or might it not be more accurate to say, at least for Germany, that there was only one "plan" all along, albeit with varying degrees of emphasis and success? Frederick was, after all, a prince, in whose veins ran the blood of some of the greatest new dynasties thrown up by the Investiture period. He saw German kingship as all other princes saw it, an honorific and almost sentimentalized office, and he clearly had no intention of attempting either the restoration of Carolingian-Ottonian tradition or the establishment of a "feudal" monarchy of the Norman and Capetian varieties. The abilities of the king of France to confederate a regionally oriented nobility had no counterpart in Germany, and none was ever intended. Frederick was, from the outset of his reign, content to restore the respect and prestige of the office, after seventy-five years of weakness and attacks, a respect that would perhaps also restore a *de facto* hereditary succession and free him to concentrate on his own *Hausmacht* and the more substantial lures of his Mediterranean interests. His relations with the lay and ecclesiastical princes were a constant search for such foundations. Munz fully realizes this, but is somewhat misleading in treating it as three distinct plans to fit a schema more appropriate to sub-Alpine considerations, rather than as one "plan" with significant variations of emphasis, technique, and symbolic success. Frederick legitimized, in feudal fashion, not a set of political structures newly formed in the 1170's but the legacy of a century or more. The Investiture struggle undermined the Saxon and Salian tradition, but it is now clearly recognized that in practice kingship more nearly resembled multi-tiered lordship, so that Frederick's feudalization marked not so much the beginnings of a new epoch as the "logical" culmination of an older one.[19]

German historians are usually too prone to read history in the light of modern legal concepts and of their own concerns with administrative institutions, governmental centralization, and political unity. These were no more "national" interests in the twelfth and thirteenth cen-

147

turies than they had been in the days of Charlemagne. Frederick Barbarossa, no less than Frederick II, was out, not to undermine the princes, but to strengthen them by creating an orderly and comprehensive framework within which they could safely exercise their independence. At best, this could produce a paper confederation, wholly foreign to the spirit and substance of contemporary kingship in France. Nothing is more instructive in this regard than to compare what Philip Augustus did with his overmighty prince, John, Duke of Normandy, with what Frederick accomplished in his relations with Henry the Lion and his peers. Frederick neither envisioned nor intended any semblance of centralized, bureaucratic authority; one cannot analyze his "government," for there was none. The basic consistency of Hohenstaufen policy in Germany in this sense should not be underestimated. To restore a certain measure of respect, to acquire territory and *ministeriales*, to re-establish hereditary succession: these were not only the solid achievements of Frederick Barbarossa, but also the genuine objectives of Frederick II, within an even more limited sphere of possible action given the results of the warfare that separated their reigns. The Italian orientation of Frederick II was more specifically Sicilian than Lombard-Tuscan, but in some respects this represents a difference of degree, not of kind, as compared with Barbarossa. Similarly, if in the mid- and late thirteenth century the fisc, the royal *ministeriales*, and hereditary monarchy disappeared in Germany, this did not amount to a radical alteration of the bases of kingship or an essential change in the authority of the office. The differentiation between Germany and the western kingdoms was not newly formed in the thirteenth century. But there is nothing to be gained by blaming Barbarossa, any more than his successors, for failing to achieve what the kings of France or England or Sicily achieved. The Hohenstaufen speeded up, ratified, and sat in majesty on the triumph of the princes. Since this is what they wanted, it follows that their policies in Germany were both successful and realistic.[20]

In Italy, Frederick's actions do represent a certain "archaism" which Munz' arguments to the contrary fail to dispel entirely. There was an emphasis on externalized appearances, an outward grandeur and formalism, although it hardly amounted to Heer's caricature of the Hohenstaufen monolith flying in the face of all that was new, ennobling, and liberating.[21] In Lombardy Frederick tried to reverse urban particularism by military action, with consistently disastrous results. In Germany he was much more successful, for there he accepted and worked with a rural princely particularism. To accept and to benefit from it, in both cases, meant having little to do. But not so in Italy, and the result was failure. Further, the restoration of imperial dignity did give a more substantial programmatic effect to Romanist-universal-ist rhetoric than Munz allows. In one sense, Frederick certainly viewed the empire as a distinct territorial unit, with his own Burgundian-Swabian-Lombard territorial dominions as the nexus; and it is clear that he harbored no designs on the other independent western mon-archs. But the imperial office and mission conveyed a ceremonial and psychological dimension that went beyond the fulfillment of a crusade to an activist position as papal protector, a position not open to any other king, nor even to himself as king of Germany or *rex Roma-norum*.[22] The support of anti-popes, the canonization of Charlemagne, the campaigns into Rome suggest not mere defensive reactions to the hostility and duplicity of Alexander III, but a positive initiatory atti-tude of "protecting" the papacy from itself. If the *Gesta* truly reflects the intent of the Great Design, then the anti-papalism in it was not a merely unfortunate by-product of events. One may legitimately ques-tion whether Frederick was such an unwitting tool of Rainald of Das-sel — or if he was, one must substantially qualify Munz' favorable judgment of Frederick's statesmanship and pragmatic astuteness.

Despite areas of possible disagreement in interpretation or emphasis, it is certain that Munz is to be congratulated on a signal achievement. The basic image of Frederick for English-speaking students hitherto has been found in Barraclough;[23] Munz's biography is now the indis-pensable starting point.

The books reviewed here amount to a small and impressionistic sampling of the entire corpus of recent work in medieval politics. All are marked by vigor and imagination, and in their differing ways make significant contributions to historical perception and method. Both Ganshof and Douglas convey a sense of the possibilities and merit of works of a survey or synthesis type. Ullmann, despite the criticisms that might be made, has opened lines of inquiry in supposedly familiar fields that demand the highest qualities of learning and precision, but will in turn yield rich results. Even the hackneyed tradition of political biography becomes, in the hands of Munz (and of Douglas, in his study of William the Conqueror), a freshly rewarding endeavor. The study of medieval politics is not an exhausted field, but in reality a new one, if historians will avoid the anachronisms of modern political and legal constructs and adopt a healthy suspicion of the value of rigidly rationalized analytical frameworks. Sensitivity to social dynamics, to the power of religious aspiration and imagery, and to the nuances of medieval attitudes towards law and authority are allowing long-hidden riches in the political tradition to emerge, as the studies examined here bear witness.

NOTES

1. A shorter and more popular presentation of Ullmann's views is contained in *A History of Political Thought: The Middle Ages* (Baltimore: Penguin Books, 1965).
2. "Charlemagne et les institutions de la monarchie franque," and "Charlemagne et l'administration de la justice dans la monarchie franque," in *Karl der Grosse: Lebenswerk und Nachleben*, 4 vols. (Dusseldorf, 1965–67), Vol. I, *Persönlichkeit und Geschichte*, ed. Helmut Beumann, pp. 349–93, 394–419. Cf. also Ganshof, "The Impact of Charlemagne on the Institutions of the Frankish Realm," *Speculum*, XL (1965), 47–62.
3. "Les Réussites normandes (1050–1100)," *Revue historique*, no. 237 (1967), pp. 1–16. A number of other studies are listed in my *Anglo-Norman England 1066–1154*, Conference on British Studies, Bibliographical Handbooks (Cambridge, 1969), *sub nom.*
4. "Frederick Barbarossa and the 'Holy Empire'," *Journal of Religious History*, III (1964), 20–37; "Frederick Barbarossa and Henry the Lion in 1176," *Historical Studies, Australia and New Zealand*, XII (1965–67), 1–21; "Why Did Rahewin Stop Writing the Gesta Frederici? A Further Consideration," *English Historical Review*, LXXXIV (1969), 771–79 (a reply to J. B. Gillingham, "Why Did Rahewin Stop Writing the Gesta Frederici?" ibid., LXXXIII [1968], 294–303).
5. The best starting point — and usually finishing point as well — for all aspects of Merovingian history is the work of J. M. Wallace-Hadrill, *The Long-Haired Kings and Other Studies in Frankish History* (London, 1962).
6. D. A. Bullough, "*Europae Pater*: Charlemagne and His Achievement in the Light of Recent Scholarship," *English Historical Review*, LXXXV (1970), 59–105.
7. Heinrich Fichtenau, *Das Karolingische Imperium* (Zürich, 1949); Engl. trans. Peter Munz, *The Carolingian Empire* (Oxford, 1957), chap. 4.
8. Bullough, "*Europae Pater*," pp. 92–96, points to the probable influence of Lombard practice on the development of the *inquisitio* in Frankland itself, a consideration not investigated by Ganshof.
9. Cf. J. M. Wallace-Hadrill, "The *Via Regia* of the Carolingian Age," in Beryl Smalley, ed., *Trends in Medieval Political Thought* (Oxford, 1965), pp. 22–41; *idem, The Barbarian West 400–1000*, 2nd ed. (London, 1957), pp. 127 ff.; and for the later flowering of the tradition, the two works of Robert Folz, *Le Souvenir et la légende de Charlemagne dans l'Empire germanique médiéval* (Paris, 1950) and *Études sur le culte liturgique de Charlemagne dans les églises d'Empire* (Paris, 1951).

10. Cf., e.g., M. L. W. Laistner, *Thought and Letters in Western Europe,* A.D. *500 to 900,* 2nd ed. (London, 1957), pp. 189–396 passim, with R. R. Bolgar, *The Classical Heritage and Its Beneficiaries* (Cambridge, 1954), chap. 3.

11. Percy Ernst Schramm, *Kaiser, Könige und Päpste: Gesammelte Aufsätze zur Geschichte des Mittelalters,* 3 vols. to date (Stuttgart, 1968–   ); *idem, Der König von Frankreich: Das Wesen der Monarchie vom 9. bis zum 16. Jahrhunderts,* 2 vols. (Weimar, 1939); Ernst H. Kantorowicz, *Laudes Regiae: A Study in Liturgical Acclamations and Mediaeval Ruler Worship* (Berkeley and Los Angeles, 1946); C. A. Bouman, *Sacring and Crowning: The Development of the Latin Ritual for the Anointing of Kings and the Coronation of an Emperor Before the Eleventh Century* (Groningen, 1957); Karl F. Morrison, *The Two Kingdoms: Ecclesiology in Carolingian Political Thought* (Princeton, 1964). The last is largely concerned with Hincmar of Rheims, but Ullmann (deliberately?) makes no reference to it in his discussion of the archbishop. See also Morrison, *Tradition and Authority in the Western Church 300–1140* (Princeton, 1969), esp. chap. 9 and appendixes A and B, for further elaboration of points of disagreement with Ullmann (whose book under review here appeared, of course, too late for incorporation in Morrison's).

12. For Byzantium, see, above all, Paul J. Alexander, "The Strength of Empire and Capital as Seen Through Byzantine Eyes," *Speculum,* XXXVII (1962), 339–57; and for Gregory's treatment of Clovis, the brilliant assessment in Wallace-Hadrill, *Long-Haired Kings,* chap. 3, esp. p. 66, and chap. 7, esp. pp. 167–79.

13. Cf. the remarks of Kantorowicz, *Laudes Regiae,* pp. vii–viii, who points out that insofar as the celebration of the ruler is concerned, the early Middle Ages much more closely resembles antiquity than the later medieval period. See, in general, *La regalità sacra: Contributi al tema dell' VIII Congresso Internazionale di storia delle religione (Roma, Aprile 1955);* "Studies in the History of Religion," Supplements to *Numen,* IV (Leyden, 1959); and Francis Dvornik, *Early Christian and Byzantine Political Philosophy: Origins and Background,* Dumbarton Oaks Studies, no. 9, 2 vols. (Washington, 1966).

14. Ullmann's views on the irresistible application of early papal ideas on emperorship in subsequent centuries are even more fully and vigorously expounded in his paper "Reflections on the Medieval Empire," *Transactions of the Royal Historical Society,* 5th ser., XIV (1964), 89–108.

15. Gaines Post, *Studies in Medieval Legal Thought* (Princeton, 1964), p. 561 (the theme constantly recurs in this collection of largely previously published articles). Cf. also Brian Tierney, " 'The Prince Is Not Bound by the Laws': Accursius and the Origins of the Modern State," *Comparative Studies in Society and History,* V (1963), 378–400: of basic importance not only for the innovative importance of Roman law ideas, but also for the proper interpretation of those ideas and the inferences that can be drawn from them.

16. Evelyn M. Jamison, "The Sicilian Norman Kingdom in the Mind of Anglo-Norman Contemporaries," *Proceedings of the British Academy,* XXIV (1938), 237–85; Charles Homer Haskins, "England and Sicily in the Twelfth Century," *English Historical Review,* XXVI (1911), 433–47, 641–65.

17. Cf. his criticisms of modern German legally-oriented scholars such as Theodore Mayer (p. 108, n. 1); Ruth Hildebrand and her critics (pp. 340–41, nn.); and Heinrich Mitteis (p. 353, n. 2; 356, n. 2).
18. See especially pp. 129–40 and the separate article on Rahewin (see n. 4). Munz is particularly concerned to demonstrate the inadequacy of the interpretation of Peter Rassow, *Honor Imperii: Die neue Politik Friedrich Barbarossas, 1152–1159*, 2nd ed. (Munich, 1961). However convincing Munz' account of Otto and Rahewin might be, his assertions (p. 157), that the Italian chronicle of Otto Morena represents a similar rewriting of history on behalf of the Great Design, and at the behest of Rainald, are presented without proof or adequate elaboration.
19. Karl Bosl, "Herrscher und Beherrschte im deutschen Reich des 10.–12. Jahrhunderts," in his *Frühformen der Gesellschaft im mittelalterlichen Europa* (Munich, 1964), pp. 135–55, with references to other scholarship, in particular the work of Walter Schlesinger.
20. From the recent literature, mention should be made of Erich Klingelhöfer, *Die Reichsgesetze von 1220, 1231/32 und 1235: Ihr Werden und Ihre Wirkung im deutschen Staat Friedrichs II* (Weimar, 1955); Karl Bosl, *Die Reichsministerialität der Salier und Staufer*, Schriften der Monumenta Germaniae historica, no. 10, 2 vols. (Stuttgart, 1950–51); Werner Goez, *Der Liehezwang: Eine Untersuchung zur Geschichte des deutschen Lehnrechtes* (Tubingen, 1962), as examples of works which tend to emphasize continuities rather than radical discontinuities in Hohenstaufen rule, although the first two overestimate the importance and success of centralized statecraft.
21. Friedrich Heer, *Die Tragödie des heiligen Reiches* (Vienna, 1952) and *Aufgang Europas* (Vienna, 1949). Munz, "Frederick Barbarossa and the 'Holy Empire'," (n. 4), 20–24, provides an extended summary and critique of Heer's views.
22. Munz unfortunately does not analyze Frederick's titles or their legal and ideological connotations. For the origin of the *rex Romanorum* designation, cf. Rudolf Buchner, "Der Titel rex Romanorum in deutschen Königsurkunden des 11. Jahrhunderts," *Deutsches Archiv*, XIX (1963), 327–38.
23. Geoffrey Barraclough, *The Origins of Modern Germany*, 2nd ed. (Oxford, 1947), pp. 162–95; *Medieval Germany 911–1250: Essays by German Historians*, 2 vols. (Oxford, 1938), Vol. I, *Introduction*, pp. 76–79, 101–14; "Frederick Barbarossa and the Twelfth Century," in his *History in a Changing World* (Oxford, 1957), pp. 73–96. The last two studies are more careful and qualified in their enthusiasm for Frederick than the first, but are less widely known.

Latin Palaeography in the Later Middle Ages

SOME RECENT CONTRIBUTIONS

Braxton Ross

M. B. Parkes. *English Cursive Book Hands 1250–1500*. Oxford Palaeographical Handbooks. Oxford: Clarendon Press, 1969. Pp. xxxii, 24, 24 plates.

S. Harrison Thomson. *Latin Bookhands of the Later Middle Ages 1100–1500*. Cambridge: Cambridge University Press, 1969. Pp. xiv, 137, 132 plates.

Joachim Kirchner, *Scriptura Gothica Libraria a Saeculo XII usque ad Finem Medii Aevi LXXXVII Imaginibus Illustrata*. Munich and Vienna; Rudolph Oldenbourg, 1966. Pp. 81, 66 plates.

PALAEOGRAPHY STRODE FORTH into the twentieth century with the giant steps of such scholars as Léopold Delisle, M. R. James, and Ludwig Traube. In the years since, investigation into the history of book script in the earlier Middle Ages and Renaissance has continued to progress, though in perhaps less spectacular fashion.[1] But despite this general advance and despite a few important studies on "Gothic" writing and on the university book trade, palaeographers have penetrated the obscurity of the later Middle Ages but slowly. Today, however, there are glimmers of light which promise a brighter future. The first of these is the Colloque international de Paléographie, which met in Paris in 1953 under the auspices of the Centre national de la Recherche scientifique. The Colloque founded a catalogue of dated Latin manuscripts,[2] provided for a Comité international de Paléographie, and a year later the papers read to the Colloque were published under the title *Nomenclature des écritures livresques du IXe au XVIe siècle*.[3] Each of these steps has contributed materially to later medieval palaeography. Particularly to be mentioned here is the paper of Professor Lieftinck, "Pour une nomenclature de l'écriture de la periode dite gothique," which he followed up with some revisions in the introduction to his *Manuscrits datés conservés dans les Pays-Bas*. Three further contributions to later medieval palaeography have appeared more recently, and it is to them that I wish to call special attention in this essay.

Mr. Parkes' study of the types and development of English cursive book hands addresses itself primarily to palaeographers; nevertheless, it is not too much to say that nearly everyone who works in the wider fields of manuscripts written by English scribes in the period from 1250 to 1500 will profit from its discussions and facsimiles.

Scribes of the last three or four medieval centuries copied books, broadly speaking, in two kinds of script: Littera Textualis (Gothic Textura) and Littera Cursiva (Gothic Cursive). The latter, as used in books, has been little studied, even though it is the script of much or most literature (especially the vernacular), philosophy, theology, and science in this period. This lack of research and the apparently bewildering varieties of later medieval cursive hands have forced most manuals of palaeography to skim over this subject unsatisfactorily. Mr. Parkes is concerned with both the development and the classification of English cursive scripts, and his book, I believe, sheds considerable light in one corner of a neglected area in palaeography.

Parkes identifies two principal cursive scripts in the surviving books of later medieval England. (He uses "cursive," as Lieftinck does, to indicate a category of script with certain distinctive letter forms, though some scripts in this category are not written cursively.) The first is of native origin, emerging out of English documentary hands, and Parkes, broadening a term already used by N. R. Ker,[4] calls it Anglicana. He finds it in three principal varieties. The simplest form is an adaptation of the informal script used to enroll documents for reference purposes. The formal "engrossing hand" of documents actually issued became the basis of the more pretentious book script which the author calls Anglicana Formata. These two varieties of Anglicana had appeared in books before the end of the thirteenth century and lasted, with various changes, until late in the fifteenth. Anglicana Formata became the major English book hand of the fourteenth century and is the script of a number of famous and imposing extant manuscripts written around 1400, including the Ellesmere Chaucer and British Museum, Cotton Vespasian B. XVI of the C-text of *Piers Plowman*. A third and calligraphic variety of Anglicana appeared during the fourteenth century, and as it was developed out of a union between Anglicana and Textura, it is given the tag Bastard Anglicana.

The second principal cursive script identified by Parkes' investigation is Secretary. The author believes its ultimate origins probably lie in Italy, though it was modified by French scribes before its introduction into England during the second half of the fourteenth century. English copyists gave Secretary their own stamp and increasingly began to prefer it in the second half of the fifteenth century, as a number of English literary manuscripts still bear witness. A Bastard Secretary was developed for formal purposes by English writing masters — much as with Anglicana a century earlier — out of a union between cursive Secretary and Textura.

Many texts, it should be emphasized, were not copied in a pure script but were written by scribes drawing on more than one model. This is particularly true in England after the advent of Secretary. Furthermore, scribes often introduced personal features which give some hands a highly idiosyncratic character.

Mr. Parkes sets forth his theories about the types and history of English cursive hands in a packed introduction of thirteen pages, to which the summary above cannot do justice. Twenty-four plates exhibiting forty-eight manuscripts furnish the visual evidence. Each facsimile is accompanied on the facing page by identification of the manuscript, a statement about the circumstances of writing, palaeographical commentary, and a complete transcription. Within this format the author attempts to illustrate the development of each script and the influences operating on it. His commentaries on the plates are pertinent — especially the comparisons; the transcriptions are accurate, and the identifications and bibliography on individual scribes will be useful to those wishing to go further. The facsimiles, though they cannot compare with the hand-crafted Oxford collotypes of yore, are clear and reproduced in natural size.

The crucial questions to be asked of this book concern the types of script identified by the author and their history: do Anglicana and Secretary, with their respective varieties, correspond to the actual situation in the manuscripts? Are their origins and courses of development accurately represented in the author's narrative and in the plates he has chosen? Now, a type of script may be defined as one which has a definite set of rules governing its writing, "the model which the scribe has in his mind's eye," as the author puts it in his paragraph "A Note on Palaeographical Terms." The existence of a type of script may be demonstrated by listing a number of manuscripts which conform to a particular model. Ludwig Traube and his pupils established earlier types of Latin scripts by this method; complete lists of the surviving manuscripts of a given type, moreover, form the ideal basis for an analysis of the script's origin and development. In the current stage of palaeography, however, this technique is less practical for the central and later Middle Ages, from which manuscripts survive in much greater and less manageable numbers than from earlier periods. In any case, though Mr. Parkes often cites several manuscripts to illustrate his discussion or the work of a scribe, he does not use lists of script types as his point of departure.

Another approach is to search individual manuscripts for evidence indicating the types of scripts of which the scribes themselves were clearly conscious. This is the sort of evidence on which Mr. Parkes has chiefly relied. He offers, in the first place, four to six facsimiles to illustrate each type and its development. Five facsimiles showing specimens from the first century of Secretary script in English documents support the presentation of Secretary Book Hand and its history. In the second place, Mr. Parkes furnishes three further series of plates: "The Handwriting of University Scribes," "Developments in the Hierarchy of Scripts," and "The Handwriting of Individual Scribes." Their evidence rounds out the case from different angles with corroborative testimony of various kinds. Among other things, they show how certain scribes wrote more than one script, how they distinguished between the scripts in their repertoire, and how they ranked them in importance. Much can be learned from the study of such facsimiles (note also Plate 2 in this connection). When, for example, the first scribe of the manuscript in Plate 19 (ii) wanted to distinguish between Latin lemmata of the Psalter and Richard Rolle's commentary, he penned the former in Textura and the latter in a version of Anglicana Formata. His colleague, who took over in the middle of the page shown in the facsimile, achieved the same thing by writing the lemmata in a Bastard Secretary and the commentary in the less formal ordinary Secretary. The three facsimiles of Plate 21 suggest how the ingrained habits of a scribe may overcome his more formal first intentions: he began copying his text in a calligraphic Secretary, but already on fol. 2^v he was writing a much less formal Secretary that includes some Anglicana forms, and by fol. 30^v he had abandoned Secretary entirely for a current, sprawling Anglicana.

Mr. Parkes' kind of evidence is instructive and convincing. My own examination of numerous facsimiles and manuscripts, including alphabets penned on fly-leaves, suggests that what the scribes on his plates have to tell us will not be seriously contradicted, though we may eventually come to understand them more precisely and in a fuller context. My experience also urges me to emphasize the author's statement that "by far the greater number of manuscripts produced in England during the fifteenth century were written in hands which contain forms and features drawn from more than one script. Not all these mixed hands were produced by accident" (pp. xxiv f.). The raw material for the other, the "Traube," kind of evidence is gradually being accumulated in the catalogues of dated Latin manuscripts mentioned above. Though it may be necessary to have this series in hand before the definitive types of scripts and their histories can be established, the catalogues themselves will not attain this end. Books like that of Mr. Parkes will still be necessary, and coming as it does at this stage in our progress, his analysis can serve admirably both as an exemplar to imitate and a model to test.

S. Harrison Thomson's book is a unique contribution of quite a different sort. As a guide to Latin literary codices copied in Europe and England between 1100 and 1500, it places abundant resources at the disposal of those who work with manuscripts and who wish to estimate their dates and places of origin. Much experience lies behind Professor Thomson's descriptions, and they bring real grist to the palaeographer's mill; the book, however, speaks even more to other users of manuscripts: editors of texts, historians, art historians, and students of medieval Latin and vernacular literature.

Latin Bookhands furnishes 132 palaeographical guideposts, manuscripts whose places and dates of writing are more or less firmly fixed by non-palaeographical evidence. Since most medieval manuscripts bear no explicit indication of either where or when they were copied, those few of certain origin become the standards of comparison against which the rest are judged. Twenty-four to twenty-eight manuscripts represent France, the Holy Roman Empire, Italy, Britain, and Iberia, with roughly six or seven allotted to each century within those regions. This distribution represents the Latin west and allows an average interval between manuscripts of about fifteen to twenty years, which, since script generally is slow to change, seems adequate for a volume of this scope. There is need, however, for indicators beyond those of place and date. Scribes of different training and books of varied content and purpose need to have their place. Here the choice is difficult. Professor Thomson gives place to monastic, university, city-bred, and provincial scribes, to a variety of formal and informal types of writing, and to books containing ancient and patristic authors, philosophy, theology, law, the Bible, religious writings, science, medicine, literature, and other texts. There is the calligraphic product of the professional scribe, the chancery-influenced script of the trained clerk, and the scrawl of the scholar writing for his own use. Many copyists, some of whom are well known, are identified by name: Albert the Great, Robert Grosseteste, Thomas Aquinas (the author makes a good case that Thomas wrote with his left hand), Petrarch, and John Hus. Generous treatment is given to the manuscripts, including an individual plate for each. The facsimiles are in natural size. Reproducing a full manuscript page or opening whenever the ample format (9½ × 14 inches) permits, they illustrate and at the same time verify the author's commentary; they will reward study and comparison. Each is accompanied on the opposite page by evidence of the manuscript's origin, a palaeographical description, and a transcription of some twenty lines.

The evidence of origin, or rather its interpretation, is the foundation on which this book rests. This evidence most commonly consists of a colophon in which the scribe states when he finished his work and frequently where he wrote, although contents, additions in the vernacular, and later history may help to establish or confirm place and date. Experienced and careful judgment is required to decide if the colophons are original, since scribal statements and notes by readers are often taken over from model to copy without change. Evidence for the place of writing can be especially elusive. In a few of Thomson's cases, we must rely on the persuasive, though not certain, grounds of later history (e.g., nos. 4, 26, 56). It is not clear why either Lilleshall or Westderham is suggested as a probable origin of no. 108; both places seem associated with the texts rather than with the scribes, although the manuscript is doubtless English. Experts may question one or two other attributions; but on the whole, the author exercises sure judgment and his set of guides is trustworthy.

The distinguished contribution of *Latin Bookhands* is its manuscript descriptions. With remarkable skill at seeing the process from the scribe's point of view, Professor Thomson describes how letters were formed, and discusses abbreviations, orthography, decoration, and other characteristic or noteworthy palaeographical features. Descriptions emphasize, first, features characteristic of the place or region of writing; secondly, traits indicative of date; and lastly, the peculiar and personal habits of the scribe. Classical and other scholars will recognize this as a sound order of priorities. In the same way as the archaeologist, the user of manuscripts must determine, or at least estimate, the home of his artifact before he can make proper comparisons to establish or to judge its approximate date. Thomson finds that regional features fall roughly into the five areas already mentioned — France, Germany, Italy, Britain, and Iberia (with some natural cross-fertilization in border areas) — and lists the outstanding regional features of each manuscript. The student must beware, as the author does, of relying exclusively on script or on one or two features alone. "Non ex sola scriptura, neque ex uno characterismo, sed ex omnibus simul . . . pronuntiandum" is the still-valid principle urged in the eighteenth century by the father of palaeography, Dom Jean Mabillon. One may note, for example, that an *r* whose shoulder fails to touch the upright, "a frequent occurrence in French MSS" (no. 8), is also typical of some English hands (nos. 97, 98, and 102) including that of Matthew Paris (N. Denholm-Young, *Handwriting in England and Wales*, Plate 12) and that Italian spellings are very much like Spanish. It is when these details are found with others indicative of the same region that they become significant. Thomson rightly emphasizes abbreviations and abbreviation-marks: the Spanish love of consonants (apstll = apostoli, etc.); the different forms of reversed *c* for *con* in France, Germany, and Italy; the distinctive flourishes for *r, er, re*, etc., used in England, Germany, and Italy; the various forms assumed by the tironian symbol for *et*, and others.

Thomson also submits criteria for dating manuscripts. They too must be taken together and, further, must be considered with the place of copying in mind (e.g., the tironian symbol for *et* appears in England, France, and Italy at about the same time, but it is crossed sooner in Paris than in the French provinces, while in Italy it tends to remain uncrossed in all periods). Dating is further complicated by the fact that some scribes had long careers and failed to keep up with changing styles. One might mention the scribe of no. 6 from whose pen manuscripts survive over a period of a quarter of a century; as Mlle. d'Alverny shows in the article cited by Thomson, his hand seems to have become progressively more archaic.

The possibilities of description are by no means exhausted by the author, and some will perhaps lament the lack of data on such features as ruling, quire-marks and catchwords, or methods of correction. On the whole, however, the author's restraint seems sensible for a volume of this scope and, moreover, offers the student an invitation to delve for himself. Is the "two-storied," double-looped *a* of the formal book hand seldom to be found south of the Alps, as Thomson's plates suggest? Is it characteristic of this hand in the north from ca. 1275 onwards? What is the history of the long *i* in Spanish writing? While it occurs irregularly but frequently in this period, as the author notes, it was a regular feature of ancient Spanish writing.

Although this book does not delineate the history of script in a formal way, students of these more purely palaeographical matters may wish to note the following: Professor Thomson calls attention to ancient influences in script, abbreviations, and lack of spacing between words in twelfth-century Italy (no. 57) — graphic evidence of the continuity of culture there; he sees cursive school hands in Italy as deriving mainly from Italian notarial script, in contrast to French academic hands, which are directly related to formal Gothic (nos. 72, 76, 78); he adds his voice to those who have found scripts akin to French "lettre bâtarde" developing independently in other parts of Europe (nos. 72, 73, 97, 100); and his no. 82 reminds us that humanist scripts had not taken over completely in Italy as late as 1485, even for humanist texts.

No one who ponders the resources of this volume can fail to return to his manuscripts with fresh eyes. For this we can say with one of the author's beloved scribes (no. 18): "Vinum scriptori tradatur de meliori."

In *Scriptura Gothica Libraria* Joachim Kirchner proposes to illustrate the origins and development of various scripts and to point out their regional differences, purposes which overlap those of Parkes and Thomson. Professor Kirchner, depending more on his plates, offers less description and commentary. Some may prefer this approach, with its greater emphasis on allowing the evidence to speak for itself; I feel, however, that the other two books are more instructive and likely to have greater impact, because their narrower fields of concentration permit them to pursue their subjects in greater detail. Whatever the substance of these limitations, it is a book to be recommended on several counts, as I hope the following will make clear.

Scriptura Gothica Libraria seeks to serve as a "fidus dux" to the book scripts of the later Middle Ages. As guideposts it offers eighty-seven facsimiles in natural size of dated manuscripts, many also of known provenance. The plates are preceded by the section "Transcriptiones paginarum litteris textualibus scriptuarum," which also gives for each manuscript identifying information, the author's label for the script, and evidence for the date and place of origin. There is a preface and a short introduction entitled "Brevis notitia de formis et nomenclatura scriptuarum, quae in tabulis afferuntur."

Professor Kirchner brings great learning to this work, as his comments and plates quickly make evident. In the years since the publication in 1928 of his book *Die gotischen Schriftarten* (his *Scriptura Latina Libraria* appeared in 1955), Professor Kirchner has become even more aware of the importance of setting forth for the reader the development of scripts as they were written in particular regions or nations. "Not only the characteristics of each period ought to be exhibited," he writes in the preface of *Scriptura Gothica Libraria* (p. 5), "but also those in which the scripts of individual nations and regions are different."

To accomplish these purposes the author has arranged the plates chronologically in two series, Litterae Textuales and Litterae Notulae, Bastardae, Cursivae, and has devoted the introduction to commenting on the scripts they present. The division into two general types of script is a sensible decision, one with which most palaeographers would agree. The second category would be called simply Littera Cursiva by many; Professor Kirchner uses the medieval term Notula to indicate the hands most obviously derived from documentary script and Bastarda to designate the calligraphic forms of Cursiva to which scribes gave first place in the hierarchy of scripts. Just how the author distinguishes between Textualis and Cursiva does not seem to be made entirely clear, a fuzziness which is reflected in the misplacing, in my opinion, of Plate 28 and perhaps Plates 34a and 34b among the Textuales. The author's preface and "Brevis notitia" consist mostly of general observations, a number of which are illuminating and to the point (the observations on Bastarda, pp. 5 and 13, the introductory remarks on Notula, pp. 11 f., for example). There is much to be said for trying to distinguish manuscripts by their general appearance — angularity, rotundity, compactness, natural or imitative forms, etc. On the other hand medieval manuscripts contain significant features discoverable only by paying attention to what E. A. Lowe called "nugae palaeographicae" — trifles. In this respect, more might be expected of so experienced a palaeographer. His comments relating to Plate 10 are typical: British scribes of the thirteenth century used many abbreviations; vertical minim strokes become angular at this stage in the development of Scriptura Gothica (p. 9). It so happens that the manuscript page shown on Plate 10 was written at St. Albans by Matthew Paris, whose distinctive script is well known. Here it would have served the author's purpose better, I think, to have added a word about the peculiar broken-backed hand of the famous chronicler and about the distinctively English "trailing-headed *a*" and forked ascenders (the latter characteristic of contemporary English documents).

What finally emerges from this book is a valuable collection of palaeographical specimens and general observations. If the author falls somewhat short of his aim to identify the regional and temporal features in the development of later medieval book scripts, it is owing in large part to the presently inadequate state of our knowledge. Professor Kirchner has set his sights high; he has made a useful contribution.

While these three volumes teach us much about the ways of later medieval scribes and their books, they should serve as well to guide others in pursuing the history of Latin scripts in this period. Mr. Parkes' book is a model study after the best traditions of Latin palaeography, one which investigators of continental Cursivae will want to consult for information and method. It justifies once again the decision taken in 1952 at The Clarendon Press to replace Sir E. M. Thompson's classic work, *An Introduction to Greek and Latin Palaeography*, with a new series rather than with a single volume. Likewise following sound precedents, and apparently inspired by the manuscript descriptions of E. A. Lowe's *Codices Latini Antiquiores*, Professor Thomson has given us a work to which medievalists and especially editors of texts will long turn with profit. His book is a more personal one which will be less easy to imitate, because, as the readers of *Medievalia et Humanistica* under his editorship know, it is the product of an almost unique career in the several disciplines of palaeography, textual criticism, history, and journal editing. Few recent American scholars — among them B. L. Ullman, to whom *Latin Bookhands* is dedicated — have probed man's past so deeply in so broad a compass. In one sense, therefore, the merit of Professor Thomson's book is not only its informative value but also its ability to teach one how to explore medieval handwriting for oneself.

All three books make clear how much remains to be unearthed among the manuscripts of the later Middle Ages, especially among those written in hands derived from cursive. Because it is always closer to the marketplace and the chancery, cursive handwriting, unlike more formal scripts, refuses to be petrified into archaic or imitative forms, tends to be dynamic, and reflects something of the scribe and his training. This vitality and individuality carry over in one degree or another to the later medieval adaptations of cursive used in books, the so-called Litterae Cursivae. For this period, when important texts were increasingly copied in a variety of these adaptations, one of the lessons to be learned from Mr. Parkes, Professor Thomson, and Professor Kirchner is that more research among the Litterae Cursivae is desirable. Their books suggest to me that the most fruitful lines of investigation will take into account the importance of single regions or types and the varying but significant relationship of book script to the writing of documents.

NOTES

1. Professor Julian Brown surveys the notable publications in palaeography over the last thirty-five years in his introduction to the latest printing of B. L. Ullman, *Ancient Writing and Its Influence* (Cambridge, Mass., and London: M.I.T. Press, 1969).
2. C. Samaran-R. Marichal, *Catalogue des manuscrits en écriture latine portant des indications de date, de lieu ou de copiste*, I, II, V, VI (Paris, 1959–) for manuscripts preserved in French libraries, and G. I. Lieftinck, *Manuscrits datés conservés dans les Pays-Bas*, I (Amsterdam, 1964), have appeared.
3. The papers were presented by Professors B. Bischoff, G. I. Lieftinck, and G. Battelli.
4. *Medieval Manuscripts in British Libraries, I: London* (Oxford, 1969), x f., where there are also valuable observations of palaeographical interest.

The Cataloguing of Mediaeval Manuscripts

A REVIEW ARTICLE

M. L. Colker

SEVERAL CATALOGUES DESCRIBING COLLECTIONS of mediaeval manuscripts have appeared very recently: A. L. Gabriel, *A Summary Catalogue of Microfilms of One Thousand Scientific Manuscripts in the Ambrosiana Library, Milan* (Notre Dame, Indiana, 1968); J. J. G. Alexander and A. C. de la Mare, *The Italian Manuscripts in the Library of Major J. R. Abbey* (New York: Praeger, 1969); N. R. Ker, *Medieval Manuscripts in British Libraries*, I: *London* (Oxford, 1969). Each of these works will be discussed in turn.

Professor Gabriel's book is an outcome of the project of the University of Notre Dame to microfilm the manuscripts of the Ambrosian Library: the book deals with codices of scientific content, the first group to be photographed.[1] According to the dust jacket, the manuscripts range from the tenth to the eighteenth centuries. But apart from a seventh-century mathematics fragment (MS 607), there are an eighth-century Isidore (MS 607), a ninth-century Solinus (MS 72), and nineteenth-century texts (MSS 748, 959). In fact, a large proportion of the manuscripts are sixteenth-century or later.

Professor Gabriel declares that he borrowed the method (and much of the material) of Antonio Ceruti, whose *Inventario* goes back to the latter half of the nineteenth century.[2] The following specimen will provide an idea of Professor Gabriel's technique:

> 654. N 104 Sup.
> > Latinus
> > 1. Chart.: O.21 × 0.16
> > 4. ff. 155
> > 5. Anno 1445
> > 6. f. 1: Q. Horatii Flacci *Ars Poetica*, notis adspersa.

f. 15: Eiusdem *Epistolae.*
f. 59: Prudentii Aurelii *Psychomachia.*** [3]
f. 135: Reformatio computi solaris et lunaris facta a mag. Bono de Lucca anno 1254.
Bibl.: Revelli, no. 250. Kristeller, 235.

As the above specimen indicates, some non-scientific writings are listed when they accompany scientific material. But the catalogue does not aim to notice all the works within every codex. Often particular works in an aggregate are singled out and the rest ignored: e.g., "Tractationes variae ad philosophiam et ad mathematicas scientias pertinentes, *inter quas* aliquot expositiones librorum Raymundi Lulli, *e.g.,* eiusdem *Artis inventivae, Librorum testamenti, Artis magnae, Artis generalis, etc.*" (MS 13; the italics are mine). It is regrettable that all the texts in a codex are not consistently reported.

The summary character of the catalogue is also evident from the absence of information on script, editions, decoration, the history of the manuscript, and the like. Initia are often omitted, even when they are needed for the potential identification of a text.[4] Thus, the catalogue discloses nothing further about *De aqua tractatulus* (MS 145), *Versus de ponderibus et mensuris* (MS 591), *De utilitatibus chilindri* (MS 575), *Lapidarius* and *Carmina medicinalia* (MS 916). Particularly vague are the headings *Incerti Tractatus philosophicus* and *Incerti scientiae tractatus* (MS 924), without initia or description of contents.[5]

The book does not ordinarily make clear whether an author's name and the title of his work are present in the manuscript or are supplied.[6] Nor is it always possible to find on what page a text ends. Rarely is a century divided so that one may learn that a codex was produced, say, in the second half of the thirteenth century or in the mid-fifteenth century. In cases where different parts of a codex are of different ages, the catalogue fails to show which text belongs to what century. MS 947 is "partim anno 1488," but which part is so dated? No explanation is given for the approximate dates "circa 1286" (MS 752), "fortasse ca. annum 1488" (MS 431), "ante an. 1358" (MS 479), "circa 1496" (MS 508), "circa annum 1429" (MS 576).[7]

Professor Gabriel provides a subject index and author index but no index of initia.

By contrast with the summary catalogue, that of Alexander and de la Mare is heavily detailed, with emphasis on script and decoration.

The authors describe for the first time the collection of manuscripts, of Italian origin, once belonging to Major J. R. Abbey. This collection is strong in manuscripts that can be dated and localized. In all, there are 63 codices, chiefly of the Renaissance: only five were written before 1400 — the earliest are three of the twelfth century. Most of the texts are from Florence and Tuscany.

The catalogue offers an introduction summarizing the development of humanistic script and decoration according to the latest studies. Each manuscript is represented by at least one black and white photograph,[8] and there are six color plates. The descriptions often include extremely valuable references to manuscripts executed by the same scribe or in a similar style of writing or decoration. Here is a sample description:

45. J.A. 3206
[Plates LVI*b*, LVII*a*]

In Latin, on parchment, written in Venice in the late fifteenth century: 232 x 137 (144 x 70) mm.: 65 + i leaves: 30 long lines ruled in dry point: collation, the manuscript has been rebound and it is impossible to recover the collation. Some leaves appear to be guarded. There are no catchwords. Modern binding.

2° *folio*: Jus nullum

CONTENTS. Juvenal, Satires.
   (f.1, blue capitals): "Junii Juvenalis Aquinatis Satyrarum Liber Primus" *beg.* (gold capitals): Semper ego auditor.**

SCRIPT. Written in a thin, distinctive, rather uneven hand; there is some fusion of round letters and the ampersand and minuscule "a" are both unusual. The same scribe wrote the first part of a Horace now in Philadelphia Free Library, MS. E.235.**

DECORATION. On f. 1 there is an initial "S" in plain gold on a square ground of very dark blue outlined in gold.**

PROVENANCE. On f. 1 are the unidentified arms, azure a tower argent.**

Such an effort at full presentation must be applauded,[9] and it may seem harsh to suggest that occasionally there be greater economy: I refer not to the blank space, sometimes three-fourths of a page, between descriptions, but to the language. The wording of catalogues should be telegraphic,[10] without any waste words to slow down the user. Thus, "In Latin, on parchment, written in Italy at Naples in the late fifteenth century" (MS 90) can be effectively trimmed to "Parch-

167

ment. Naples, late 15 cent." — since almost all the texts are Latin, only the vernacular tongues should be named.[11] "Collation" as a label is unnecessary: when something like $1^{10}-12^{10}$ is seen, a reader recognizes instantly what this is.[12] For complete texts there is no reason to employ "beg." and "ends" if both extremes of text are quoted with a dash between them. It is pointless to print the beginning and end of each of the five books of Cicero's *Tusculan Disputations* (MS 42).

On the other hand, there are a few instances of skimpiness. "Dicit dominus in sancto evangelio," a familiar start for a sermon, and the formulaic conclusion, "Quod ipse vobis concedat qui cum patre," (MS 1) are too short to be very serviceable. Jejune are the conclusions "misit" and "cooperetur" (MS 1). Initia for the less known "Vergilian" poems (MS 22), e.g., *De vino et venere* and *De livore*, are not given, nor do initia or Stegmüller [13] numbers identify the Biblical prologues of MS 4. Sometimes, the brief titles for the general contents of a codex are too exclusive: Godfrey of Winchester must stand with Martial (MS 35) and Sidonius Apollinaris with Cassiodorus (MS 59). No index of initia appears.

Usually the articles of a codex are distinguished in the catalogue by capital letters in alphabetic sequence, but in MSS 41 and 46 large roman numerals are found, and it is not obvious whether one of these systems is meant to indicate, as is done elsewhere, separate manuscripts that were bound together.

While Professor Gabriel's work is particularly concerned with scientific texts and the catalogue of Mr. Alexander and Miss de la Mare emphasizes the script and decoration of manuscripts written in Italy, Mr. N. R. Ker's book presents a general catalogue of miscellaneous mediaeval manuscripts in smaller English collections. The first of probably three volumes notices about 700 codices in 47 institutions (not 42 as the dust jacket says) of the London area, arranged alphabetically from Birkbeck College to Dr. Williams' Library.

Mr. Ker uses several types of description, ranging from a highly detailed form to a severely summary listing (where catalogues already exist or are in progress). Here is an example of the longer style, exercised for a codex in the Institution of Electrical Engineers:

Thompson Collection, 2.   *J. de Pecham, etc*·   s. xiv

1. ff. 2–36ᵛ Incipit perspectiua. Inter phisice considerationis studia . . . in hoc philosopho contradicere non uerentur. Ex-

plicit perspectiua fratris Iohannis de pethano cantuariensis quondam archiepiscopi.

Printed first *c.* 1482 and often later. Three books of 84, 46, and 20 chapters.

2. ff. 36ᵛ–55ᵛ Incipit tractatus de spera de sacrobosco c. primum. Tractatum de spera quatuor capitula distinguimus . . . tota mundi machina cito dissolueretur. Explicit.

Ed. L. Thorndike, *The Sphere of Sacrobosco and Its Commentators,* 1949, pp. 76–117.**

ff. iii + 80 + iii, foliated (i, ii), 1–82, (83, 84). ff. 1, 82 are waste blanks of the main manuscript. 134 x 95 mm. Written space 70 x 57 mm. 2 cols. 28 lines. Collation of ff. 2-81: 1–8¹⁰. Initials 2-line. blue or red. Binding of s. xx. Secundo folio *sufficeret.*

Written in Italy. 'Of a house painter at Urbino Oct. 23 1860 J.C.R.,' f. 1.**

The short descriptions can be short indeed as in the case of a Wellcome Historical Medical Library codex:

4. s. xii med. Adelard of Bath, Quaestiones naturales. ff. 25. 190 x 105 mm. Written probably in England.

There is also a medium-sized treatment: see the following example of a Gray's Inn book:

23. s. xiv. 1. ff. 1–143 Abeuntium per hunc mundum . . . ad nupcias cum domino ihesu cristo Amen. Explicit expliceat ludere scriptor eat: a numbered table, Abire–Zelus, follows on ff. 143ᵛ–4. 2. ff. 145–78ᵛ Dieta salutis. Hec est via . . . ductor illius choree Ihesus . . . Amen. Explicit.** ff. 191. Quires of twelve leaves, wanting 16¹², a blank. Written space *c.* 220–200 x 150–140 mm. Written in England.

1. Nicholas de Gorran, Distinctiones. Stegmüller, no. 5740.
2. Probably by William de Lanicea (or Lavicea), O.F.M. Printed often among the works of Bonaventura, e.g. in ed. Rome, 1596.**

All three of Mr. Ker's systems differ not only in length but also in arrangement. Ideally, a catalogue should offer a fixed order so that the reader may expect to find his information without undue hunting. The third method above is awkward inasmuch as texts are identified in a group only after both initia and the physical characteristics of the codex, etc.

There is diversity, too, in smaller matters. Substantial initia are generally given, but sometimes they are lacking, even in the long treatments. So, a text on urines (Royal College of Physicians MS 229) and thirty-six sermons (St. Paul's Cathedral MS 8) are noticed without initia or identification. Ker sometimes mentions editions for his texts, sometimes does not, as in the cases of Raymund de Pennaforti (p. 7), Guido de Colonna (p. 88), and Peter Comestor (p. 129), and no edition is ever mentioned for the Dictionary of Hebrew Names which accompanies Bibles (pp. 4, 95, etc.). Sometimes editions are cited fully, sometimes by date alone (e.g., pp. 16, 89). Thorndike and Kibre [14] are frequently cited but never with a specific page reference. Mr. Ker often indicates the size of colored initials (e.g., "red initials, 4-line and 2-line" on p. 361) and sometimes does not (e.g., pp. 64, 244). Apart from the usual Biblical and liturgical miniatures, he normally names the themes of pictures but does not do so for the thirty-five historiated initials in a fifteenth-century Pliny the Elder (p. 388). Collations, when given, are almost always given in full, but sometimes are not, and no statement of any problem encountered, such as tight binding, is given (cf. pp. 64, 126, 130).

Mr. Ker reports nothing about watermarks, feeling that knowledge about them has not progressed far enough to make this reporting worthwhile (p. vii). Yet even rough approximations to the watermarks in Briquet [15] might benefit a future investigator, and an index of these motifs, with Briquet numbers, would be helpful to scholars comparing paper manuscripts.

Each of the three very recent books discussed above represents a distinctive kind of catalogue. Professor Gabriel's work is in the tradition of the nineteenth- and early twentieth-century summary catalogues — one thinks of certain endeavors, for example, of Léopold Delisle and T. K. Abbott.[16] Summary catalogues, despite their lean information, serve a purpose in making known texts with which scholars might not otherwise become readily familiar: these catalogues fill a gap until they are replaced by their more detailed successors. The work of Mr. Alexander and Miss de la Mare, emphasizing script and decoration and luxuriously produced, recalls the best Sotheby descriptions and in some measure the specialized palaeographic catalogues like E. A. Lowe's *Codices Latini antiquiores* (Oxford, 1934sqq.) and *Catalogue des manuscrits en écriture latine portant des indications de date, de lieu, ou de copiste* (1959sqq.) Such catalogues, deepening our knowledge of palaeography and art history, will be ever more in demand.

Most urgently needed are catalogues of general collections of mediaeval manuscripts: not only in Europe but also in the United States there are many poorly catalogued and only partially catalogued collections. The kind of catalogue suited for these collections should pursue a style similar to that of Mr. Ker's longer descriptions and contain all the essential information on the textual contents, on the physical appearance, and the history of the codex. There should be immediacy of communication without the clutter of unnecessary language but with a fixed arrangement for the information presented.

APPENDIX

Mr. Ker's excellent longer descriptions recall the compact fullness of those by Professor R. A. B. Mynors' *Catalogue of the Manuscripts of Balliol College Oxford* (Oxford, 1963).[17] I too have been much influenced by Professor Mynors, and have adapted his method in preparing a catalogue of the mediaeval Latin manuscripts at the University of Dublin. Below is a description of a codex in this collection:

303 (C.3.21)   England, 12/13 cent.

1–95^v. (1) Gislebertus Pictauiensis, Commentaria In Opuscula Sacra Boethii (ed. N. M. Häring, Toronto 1966, with use of this MS): 1–34^v <O>mnium que rebus percipiendis suppeditant racionum — uota supplebit.** Seuerini Boetii de trinitate liber explicit. G. Pictauiensis episcopi super Boetium de trinitate tractatus explicit. The MS is closely related to Paris BN lat. 16371 and 16341 (Häring 35).

96–100. (2) Memorandum of the trial of Gilbert at Rheims, A.D. 1148 (ed. M. L. Colker from this MS in *Mediaeval Studies*, 27 [1965] 170–183): <Q>uod diuina natura idest diuinitas — esse sed in filio. 100^v blank.**

Parchment. 100 fols. 206 x 141 (c. 195 x c.103). 34 lines. i–xii^8 xiii^4. Quires numbered. Single hand. Spaces for initials were not filled in. Binding style 2. 2nd fo.: -ligentes patrem.

1 has (a) *Glose super libros theologicos*** (early 13 cent.), (b) *Boethius insertus*** (16 cent.), (c) Jupiter symbols of John Dee, (d) cypher of Henry Savile (cf. no. 136 in Savile cat.). Colker o.c. 158–170. Häring o.c. 24–25, 35.

In a number of ways I have modified Mynors' system: for instance, antiquated classings and binding titles — the latter are normally post-mediaeval and often misleading — are omitted from the general heading; date is linked with place of origin and both items placed in the heading; identification of a text, as the first concern of most users, stands before the physical description of the codex; brackets do not enclose the names of authors and titles absent from the codex but instead, the manuscript evidence, if any, is directly revealed; readers are given the opportunity to see author and title at once, without having to read through the incipit or explicit; bibliographic references, as an integral part of the identification of a work, are put beside, and not at a distance away from, author and title, e.g.: 1–117. Petrus Comestor, Historia Scholastica (PL 198:1053–1122; Stegmüller no. 6565); the concluding words of a text are followed in very close succession by any comments on the condition and important traits of the text and by remarks on any interesting scholia — when all these features, including bibliographic references, stand in the same block as the statement of content, it is possible to avoid the too numerous little sections, and hence the broken effect, of Professor Mynors' descriptions and of Mr. Ker's longer treatment.

NOTES

1. "Scientific" is interpreted broadly to include even geography, music, architecture, and military technology, but it is difficult to see what is scientific in MS 424, described as containing only Turkish amatory songs.
2. See Gabriel, p. 14, and cf. P. O. Kristeller, *Latin Manuscript Books Before 1600* (New York, 1960), p. 155. A microfilm of the handwritten *Inventario* is kept in the Library of Congress.
3. Here and in sample descriptions below I use double asterisks whenever I cut out part of a description for the sake of brevity.
4. From initia that are given it is possible to identify some texts left unidentified in the catalogue: e.g., (MS 467) "Incerti Breviloquium de virtutibus" is the work of Iohannes Wallensis; (MS 664) "De virtutibus et scientiis carmen libris X distinctum" is the *Anticlaudianus* of Alanus de Insulis, normally in nine books; (MS 751) "De statura Caesaris" is an excerpt from Suetonius, Iul., chaps. 45–46.
5. The entry (MS 919) "Excerpta ex libris M. T. Ciceronis *De memoria*" conveys the impression that Cicero wrote a separate work called *De memoria*. Also, the title for a work in MS 121 is ungrammatical: "De moribus hominum et maxime ludum scachorum scientiam et maxime nobilium."
6. Titles that are additions by later hands are likewise not indicated as such in the catalogue.
7. MS 86 cannot be thirteenth century since it contains poetry by Antonius Luscus, who was born in the latter half of the fourteenth century. MS 74 is said to have been written in 1451, yet an item in the codex bears the date 1455. A portion of MS 495, generally eleventh century, is "serius scripta," but there is no indication as to what is meant by "serius."
8. Plate LIII (a) reproduces f. 131, not 131ᵛ, of the description, contrary to the label of the plate.
9. Yet there are a fair number of slips in transcription, as one can judge by comparing the plates with what is reported. The tail of caudate *e* was now and then missed, as in *evangelio* (p. 4); *epistole* (second *e*, p. 116); *preful-*

gidi (p. 116); *Flandrie* (p. 164). There are also these misreadings (the correct form is in parentheses): p. 44 *Properti* (*Propertii*); 75 *diui* (*diua*), 95 *epigrammaton* (*epigramaton*) in the explicit; 116 *Hieronimi* (*Hieronymi*); 117 *congregationis* (*congregacionis*); 131 *G. Iulii Caesaris* (*G. Iulii Caesaris*; the *G* is the same as in *Gallico* below). More serious are (p. 41), in the date of the codex, the ungrammatical *hora xxus* for *hora xxiii'a* (as the plate clearly shows) and (p. 116) *scripturam* for *scripturarum*. Objectionable is the use of *j* for *i* where the *j* is both unauthentic and unnecessary, e.g., *ejus* (p. 65), *Juvenalis* (p. 127). The word *totiens* (p. 151) should not be partly bracketed as if the *iens* is an error: *totiens* is good mediaeval Latin. The letters *ae* in *aeditum* (p. 79) are wrongly represented as a ligature.

10. Cf. E. A. Lowe, *Codices Latini antiquiores*, I (Oxford, 1934), viii.
11. It is not quite right to speak of MS 25 as in Italian (only) when a couple of texts, albeit small, are in Latin.
12. The collation given for MS 60 is inaccurate, reckoning to 1 + 100, not 1 + 90, leaves.
13. F. Stegmüller, *Repertorium biblicum medii aevi* (Madrid, 1950sqq.).
14. Lynn Thorndike and Pearl Kibre, *A Catalogue of Mediaeval Scientific Writings in Latin*, 2nd ed. (Cambridge, Mass., 1963).
15. C. M. Briquet, *Les filigranes* (Paris, 1907).
16. On L. Delisle's sundry inventories see Kristeller, *op. cit.*, p. 174. T. K. Abbott, *Catalogue of the Manuscripts in the Library of Trinity College, Dublin* (Dublin, 1900).
17. Mr. Ker, p. xiii, expresses an indebtedness to Professor Mynors' catalogue, "which made me change some of my methods."

Corpus der italienischen Zeichnungen 1300-1450

A REVIEW ARTICLE

Bernhard Bischoff

Bernhard Degenhart and Annegrit Schmitt, *Corpus der italienischen Zeich-nungen 1300–1450*. Part I: Süd- und Mittelitalien, Vols. 1 and 2, text (liv and 268 pp.; 407 illustrations; iv and 444 pp., 665 illustrations); Vols. 3 and 4, plates (iv pp., 195 pl. with 697 illustrations; iv pp., 248 pl., with 853 illustrations). Berlin: Gebrüder Mann Verlag, 1968. 950,-DM.

IT MAY BE SURPRISING that in a series dedicated to literary and humanistic studies attention is drawn to a publication which obviously is intended for the art historian. Yet in this study, which apart from its professional value may give great aesthetic delight to every friend of ancient art, hundreds of manuscripts are referred to and new light cast on the transmission of numerous literary texts. Hence it would be a great pity if students of the Middle Ages were to pass unmindfully by the great treasure which has here been displayed.

Since the fifteenth century the drawing has been regarded in Europe as one of the main types of artistic expression. The roots of the development leading to the autonomy of the drawing reach far back into the Middle Ages. One of them is the graphic illustration of manuscripts. Just as in the collections of motives in *Musterbücher* and the sketches of painters and sculptors, drawing in manuscripts has undergone growing technical refinement and gradual liberation. It is especially in manuscript drawings that the range of items represented that have been mastered as *sujets* of art has been increased.

In the culture of the period covered in this study the manuscript plays a leading part. These volumes contain and comment on several hundred illustrations from manuscripts of over forty different literary works in Latin and Italian. I shall discuss several characteristic groups of these.

After a cycle of pictures elucidating a paraphrase of the Biblical story of creation, the series of illustrated literary works begins with the poems of two contemporaries of Dante: the *Tesoretto* by Brunetto Latini (Plates 34b–37) and the allegorical *Documenti* by Francesco da Barberino (Plates 29–33), who had outlined the drawings for his work himself. The *Divina Commedia* is the opus which appears most frequently in this study; starting with a manuscript from Naples of 1323 (Plate 43) it is represented no less than sixteen times, including the commentaries. Not only do the human figures and the demonic and heavenly beings whom Dante meets in the regions of the other world appear, but the construction of these regions has been depicted as well (e.g., Plate 206), and a Florentine artist of the early fifteenth century has even represented in an imposing sketch (Plate 207a) the metaphor of the ship at the beginning of the *Purgatorio*.

It is charming to find Boccaccio among the illustrators of Dante. One of the three copies of the *Divina Commedia* which he had made during the last years of his life is embellished with seven compositions to the *Inferno* — among these Francesca and Paolo — in tender, somewhat timid drawings (Plates 113–114b). With more vivid characterization he drew a few single figures from the *Decamerone*, which disguise in ornamental fashion the catchwords in the autograph now in Berlin (Plate 114c–k). A more complete type of illustration of the *Decamerone* was already begun during Boccaccio's lifetime: at first a scene with several figures was placed at the beginning of each day (Plates 109–112), and in the fifteenth century the *Ninfale Fiesolano* and the *Teseide* were also depicted. It is not impossible that novelistic or anecdotal motives provided the inspiration for some of the representations in the Neapolitan sketchbook of the Morgan Library (Plate 132ff.), which originated not long after Boccaccio's death.

Other mediaeval works which have challenged illustrators again and again because of their richness in action are chronicles and romances, among the latter the story of Troy by Guido of Colonna. Some older literary texts seem to have been embellished with pictures only after they had been translated into Italian, e.g., Ovid's *Eroide*, Pseudo-Ovid's *De pulce* (Plates 208e–210d), and *Geta e Birria*, a version of the Amphitryo theme (based on the poem by Vitalis of Blois) that has been enlivened with scenic illustrations (Plates 373c–374b). Very remarkable in its pointed characterization and in the selection of *sujets* is a Latin Justinus with illustrations by Giovanni de' Castaldi da Fano (pp. 346–348c).

Of religious literature illustrated with drawings the *Corpus* presents, along with Biblical narratives and saints' legends, several edifying vernacular versions of the history of the Franciscan order. A series of illustrated manuscripts with the poem *De balneis Puteolanis* by Peter of Eboli demands particular attention among the scholarly litera ture here under consideration: this "tourist guide" continued to be copied in Naples up to the fifteenth century. Professors Degenhart and Schmitt devote a special study to the prophecies concerning the popes which consist of impressive patternlike pictures, lengthy predictions, and short mottos. One of the longer cycles of thirty drawings which begins with Nicholas III has been reproduced entirely (Plates 167– 170), with plenty of material for purposes of comparison, demonstrating the international spread of these pictures and showing the stylistic changes they underwent as they passed from one country to another.

The source material covers the period up to around 1470. One of the last examples worthy of special notice is an extensive series of pictures by a Florentine artist, which however is not accompanied by any continuous text (Plates 385–439a). In 128 masterly figures with almost operatic costumes, surrounded with characteristic scenery, and a few representations of towns and monumental buildings, the artist has collected from mythology and history what had seemed essential in a still partly mediaeval, if partly humanistic, education. It is unfortunate that the sequence breaks off with Milo of Croton. This type of historical picture gallery, to whose ancestors belong the *neuf preux* and a cycle of the Sibyls, is examined in a special essay. Mention should also be made of the references for the transmission of the portrait drawings of Dante, Petrarch, and Boccaccio (pp. xxixf., 196 f., 283), and of the observations on the style of Petrarch's famous sketch of Vaucluse (pp. 130 f., Plate 101c).

This monumental study, which is of great significance for the cultural history of Naples and its court as well as of the other leading centres, will be continued with the publication of drawings from northern Italy, where in the field of illustrated literature other genera maintain priority (see p. viii). The corpus will be terminated by a third part which is to be devoted to mediaeval Italian drawings up to 1300.

The Future of Medieval History*

Joseph R. Strayer

MEDIEVAL HISTORY is facing a time of troubles. In many colleges, course enrollments are declining. In many universities few students begin graduate work in medieval history, and even fewer finish it: they drift off into other fields. The decline is gradual, not abrupt; we can keep going at close to our present rate for another decade or so. But I wonder if the teachers of medieval history who are just beginning their careers will have as many excellent students as my contemporaries did and, indeed, if they will have any students at all by the year 2000. The generation of Charles Homer Haskins simply took it for granted that any civilized man would study medieval history. They could not conceive of a college, or even a high school curriculum, in which medieval history did not occupy a prominent place. My generation realized that a little persuasion was necessary and that a little time had to be surrendered to other periods of history, but we were sure that we could convince our colleagues and our students that medieval history deserved to have a key position in a liberal arts program. The new generation of medievalists will have to fight to keep medieval history in the curriculum at all, and, if it is retained, to keep it from being shoved into the back corner along with Sanskrit, Assyriology, and other subjects that are kept alive only through the efforts of a handful of specialists.

Part of our trouble results from forces that have been building up for a long time. There is so much more history now than there was in the 1920's — new approaches to history, new topics in history, new areas whose history must be investigated. Even if we had an absolutely fair share of the time available for the study of history it would be a small share — far smaller than it was in those simple days when a fully developed college program included only ancient, medieval, modern, and American history. And as far as graduate

*This paper was read at the meeting of the Midwest Medieval Conference at the University of Illinois (Champaign) on 15 November 1969.

179

students are concerned, we suffer from the steady decline in the study of the classics over the last forty years. Few entering students really know Latin, not to mention Greek, and they are usually far from proficient in modern languages. And it is a real strain to learn two or three languages while acquiring the knowledge and techniques needed by a professional historian; there are easier ways to get a degree.

We could adjust to these long-range changes if we were not faced with other pressures. The vast increase in the number of students could compensate for the decline in the percentage of students taking medieval history. After all, five percent of a million is exactly equal to twenty-five percent of two hundred thousand. The language problem is not insuperable; methods of language teaching are improving, and in many fields, for example Russian studies, students seem willing to devote at least as much time to languages as is required for medieval studies. What has made a manageable problem almost unmanageable is a relatively sudden shift in attitudes toward history by some of our colleagues and by many of our students.

The more radical form of this shift is to deny that any field of history has any value. We live in an entirely new world; change in the last few decades has been so rapid that the past has become irrelevant. Human behavior can be understood only in terms of the present, because our society is completely different from any society that ever existed before. Nothing useful, nothing that would help in solving current problems, can be found in the historical record. History is simply a rather dull form of literature.

A less extreme version of the same idea admits that there is some value in the study of past societies, but minimizes the importance of observing continuity and growth. History is valuable only in slow motion and under extreme magnification. Societies can be understood only through knowledge of their structures. There is little to be learned by examining the origins and the development of any pattern of social relationships. What is important is to examine the pattern in one place at some fixed moment in time. If we really understood all the relationships that existed in one community at one time we would be close to formulating a science of society. Such a science would be worth far more than the fruitless speculations about causation and change that grow out of attempts to survey long periods and wide areas.

Whether they accept the extreme or the less extreme position, those who hold these ideas are not likely to find themselves attracted by medieval history. When even the nineteenth century is irrelevant, the Middle Ages are incredibly remote. Industrial man has nothing in common with medieval man. And even if there were any sense in studying medieval society, the idea might as well be abandoned, because medieval society cannot be investigated in a satisfactory way. Lack of detailed information, especially quantifiable information, makes it impossible to use the new sociological and statistical techniques that are necessary if reliable results are to be achieved. Medievalists have nothing important to say; they simply amuse themselves collecting trivial information that cannot interest any sensible person.

This is the case against us. How much truth is there in it? What can we do about it?

There is some truth in it. Medievalists have spent time on trivial problems; they have accumulated odds and ends of esoteric learning of interest only to themselves; they have been rather supercilious toward those who know little about their field. Even their virtues have become faults. They love their period so much that they cannot understand — and hence find it hard to teach   those who lack their enthusiasm. They are rightly proud of the techniques that they have developed for dealing with very difficult materials, but the techniques have sometimes become ends in themselves. It is certainly good for a medievalist to edit a text; he will learn a great many things, including how carelessly he has read texts before. Again, it is essential to have critical editions of many texts. But to keep on editing texts without meditating on their meaning, or to edit a text just because it exists, without considering whether it is worth the effort, are not acts that win medievalists the esteem of their colleagues in other fields. Even worse, our fascination with the old techniques has often prevented us from using new techniques that would increase our knowledge of medieval society and make that knowledge seem more relevant to the new generation of students. We should never forget our greatest danger: we began as antiquarians and we could end as antiquarians.

But even admitting these weaknesses in medievalists, I believe that medieval history does have relevance in the modern world — perhaps more relevance than more recent and more tranquil periods such as the Victorian Age. To take a major point: the trouble with the world today is not so much rapid change as uneven change. Our thinking has not caught up with the increase in our productive capacity,

181

whether the product be new scientific theory, new technology, or new means of destruction. This is not an unknown problem in medieval history. More important, two-thirds of the world has not yet entered the new age which is supposed to make all previous experience irrelevant. This two-thirds of the world is politely called "underdeveloped." That is, it is very much in the position of western Europe in the Middle Ages, trying to build complex social-political-economic structures on a primitive agricultural basis, trying to absorb ideas and techniques from more advanced societies. As many historians have pointed out in recent years, Europe offers the first example of modernization, and the key period in the process comes during the Middle Ages. State-building, urbanization, the impact of new technologies, changing class structures, the search for a way to reconcile new interests and old beliefs — every problem that perplexes a developing society today can be found in the Middle Ages. Moreover, these problems can be studied with greater precision than is possible in dealing with a contemporary or nearly contemporary society. The rate of change was slower and easier to observe. The impulses that traveled along the nerves of the medieval body politic moved so gradually that sequences that are now telescoped into a few years were then spread out over decades, and can thus be examined at leisure. The number of people involved in any important development was very small. We can study them as individuals and avoid the error of making group ideas and group actions seem more uniform than they really were. For example, it is possible to know something about the life and work of almost every man who wrote on scientific topics between 1200 and 1300. Or, to go from the extreme of abstraction to the extreme of action, it is possible to learn a great deal about participants in urban uprisings. Usually only a few hundred men took part in these affairs; if local records are good we can determine the occupation, social standing, and often the wealth of many of the individuals involved.

The anti-historian can say, of course, that historical parallels, like those of geometry, never meet, and that reasoning by analogy is a poor form of reasoning. This is true enough; the trouble is that in dealing with human relationships no better form of reasoning is available. Faced with a new or changing situation, we all act on the basis of past experience; consciously or unconsciously, we all use analogies. If we are going to use analogies in spite of ourselves, then it is important that the analogies fit as closely as possible, and an analogy drawn from the Middle Ages will often fit better than one drawn from a more recent period. It is less likely to be distorted by passion and by prejudice. The Norman conquest of England was an act of imperialism; it is much easier to examine the consequences of this act dispassionately than the consequences of the French conquest of Indochina.

There is also a wider range of human experience to draw on if we take our analogies from the Middle Ages rather than from modern history. While the number of mistakes that human beings can make in their relations with each other is not infinite, it is very large, and some kinds of mistakes are repeated only after long intervals. We are apt to concentrate on avoiding the errors of our fathers and by doing so fail to avoid the errors of earlier generations. When I first read about the Albigensian Crusade, some fifty years ago, I would have said that this was one type of evil that could not occur in the twentieth century. Now I wonder if we should not be re-examining the causes of the Fall of Rome.

Without being so apocalyptic, there are other types of error that are particularly well illustrated by events in medieval history. There is the error of trying to extend central authority over distant regions that feel no ties with the center (the Holy Roman Empire). There is the error of trying to impose alien institutions on a people who have had no previous experience with such institutions (the English in Ireland). There is the error of imitating external forms and failing to understand the actual functioning of a political system (Frederick Barbarossa's attempt to systematize German feudalism). There is the error of trying to speed up a process that is already developing about as fast as conditions permit (Philip the Fair and royal power), and the error of trying to slow down a process that is irreversible (the English in the last stages of the Hundred Years' War).

But enough of errors and mistakes. The Middle Ages were also a period of amazing success — a period in which a poor, rejected, outlying fragment of the old Mediterranean world caught up to and surpassed not only its ancestral civilization but also the neighboring civilizations that had descended from the common ancestor. The mistakes are not only obvious, especially in political and economic affairs: they are also easily explainable. The successes are just as obvious, but are much harder to explain. How did Europe, with very little outside help, stabilize its political system, expand its economy, absorb or create new technologies and new tools of thought? If we really knew the answer to this question we would have discovered a formula that students of the developing nations have not yet found. And I suspect that the answer lies more in the realm of ideals, beliefs, habits of mind, than it does in the realm of economic and political organization.

Having said this, I must immediately add that political and institutional history is still important. Politics supplies a framework within which other forces operate and affects the ways in which they operate. The physical security provided by an effective political system does not guarantee rapid development, but its absence certainly works against development. The exact date of the coronation of Hugh Capet may not be important (though Lemarignier has given good reasons for thinking it was),[1] but the establishment of the Capetian dynasty affected the subsequent history of all of Europe. The arguments about when circuit judges first appeared in England may seem trivial, but the fact that circuit judges were used extensively in twelfth-century England made England different from all other European countries. The petty wars of thirteenth-century Italy are of interest only to the specialist, but the fact that the papacy became involved in these wars did more to weaken and discredit the Church than any heresy.

We have solved many of the problems of medieval political history, and we have the techniques and the materials to solve most of those that remain. We have done less well with social-economic history, and especially with the kind of social-economic history that would enable us to understand the way of life and the habits of mind of the middle and lower classes of European society. We have avoided significant problems, because we have thought that materials were lacking and that modern statistical methods could not be applied to the materials that do exist. We were wrong on both counts. There is a vast amount of material that has scarcely been used — 600 unpublished cartularies in France alone, to say nothing of the thousands of uninventoried items in departmental and municipal archives. Or, to take another example, it is only in the last few years that Professor Goitein has shown us how the thousands of documents of the Cairo Geniza reveal the mentality and business practices of Mediterranean traders.[2]

Moreover, we have never exploited our materials as fully as we should have done. Through simple statistical methods we can squeeze much more out of our texts than we realized. One document proves nothing, but if one searches for the presence (or absence) of certain traits through thousands of documents, one can arrive at solid conclusions. Thus Kosminsky has enlightened us about the size of peasant holdings in England,[3] Herlihy about economic conditions in Italian rural areas,[4] Fossier about the settlement and exploitation of the land in Picardy.[5] It is amazing how much can be learned just by counting, and modern techniques make counting much easier than it used to be.

Again, while it is nearly impossible for a medievalist to write a meaningful biography of an individual, it is possible to write a sort of collective biography of a class or a group by assembling hundreds of scraps of evidence. This kind of work is often more useful than the individual biography; it can reveal the texture of a society. The possibilities were demonstrated long ago by scholars such as Duby,[6] and some of my own students have used this method with considerable success.[7] A collection of collective biographies would be even more informative. To take only one example, we already know enough about the French civil service between 1250 and 1350 to say that the whole group — judges and lawyers, financial officials and provincial governors — was drawn from a rather narrow segment of the population. The lower upper and upper middle classes were heavily represented, but few officials came from the great noble families or from the artisans of the towns, and even fewer from the peasantry. There was also a geographical restriction. The old royal domain was the favorite recruiting ground; Burgundy and the Center were acceptable sources of manpower; Normandy, and even more Languedoc, were looked on with suspicion. Knowledge of the social and geographic origins of royal officials in turn explains some of the characteristics of French government during the period.

In short, we can now discover many new facts and frame many new hypotheses about the social-economic history of the Middle Ages. We can quantify more than we thought we could, and we can have a good time doing it. The kind of work I have been talking about has all the fascination of a good puzzle, and it involves the use of all the new, and therefore popular, techniques of the social scientist.

I am still worried, however. A shift toward social-economic history may satisfy our graduate students, but it will not necessarily attract a wider audience. Undergraduates and the reading public may still think of medieval history as an esoteric game. To calculate the population of Périgueux in the fourteenth century is no more interesting to the ordinary student than to establish the date of the coronation of Hugh Capet. We may find that we have merely exchanged one kind of private amusement for another, and that the new activity seems no

185

more relevant than the old. Why do we want these new facts and new hypotheses? How are we going to use them?

We need the new material, first, because a lot of our old generalizations (and some not so old) are erroneous and incomplete and, secondly, because many potentially useful generalizations have never been made. And it is these incomplete or nonexistent generalizations that might help us understand the developing part of the world.

To take one of the toughest problems first, it is hard to realize how incredibly backward European agriculture was in the eighth and ninth centuries, what a tremendous effort it took to increase production, how slow growth was. We can identify some of the significant innovations, but we are apt to exaggerate the speed with which they were adopted, e.g., use of water power, planting of field peas. Other problems have barely been touched. How was the appalling shortage of tools that is so apparent in Carolingian documents remedied? Who made the tools? Where did the iron come from? Even though only minimal quantities were needed, not every region produced its own iron. Did more iron in west Germany mean more wheat in eastern France? If it did, how were the exchanges arranged?

The last question raises another problem — that of early medieval commerce. We could probably find out more about the volume and character of trade in northern Europe. We are finding out a great deal more about Mediterranean trade and about the influence of Moslem and Jewish commercial law and practice on Europeans, especially on Italians. Italian businessmen may have borrowed more and invented less than we thought. On the other hand, because of this borrowing, Italian commercial and financial operations may have been quite sophisticated at a surprisingly early date.

To shift to another area, we do not know enough about medieval elites. We talk about the nobility or about the patriciate, but these words had different meanings for each generation and for each district. We have some excellent local studies; we need many more. And the allied question of social mobility, while not neglected, has certainly not received its final answer.

Two, at least, of the medieval elites — the clergy and the upper bourgeoisie — were educated elites. We know very little about the schools or the teaching methods that prepared men for a business life. We know a great deal about the universities, but how were boys prepared for university work? And what about the vast army of clerks — men who were technically in holy orders, men who could rise to the highest positions in Church and state? Most of these men did not attend universities, yet they were educated, often well educated. How was this done? How was it done without elaborate educational organization or great expense?

Why — to combine an educational problem with one that requires an appraisal of the basic characteristics of western civilization — why did European scholars continue the study of science and mathematics when such studies were being abandoned by every other civilized society? All the reasons that have been given for the loss of interest in science by other people — lack of practical results, undue respect for ancient authorities, the rise of mysticism, dislocations caused by invasions and civil wars — apply to Europe. Moreover, it cannot be claimed that the achievements of medieval scholars in the field of science were so spectacular that interest in science was bound to persist, however unfavorable the environment. Obviously the scientific tradition persisted in Europe because it was part of a broader cultural tradition, but why and how did it become a necessary part of that tradition?

One final question, which brings us around the circle from economic, social, and cultural history back to political history. Medieval men had a strong sense of community, but the idea of community covered everything from the peasant village to the Commonwealth of Christianity. What were the different communities; how strong a pull did each one have; how did this attraction vary from generation to generation and from place to place? What were the *gentes*, the "nations," of the early Middle Ages? The words can be taken in their literal sense if we are talking about a people like the Saxons, but how about the Aquitanians? How did a man know that he was an Aquitanian; what did it mean to him *if* he knew? How did these early ethnic or semi-ethnic loyalties become territorial loyalties, and why were some territorial loyalties more persistent than others? What is the difference between provincial loyalty, which everyone admits was strong, and national loyalty, which everyone says was nonexistent? Was England, given its size and population, anything more than a large province? And if we think of medieval England as a large province, does this help to explain some of the peculiarities of English history?

Everyone can probably think of other — and better — questions. The ones I have given are merely samples of the sort of work that needs to be done. If we do this kind of work, we are certainly going to be busy, and we may become schizophrenic. On the one hand, we

187

need a vast amount of detailed knowledge that is not now available. On the other hand, we must find meaning in this detailed knowledge as we accumulate it. It is not easy to do both tasks at the same time, either as individuals or as a group. But both tasks must be done, and must be done simultaneously. If we merely accumulate, we shall sink into the pit of antiquarianism. If we generalize without finding new material and reworking old material, we shall soon discover that we have nothing to say to coming generations of students. But if we have both new knowledge and new ideas about medieval society we might be able to give our students some insights into the problems of a troubled world.

NOTES

1. J. F. Lemarignier, "Autour de la date du sacre d'Hugues Capet," *Miscellanea Medievalia in Memoriam Jan Frederik Niemayer* (Groningen, 1967), pp. 125–35.
2. S. D. Goitein, *A Mediterranean Society: The Jewish Communities of the Arab World as Portrayed in the Documents of the Cairo Geniza*, Vol. I (Berkeley, 1967).
3. E. A. Kosminsky, *Studies in the Agrarian History of England* (Oxford, 1956).
4. David Herlihy, "The Agrarian Revolution in Southern France and Italy, 801–1150," *Speculum*, XXXIII (1958), 23–41.
5. Robert Fossier, *La Terre et les hommes en Picardie*. 2 vols. (Paris, 1968).
6. Georges Duby, *La Société aux XIe et XIIe siècles dans la région mâconnaise* (Paris, 1953). Another excellent example of the value of this method may be found in Bernard Guenée, *Tribunaux et gens de justice dans le bailliage de Senlis à la fin du moyen âge* (Paris, 1963).
7. John Freed, "The Mendicant Orders in Germany 1219–1273"; Rhiman Rotz, "Urban Unrest in Hamburg and Braunschweig at the End of the 14th Century"; Jan Rogozinski, "The Lawyers of Lower Languedoc." All three theses are deposited in the Princeton University Library.

BOOKS RECEIVED

This list was compiled from the books received between 1 January 1970 and 15 May 1971. The publishers and the editorial board would appreciate your mentioning *Medievalia et Humanistica* when ordering.

Don Cameron Allen. *Mysteriously Meant: The Rediscovery of Pagan Symbolism and Allegorical Interpretation in the Renaissance.* Baltimore: The Johns Hopkins Press, 1971. Pp. x, 354. $12.00.

Anglo-Norman England 1066–1154 (Conference on British Studies Bibliographical Handbooks), comp. Michael Altschul. Cambridge: Cambridge University Press, 1969. Pp. xii, 83. $5.95.

Frank Barlow. *Edward the Confessor.* Berkeley and Los Angeles: University of California Press, 1970. Pp. xxviii, 375, 16 illustrations, 4 maps, 2 genealogical tables. $10.95.

Charles Béné. *Erasme et Saint Augustin ou Influence de Saint Augustin sur L'Humanisme* (Université de Paris Faculté des Lettres et Sciences Humaines). Geneva: Libraire Droz, 1969. Pp. 472.

Davis Bitton. *The French Nobility in Crisis.* Stanford, Cal.: Stanford University Press, 1969. Pp. vii, 178. $6.50.

Morton W. Bloomfield. *The Interpretation of Narrative: Theory and Practice* (Harvard English Studies I). Cambridge, Mass.: Harvard University Press, 1970. Pp. 287. $6.00.

William M. Bowsky. *The Finance of the Commune of Siena: 1287–1355.* London: Oxford University Press, 1971. Pp. xx, 379, 3 plates, 3 maps. $16.00.

John D. Boyd, S.J. *The Function of Mimesis and Its Decline.* Cambridge, Mass.: Harvard University Press, 1968. Pp. xiv, 317. $7.50.

Robert Brentano. *Two Churches: England and Italy in the Thirteenth Century.* Princeton: Princeton University Press, 1968. Pp. xii, 372. $11.00.

Bulletin de Philosophie Médiévale, édité par la Société Internationale pour l'Étude de la Philosophie Médiévale, 7e. Louvain: Secretariat de la S.I.E.P.M., 1965. Pp. 202. $6.00.

Domenico Caccamo. *Eretici italiani in Moravia, Polonia, Transilvania* (1558–1611). Florence and Chicago: The Newberry Library, 1970. Pp. 286, 2 illustrations. 10,000 lire.

Hans von Campenhausen. *Ecclesiastical Authority and Spiritual Power in the Church of the First Three Centuries,* trans. J. A. Baker. Stanford, Cal.: Stanford University Press, 1969. Pp. vi, 308. $8.95.

Hans von Campenhausen. *The Fathers of the Latin Church,* trans. Manfred Hoffman. Stanford, Cal.: Stanford University Press, 1969. Pp. vi, 328. $6.50.

M. D. Chenu, O. P. *L'Eveil de la Conscience dans la Civilisation Médiévale* (Conférence Albert-Le-Grand 1968). Montreal and Paris: Institut d'Études Médiévales, 1969. Pp. 81.

Christianity in Britain, 300–700 (Papers Presented to the Conference on Christianity in Roman and Sub-Roman Britain Held at the University of Nottingham 17–20 April 1967), ed. M. W. Barley and R. P. C. Hanson. Leicester: Leicester University Press, 1968. Pp. 221, 6 plates. $8.00.

Pierre Courcelle. *La Consolation de Philosophie dans la Tradition Littéraire, Antécédents et Postérité de Boèce.* Paris: Études Augustiniennes, 1967. Pp. 449, 132 plates.

Pierre Courcelle. *Late Latin Writers and Their Greek Sources,* trans. Harry E. Wedeck. Cambridge, Mass.: Harvard University Press, 1969. Pp. x, 467. $15.00.

Dante Alighieri. *The Divine Comedy,* Vol. 1, Italian Text and Translation; Vol. 2, Commentary. Trans. Charles S. Singleton. Princeton: Princeton University Press, 1970. Pp. 382 and 683. $25.00 the set.

Dante Alighieri. Inferno: *The Italian Text with Translation and Notes,* by Allan Gilbert. Durham, N.C.: Duke University Press, 1969. Pp. xlvi, 373. $12.50.

Colin Davies. *The Emergence of Western Society: European and English History 300–1200.* New York: Humanities Press, 1970. Pp. 403, 18 plates. $6.00 cloth, $4.50 paper.

Philippe Dollinger. *The German Hansa,* trans. D. S. Ault and S. H. Steinberg. Stanford, Cal.: Stanford University Press, 1970. Pp. xxii, 474, 3 maps. $15.00.

Mortimer J. Donovan. *The Breton Lay: A Guide to Varieties.* Notre Dame, Ind.: University of Notre Dame Press, 1969. Pp. xiii, 267. $7.95.

Charles L. Eastlake. *A History of the Gothic Revival.* New York: The Humanities Press, 1970. Pp. xvi, 372, 26 plates. $16.50.

Robert Forster and Jack P. Greene. *Preconditions of Revolution in Early Modern Europe.* Baltimore and London: The Johns Hopkins Press, 1971. Pp. 214. $8.95.

Russell Fraser. *The War Against Poetry.* Princeton: Princeton University Press, 1971. Pp. 215. $7.50.

Fulcher of Chartres. *A History of the Expedition to Jerusalem 1095–1127,* trans. Frances Rita Ryan and ed. with an Introduction by Harold S. Fink. Knoxville: University of Tennessee Press, 1969. Pp. xiv, 348. $13.50.

D. Gaborit-Chopin. *La Décoration des Manuscrits a Saint-Martial de Limoges et en Limousin du IXe au XIIe Siècle* (Mémoires et Documents, Publiés par la Société de l'École des Chartes, 17). Paris: Librairie Droz, 1969. Pp. 230, 128 plates.

Lionel Gossman. *Men and Masks: A Study of Molière.* Baltimore: The Johns Hopkins Press, 1969. Pp. x, 310. $2.45 paper.

Paul F. Grendler. *Critics of the Italian World 1530–1560: Anton Francesco Doni, Nicolò Franco, and Ortensio Lando.* Madison & London: University of Wisconsin Press, 1969. Pp. xii, 282. $10.00.

Guillaume de Lorris and Jean de Meun. *The Romance of the Rose,* trans. Charles Dahlberg. Princeton: Princeton University Press, 1971. Pp. 449, illustrations 64. $16.50.

M. B. Hackett. *The Original Statutes of Cambridge University: The Text and Its History.* Cambridge: Cambridge University Press, 1970. Pp. xix, 398. $16.50.

John Halkett. *Milton and the Idea of Matrimony: A Study of the Divorce Tracts and* Paradise Lost. New Haven: Yale University Press, 1970. Pp. ix, 162. $6.50.

O. B. Hardison, Jr. *Christian Rite and Christian Drama in the Middle Ages: Essays in the Origin and Early History of Modern Drama.* Baltimore: The Johns Hopkins Press, 1969. Pp. xi, 238. $2.45 paper.

Nikolaus M. Häring, S.A.C., ed. *The Commentaries on Boethius by Gilbert of Poitiers.* Toronto: Pontifical Institute of Mediaeval Studies, 1966. Pp. xiv, 437. $9.00.

Geoffrey Harlow. *Year's Work in English Studies.* Vol. 49, 1968. New York: Humanities Press, Inc., 1971. Pp. 456. $7.50.

Marvin T. Herrick. *Italian Comedy in the Renaissance.* Urbana: The University of Illinois Press, 1966. Pp. vi, 238. $1.75 paper.

Marvin T. Herrick. *Italian Tragedy in the Renaissance.* Urbana: The University of Illinois Press. Pp. vi, 315.

Delbert R. Hillers. *Covenant: The History of a Biblical Idea.* Baltimore: The Johns Hopkins Press, 1969. Pp. xii, 194. $7.00 cloth, $1.95 paper.

Bede Jarrett, O.P. *Social Theories of the Middle Ages, 1200–1500.* London: Frank Cass and Co. Ltd., 1926; rpt. 1968.

Robert Javelet. *Image et Ressemblance au Douzième Siècle de Saint Anselme à Alain de Lille.* Vol. 1: Texte; II: Notes. Strasbourg: Université de Strasbourg, 1967. Pp. xxiii, 467; xl, 383.

Robbin S. Johnson. *More's Utopia: Ideal and Illusion.* New Haven: Yale University Press, 1969. Pp. xi, 166. $6.00.

David Knowles. *Thomas Becket.* Stanford: Stanford University Press, 1971. Pp. 183, 2 illustrations. $6.95.

Benoît Lacroix, O.P. *L'Historien au moyen âge.* Montreal: Institut d'études médiévales; Paris: Librarie J. Vrin, 1971. Pp. 304. $8.00.

John L. Lievsay, ed. *Medieval and Renaissance Studies* (Proceedings of the Southeastern Institute of Medieval and Renaissance Studies, Summer 1966, Medieval and Renaissance Series, no. 2). Durham, N.C.: Duke University Press, 1968. Pp. viii, 174, 12 plates. $6.00.

John L. Lievsay, ed. *Medieval and Renaissance Studies Number 4* (Proceedings of the Southeastern Institute of Medieval and Renaissance Studies, Summer 1968). Durham, N.C.: Duke University Press, 1970. Pp. 183. $8.00.

Peter Llewellyn. *Rome in the Dark Ages.* New York and Washington: Praeger Publishers, 1970. Pp. 324, 3 illustrations. $10.00.

F. Donald Logan. *Excommunication and the Secular Arm in Medieval England: A Study in Legal Procedure from the Thirteenth to the Sixteenth Century* (Studies and Texts 15). Toronto: Pontifical Institute of Mediaeval Studies, 1968. Pp. 239. $8.00.

D. E. Luscombe. *The School of Peter Abelard: The Influence of Abelard's Thought in the Early Scholastic Period* (Cambridge Studies in Medieval Life and Thought, 2nd ser., 14). Cambridge: Cambridge University Press, 1969. Pp. xiii, 360. $12.50.

C. Mallary Masters. *Rabelaisian Dialectic and the Platonic-Hermetic Tradition.* Albany: State University of New York Press, 1969. Pp. xi, 152. $6.00.

Millard Meiss. *French Painting in the Time of Jean de Berry: The Late Fourteenth Century and the Patronage of the Duke.* New York: Phaidon Publishing Inc., 2nd ed., 1969. Text volume xi, 453 pp.

Ralph Merrifield. *Roman London.* New York: Frederick A. Praeger, 1969. Pp. xii, 222, 63 illustrations. $9.50.

Philippe de Mézières. *Le Songe Du Vieil Pelerin,* ed. G. W. Coopland. 2 vols. Cambridge: Cambridge University Press, 1969. Pp. ix, 636; 537. Set $42.50.

Alice Miskimin, ed. *Susannah: An Alliterative Poem of the Fourteenth Century.* New Haven: Yale University Press, 1969. Pp. xvii, 255. $7.50.

Jerome Mitchell. *Thomas Hoccleve: A Study in Early Fifteenth Century English Poetic.* Urbana, Chicago, London: University of Illinois Press, 1968. Pp. x, 151. $5.95.

D. G. Mowatt, ed. *Friderich von Husen* (Anglica Germanica Series 2). New York: Cambridge University Press, 1971. Pp. 212. $13.50.

Francis William Newman. *Phases of Faith.* New York: Humanities Press, 1970. Pp. xxiv, 212. $5.25.

F. X. Newman, ed. *The Meaning of Courtly Love* (Papers of the First Annual Conference of the Center for Medieval and Early Renaissance Studies, State University of New York at Binghamton, March 17–18, 1967.) Albany: State University of New York Press, 1968. Pp. x, 102. $5.00.

Robert J. O'Connell, S.J. *St. Augustine's Confessions: The Odyssey of Soul.* Cambridge, Mass.: The Belknap Press of Harvard University Press, 1969. Pp. ix, 200. $6.50.

Robert J. O'Connell, S.J. *St. Augustine's Early Theory of Man, A. D. 386–391.* Cambridge, Mass.: The Belknap Press of Harvard University Press, 1968. Pp. xxii, 301. $10.00.

Annable M. Patterson. *Hermogenes and the Renaissance: Seven Ideas of Style.* Princeton: Princeton University Press, 1970. Pp. xv, 240. $10.00.

Jean Pepin. *Dante et la tradition de l'allegorie.* Montreal: Les Publications de l'Institut d'études médiévales; Paris: Librarie J. Vrin, 1971. Pp. 164. $5.00.

R. R. Post. *The Modern Devotion: Confrontation with Reformation and Humanism* (Studies in Medieval and Reformation Thought, Volume III). Leiden: E. J. Brill, 1969. Pp. xi, 694. 92 guilders.

James Samuel Preus. *From Shadow to Promise: Old Testament Interpretation from Augustine to the Young Luther.* Cambridge, Mass: The Belknap Press of Harvard University Press, 1969. Pp. vii, 301. $7.50.

Donald E. Queller. *The Office of Ambassador in the Middle Ages.* Princeton: Princeton University Press, 1967. Pp. xi, 251. $7.50.

Camillo Renato: *Opere, documenti e testimonianze,* a cura di Antonio Rotondó (Corpus Reformatorum Italicorum, I). Florence: G. C. Sansoni Editore; Chicago: The Newberry Library, 1968. Pp. 350, 5 plates. L. 10,000.

James H. Robb, ed. *St. Thomas Aquinas: Quaestiones de Anima* (A Newly Established Edition of the Latin Text with an Introduction and Notes). Toronto: Pontifical Institute of Mediaeval Studies, 1968. Pp. 282. $9.00.

Fred C. Robinson. *Old English Literature: A Select Bibliography* (Toronto Medieval Bibliographies, Number 2). Toronto: University of Toronto, 1970. Pp. xv, 68. $3.95.

Paul Seaver. *The Puritan Lectureships: The Politics of Religious Dissent 1560–1662*. Stanford, Cal.: Stanford University Press, 1970. Pp. ix, 402. $12.50.

Jerrold E. Seigel. *Rhetoric and Philosophy in Renaissance Humanism: The Union of Eloquence and Wisdom, Petrarch to Valla*. Princeton: Princeton University Press, 1968. Pp. xvii, 268. $8.50.

Thomas F. Sheppard. *Lourmarin in the Eighteenth Century*. Baltimore and London: The Johns Hopkins Press, 1971. Pp. 248. $11.00.

James D. Simmonds, ed. *Milton Studies*, Vol. 1. Pittsburgh: University *of Pittsburgh Press*, 1969. Pp. 192. $8.95.

Joseph R. Strayer. *Medieval Statecraft and the Perspectives of History*. Princeton: Princeton University Press, 1971. Pp. 425. $13.75.

Thomas More's Prayer Book: A Facsimile Reproduction of the Annotated Pages, transcribed and translated, with an Introduction, by Louis L. Martz and Richard S. Sylvester. New Haven: Yale University Press, 1969. Pp. xlv, 206. $12.50.

A. P. Vlasto. *The Entry of the Slavs Into Christendom*. Cambridge: Cambridge University Press, 1970. Pp. xii, 435. $19.50.

Donald Weinstein. *Savonarola and Florence*. Princeton: Princeton University Press, 1971. Pp. viii, 399. $13.50.

ANNOUNCEMENTS

S.I.E.P.M., the "Société Internationale pour l'Étude de la Philosophie Médiévale," established in 1958, has as its aim bringing together people doing research in medieval philosophy or related fields. Candidates can request admission through the sponsorship of two full members; the fee is $4.00 annually. The *Bulletin de philosophie médiévale* is published annually and provides numerous items of information, and in particular a prospective bibliography (studies in preparation). The subscription rate is $6.00 (double numbers 8 and 9 are $8.00). Complete sets will be available after numbers 1, 2, and 4 have been reprinted.

The S.I.E.P.M. has organized four International Congresses of Medieval Philosophy, the last one in Montreal in 1967. The Fifth Congress will be held in Madrid-Granada, Spain, 5–12 September 1972. Further information may be obtained from the Secretary of the Society, Professor Christian Wenin, Kardinaal Mercierplein 2, B-3000 Louvain, Belgium.

The first International Congress of Neo-Latin Language and Literature was held 23–28 August 1971, at the University of Louvain, Belgium. The Congress plans to bring together scholars of various disciplines working on Neo-Latin texts or interested in the contributions of Neo-Latin authors to Western literature. Lectures and discussions will concern three main themes: (1) problems of Neo-Latin bibliography, lexicography, and editions; (2) general history of Neo-Latin literature; (3) Neo-Latin and the vernacular. Further inquiries should be addressed to Professor J. IJsewijn, Katholieke Universiteit te Leuven, Seminarium Philologiae Humanisticae, Leopoldstraat 32, B-3000 Leuven, Belgium.

The VI centenary of the death of Francesco Petrarca will be commemorated at the Folger Shakespeare Library 7–13 August 1974, with a symposium featuring lectures by outstanding Petrarch scholars throughout the world. The planning committee will be headed by Aldo S. Bernardo, Co-director of the Center for Medieval and Early Renaissance Studies of the State University of New York, Binghamton, and O. B. Hardison, Jr., Director of the Folger Shakespeare Library, Washington, D.C.

TABLE OF CONTENTS FOR FASCICULI I–XVII

FASCICULUS V
(1948)

FASCICULUS VI
(1950)

FASCICULUS IX
(1955)

FASCICULUS X
(1956)

FASCICULUS XIII
(1960)

FASCICULUS XIV
(1962)
Studia in Honorem E. A. Lowe

FASCICULUS XV
(1963)

CUMULATIVE INDEX FOR FASCICULI I–XVII